YOUTH IN TRANSITION

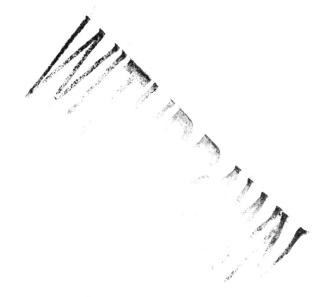

Also by Ken Roberts

Leisure in Contemporary Society

The Leisure Industries

Class in Modern Britain

Youth and Employment in Modern Britain

Youth in Transition

Eastern Europe and the West

Ken Roberts

First published 2009 by
PALGRAVE MACMILLAN

Palgrave Macmillan in the UK is an imprint of Macmillan Publishers Limited,
registered in England, company number 785998, of Houndmills, Basingstoke,
Hampshire RG21 6XS.

Palgrave Macmillan in the US is a division of St Martin's Press LLC,
175 Fifth Avenue, New York, NY 10010.

Palgrave Macmillan is the global academic imprint of the above companies
and has companies and representatives throughout the world.

Palgrave® and Macmillan® are registered trademarks in the United States,
the United Kingdom, Europe and other countries.

ISBN-13: 978-0-230-21443-9   hardback
ISBN-10: 0-230-21443-6   hardback
ISBN-13: 978-0-230-21444-6   paperback
ISBN-10: 0-230-21444-4   paperback

This book is printed on paper suitable for recycling and made from fully
managed and sustained forest sources. Logging, pulping and manufacturing
processes are expected to conform to the environmental regulations of the
country of origin.

A catalogue record for this book is available from the British Library.

A catalog record for this book is available from the Library of Congress.

10 9 8 7 6 5 4 3 2 1
18 17 16 15 14 13 12 11 10 09

Printed and bound by The Cromwell Press, Trowbridge, Wiltshire.

Contents

List of tables

List of boxes

Map of Europe

Introduction

1

This book is about global youth, but with a particular route map. We start in Eastern Europe, and then move into the rest of the world via the west. The actual start-point, of course, is a western (UK) sociologist's understanding of youth in Eastern Europe. Readers are invited to join in considering the condition of contemporary youth (some issues will be familiar if readers are youth researchers) from an unorthodox vantage point. English language books about global youth (or global anything) usually start in the west; the rest of the world is then subjected to explicit or implicit 'othering' – having its character defined from the perspective of another. Here the western gaze is filtered by focusing, initially, on youth in Eastern Europe.

That said, any westerner in Eastern Europe will inevitably look upon local youth through a western gaze. At first glance, especially if one's introduction to Eastern Europe is through universities, the young people will look familiar, and they have become more familiar during the last 20 years, since the end of communism. They are listening to familiar kinds of music, wearing familiar fashions and styling their hair in familiar ways. More and more of them are able to use English language. There have been some startling convergences. Russian girls have become slimmer, and this is not a result of food shortages. In Central Asia the young males and females have become more Eurasian in appearance. In the Caucasus formerly swarthy complexions have become lighter, especially girls' complexions. All this is alongside some striking contrasts. The university students in Eastern Europe look younger than their western counterparts. In fact they have tended to be younger. More of them have commenced university studies at 16 or 17 than has been normal in the west, and fewer have embarked on the old 5-year university diploma programmes at age 20 or above. Over the last 20 years it has become rarer for university entrants to be under 18, but they still look and appear to behave in more juvenile ways than western students. This is likely to be because they do not possess, and as younger teens have not possessed, the amounts of money that western youth spend on themselves. It is also relevant that in most East European countries university students still do not have the self-governing student unions that are an established part of western campus life. Nor do most young people in Eastern Europe gain any experience in genuine voluntary associations – sports and arts clubs, youth clubs etc. Yet in other respects Eastern Europe's young people grow up quickly. In many of the countries the most common ages of marriage throughout the 1990s and since have been 22–24, and parenthood has followed quickly. Mean ages of marriage and parenthood have risen, and those who do not marry in their early 20s are now more likely than in the past to delay until they are into their 30s, but early-20s remains a common age in much of Eastern Europe. Maybe there will be more east-west convergence during the 21st century, but who will change? Biologically, early 20s is more appropriate for becoming a parent for the first time than late 30s. It is probably peculiar western behaviour that needs to be 'othered' and given a specific socio-cultural explanation.

Eastern Europe is still much poorer than the west. All the countries of Eastern Europe are poorer than all the countries of Western Europe with one exception – Slovenia, a small country with a population of less than 2 million adjacent to Italy and Austria. Slovenia was the first region to break away from Yugoslavia, starting the process that sparked the Balkan wars of the 1990s. This has been another stark difference between the experiences of western and East European youth during the last 20 years. Western youth who have gained military experience have done so as volunteer soldiers, sailors and air force personnel. Some have fought in Afghanistan and Iraq, or have been part of peacekeeping missions in various parts of the world. Some young military personnel from NATO's new members in Eastern Europe have been part of these operations, not necessarily as volunteers. Young males are still eligible to be conscripted into military service throughout Eastern Europe (and usually try to avoid this). Many young males have fought in real wars in the Balkans and in the North and South Caucasus. During the 1990s many young males in Eastern Europe were in serious harm's way. Some were seriously wounded. Young women were widowed and their children became fatherless.

However, the most obvious east-west difference is that the East European countries remain relatively poor. Workers earn far less than in Western Europe. Young people have less to spend than their western counterparts, and they are *not* catching up. The global market economy will develop hotspots in Eastern Europe – mainly capital cities and places close to the borders of western countries. The chances are that most of Eastern Europe will be systematically under-developed by the global market economy, the fate of the third world. Since the early 1990s many East Europeans have feared that their world region could become another Latin America – a source of raw materials (like oil and gas) and cheap manufactured products for first world consumers.

However, it is not only or even mainly their lower living standards, lower disposable incomes, that separate youth in Eastern Europe and the west. The housing regimes are responsible for possibly greater differences. In Eastern Europe the rapid privatisation of the residential stock to occupiers in the 1990s is perpetuating young people's dependence on family resources to make life stage transitions into their own dwellings. Waiting to inherit an elder's property is a pre-modern practice that was consolidated under communism and is surviving under post-communism. It remains normal throughout Eastern Europe for the younger generation's transitions to head of household status to be delayed until after marriage and parenthood. This makes a huge difference. Young people in most western countries experience a period of life prior to marriage when they are free from daily parental surveillance and the accompanying control. Among other things, the East European way tends to perpetuate traditional gender divisions. Young males do not learn to care for themselves while young females share the housework with mothers and sisters. It also makes a difference that the standard residences built under communism were squalid 2 and 3 room apartments – the housing stock that the people will live in for years to come.

An aim of this book is definitely not to portray East European youth as thoroughly backward, perpetually trying to catch up with the west, though this is how many of the differences will appear to the western gaze. East Europeans are not in awe of all aspects of western ways – the amounts of money that young people spend on clothing, alcohol and drugs, and their willingness to leave elders to care for themselves. Also, there are senses in which East European youth have become hyper-modern world leaders – the latest examples of late-development effects in which the last countries to arrive leap to the head of the international procession (see Dore, 1973, 1976). The ex-communist countries have become part of the global market economy, and have established multi-party political systems, in late-20th and early-21st century conditions, most institutional baggage having been discarded. There are three important ways in which East European youth have become more advanced than their western counterparts. First, in many East European countries, rates of participation in higher education have rocketed. Old universities have expanded and new universities, including many private universities, have been created. All universities have sought to increase their budgets by admitting more fee-paying students. Alternatives for young people in Eastern Europe – jobs and vocational courses – have been dwindling. In this context, in some countries, progression from school to university has become the normal way forward. Second, on leaving full-time education many young people in Eastern Europe (generally far more than in the west) are experiencing prolonged periods of under-employment (this is defined properly below). Under-employment is now a global phenomenon in youth labour markets. In the west it is typically seen as a sign that young people need to catch up with the demands of the new knowledge economy. In Eastern Europe it is typically construed as a sign that the countries' transitions into properly functioning market economies are still incomplete. Not so: under-employment is the 21st century global normality for youth in the labour market. Third, East European youth have become leaders in their disengagement from public affairs preferring to seek private, personal solutions to their problems, whatever these problems might be.

Young people in Eastern Europe are also different – not lagging or more advanced than western youth but simply different – in experiencing their coming of age in distinctive cultural contexts. An important part of these contexts is that their countries were once communist. Today's young people have no personal experience of life under communism, but everywhere this is part of the collective memory which shapes how the present is experienced. Looking back historically, the populations in Eastern Europe are aware of what young people have lost since communism ended. The west needs to be reminded of this, especially since there is no longer a working alternative to the global, capitalist market economy. A plain fact is that communism was more generous and protective towards its young people than any western society. Nearly all young people in Eastern Europe have concluded that, even so, they prefer the present. They are progressives rather than reactionaries, but with a particular historical awareness. Western youth also have a specific historical awareness; this comes from growing up in countries with histories of being (or at least regarding themselves as) world leaders. This makes a difference to how the present is experienced, and to young people's future hopes and expectations.

There are many reasons why westerners, and not only social scientists, should be interested, maybe concerned, about trends in Eastern Europe, especially among the region's young people. Not the least of these reasons is that the west is going to be, and in fact is already

International Student

being, affected. While labour costs remain substantially lower, businesses will be tempted to direct new investment (and jobs) towards the EU's new member states. At the same time, young people from Eastern Europe will travel and compete for jobs in the west. Up to now young East Europeans with decent educational qualifications have been employed in the west doing seasonal jobs in agriculture, as low-grade hotel staff and suchlike. No one should imagine that this will continue. Students at West Europe's universities will be aware that thousands of students from Eastern Europe are now spending a semester at western institutions assisted by the EU ERASMUS programme. Their German, French or English language often reaches the standard of local students. They will be returning with degrees to compete for graduate jobs. They will be able to offer more than one language. They will have a wider knowledge of European markets and cultures than stay-at-home locals. If you are based in the west, make no mistake: what is happening in Eastern Europe, and how the region's young people are responding, is going to affect you.

Eastern Europe and the west

In this book Eastern Europe means the entire pre-1989 communist bloc. Europe in this book is not just the European Union (EU) countries – 15 up to 2004, then 25, and 27 in 2007, with the Balkan states of the former Yugoslavia, Turkey, Ukraine, Georgia and Albania somewhere in the queue for future membership. Europe, for this book's purposes, does not end at the Ural Mountains, partway across Russia, the geographical boundary that is sometimes used. Present-day Europe cannot be defined in terms of a particular religion – Christianity – and the associated culture. Nor can Europe be defined as sharing a common history – the history of Europe looks very different, and the key dates and events are different, depending on the particular country or group of countries.

The whole of Soviet space was Europeanised, lightly under the Czarist Empire, then much more thoroughly by communism which modernised agriculture everywhere on collective and state farms (except in Poland). Communism expanded the towns and cities, built factories and created modern industries, and introduced modern systems of public administration, health and education services. For this book's purposes there is simply no point in trying to work within a boundary between countries that are more or less likely, and those that look unlikely, to join the EU at some point in the future, or even according to their traditional, that is, pre-communist characteristics.

The East European countries (as defined here) shared a common experience of communism, and they have all experienced a similar post-communist transition. As explained below, there are differences among the ex-communist countries, but they share much in common simply by now being in a post-communist historical era.

'The west' in this book comprises western Europe and North America. Of course, there are differences among western countries including a great deal of American exceptionalism, and there are important differences in the character of the youth life stage between northern and southern pre-2004 EU member states. However, when set in a global context, the western countries are seen to share much in common. As noted above, standards of living were and still are much higher throughout the west than in any part of Eastern Europe except Slovenia. Capitalism and market economies, and multi-party political systems, have longer histories throughout the west than in Eastern Europe. Also, although there have been important changes in the economies, labour markets, education and much else in the western world since the mid-20th century – sufficient to inspire widespread talk and writing about 'youth's new social condition' – none of the countries has experienced as abrupt or as thorough a change as was experienced throughout Eastern Europe when communism ended.

Communism and post-communism

There were variants of communism. People in every East-Central and South-East European country, and in every former Soviet republic, will tell visitors what was distinctive about their experience of communism: most farms remaining privately-owned in Poland; the thwarted revolutions in Hungary in 1956 and in Czechoslovakia in 1968; the experiment with workers' self-management in Yugoslavia; or the industrialisation of parts of Central Asia during the Great Patriotic War (known as the Second World War in the west) when entire factories were transported lock, stock and barrel from the western parts of the Soviet Union that were at risk of, then subjected to, German occupation. Equally important, countries differ in how long they were communist – from 1917 in the case of Russia but only since 1945 in the case of the Baltic states and all the non-Soviet countries. They also differ in whether they had pre-communist histories of industrialism and multi-party democracy (histories which some have been able to recover and restart since 1989). However, over-arching all the variations, the entire communist bloc experienced the basic features of communism, namely:

- State ownership of virtually all economic assets.
- Central economic planning.
- Government by communist parties to which no organised opposition was permitted.

These were the system-defining features of communism which ended, vanished, immediately and abruptly, in 1989 in East-Central and South-East Europe, and in 1991 when the Soviet Union was dissolved.

Young people's treatment under communism was very distinctive. Their situations were 'constructed' in a standard way throughout the communist bloc. Modern youth was 'constructed' in all the countries that modernised during the 19th and 20th centuries (see Wallace and Kovacheva, 1998). 'Constructed' here means that special institutions were created for young people, together with special rules and roles that defined their proper places – in schools, training schemes, youth movements, and so on. Under communism the construction was firmer than in most other places. After or before age 16 young people were set on different educational tracks or programmes of training that led to particular kinds of employment where, in the normal course of events, they were expected to remain throughout their working lives. It was possible to break out, but it was always easiest to work with the grain.

Young people were also held in their 'proper places' by the inter-twining of family relationships and the control of housing that developed under communism. Some housing was privately owned (the proportions varied from country to country, and in the countryside private ownership was more common than in urban areas). However, there was no 'market' in dwellings. There was no way in which people could (legally) save the money that house purchase would require. There were no banks offering long-term loans for house purchase. Dwellings were sometimes exchanged, but this was most likely to happen within extended families when, for example, a widow might exchange a larger apartment for the smaller flat occupied by younger members of the family and their own children. It was possible informally to rent a room or rooms in a private dwelling, but there were no private landlords who built or otherwise accumulated properties for rent. In order to obtain their own places young people (usually couples) relied on family support. The custom and practice in most places was that the son's family was responsible for accommodating a marrying couple. Dwellings could be obtained from the socially owned stock by placing an individual's name or a couple's names on a waiting list, where the names would usually remain for years during which someone would have to pay for this privilege. Alternatively, young people could wait until a family property was vacated (usually by the death of the occupant). By then a younger individual or couple would most likely have moved in, thereby establishing their right to inherit the tenancy. Young people's housing prospects depended on maintaining strong family relationships. Separation (social separation rather than locational) from one's family was a grave disadvantage.

Young people's leisure was equally regulated. There were no commercial provisions, and there were no voluntary organisations that operated independently of the state and communist party. Opportunities to play sports, to watch films, to take part in and to watch concerts and other theatre performances, and to travel away on holiday, were under the auspices of local governments and especially the communist party youth organisations – the Pioneers for 9–16s, and the Komsomol for 16–28 year olds. These youth organisations were present in all schools and higher education institutions, and in work-places. Leisure time could be (and was) spent privately, with friends and in families. Private life was valued under communism. Its value was accentuated by the absence of voluntary associations and other features of a civil society. It was only in private (if there) that people felt able to talk and act freely. However, in the public sphere young people's leisure opportunities were very firmly constructed by the state and party. In all the above ways, under communism young people's situations were firmly and distinctively constructed.

Then, as soon as communism ended, there was a rapid process of deconstruction. The communist youth organisations simply disappeared. School attire changed from uniforms to free dressing. The new market economies began offering a wide array of goods and services, for those who could pay. Consumer cultures spread more rapidly than the money to allow people to become active consumers. Citizens gained the right to form voluntary associations to promote sports, art forms, religious causes and political programmes. However, Eastern Europe soon learnt, and has shown the world, that it takes time for strong voluntary organisations with deep and wide grassroots to develop, especially under 21st century conditions. Housing was privatised rapidly in most places. Public authorities wanted to privatise the costs of and responsibility for maintenance. Waiting lists for dwellings shortened – in most places there was no longer any point in joining one. In exchange, there were new opportunities to rent and purchase privately, but once again this depended on would-be purchasers having the money. Former links between education and employment snapped. Responsibility for finding a job (and for hiring labour) was privatised. The security with which the old system had embraced young people was replaced by the liberty, and the responsibility, of preparing then marketing 'the self' to employers who, in turn, had to learn how to behave in genuine labour markets, and also how to operate in the markets through which they needed to procure supplies and sell their goods or services.

All the above were common experiences during the immediate transition from communism. It soon became clear that it was far easier to dismantle old institutions than to create new ones. Laws can be changed in months. Building new institutions usually takes years. Cultural change – aligning people's expectations and dispositions with new institutions – is most likely to take decades. As they approach or enter their third decade of post-communism, most of the countries continue to regard themselves as in transition.

Youth's new condition in Eastern Europe

There were variants of communism, but under post-communism the countries have become much more dissimilar from one another. The old Soviet republics have become new independent states. The countries of East-Central Europe have looked west (to the European Union and NATO), and no longer appear even to care what Moscow thinks. National cultures and identities have strengthened everywhere. The national language has always become the normal language of education and of all official (state) business (controversial matters in countries such as Ukraine and Kazakhstan, which have substantial ethnic Russian minorities, especially since Russian was formerly the international language, and taught in all schools throughout the communist bloc). School syllabuses have been changed to foreground national literatures and histories. The countries differ in how far they have reformed, that is, in the extent to which state ownership and control of the economies have been relinquished, and whether political parties and presidential candidates compete for power on equal terms. The countries also differ in the severity of the shock that was experienced when dismantling communism, and the extent to which their economies have subsequently recovered. Generally, it has proved to be an advantage to be a small country adjacent to the old (pre-2004) EU. Slovenia, with less than 2 million people, and bordering Italy and Austria, has been an outstanding success story. It has also been an advantage (up to now) for a country to be well endowed with natural resources (such as oil and gas) that are in heavy demand on world markets. The Soviet Union disintegrated at a time when new, vast reserves of oil and gas were being discovered within its territory. Until 1991 these reserves, when exploited, were assets that could have benefited all Soviet citizens. In the event the reserves are benefiting the ex-Soviet republics where they happen to be located (mainly Azerbaijan, Kazakhstan, Russia and Turkmenistan). There were inter-country differences in living standards under communism but these differences now look tiny. Throughout the communist bloc there was a single communist way of life. Similar flats were built everywhere. Consumer goods were always scarce. There was full employment, and full salaries were paid regularly. By 2005 the average income in Kazakhstan (which has large oil and gas reserves) was roughly four times as high as in neighbouring Uzbekistan. Czechs have become richer than Slovaks. Hungarians have become richer than Romanians. Hence the debate that has arisen about whether post-communism has become a redundant concept.

The justification for continuing to use the term is that there have been commonalities in the countries' experiences of the transition, including how their young people have fared and how they have responded, and nowadays there is considerable overlap between the conditions and responses to these conditions of young people in Eastern Europe and in the west. In terms of many of these conditions and responses it is young people in Eastern Europe, not western youth, who are now the more advanced. Their late arrival in the capitalist, global market place has allowed the new market economies to become hyper-modern in many respects.

(i) *Young people have been prolonging their education.* As mentioned earlier, enrolments in higher education have risen sharply in most of the countries. Also, it is usually general education rather than vocationally specific courses in which the 16-plus age group now enrols.

(ii) *A period of under-employment has become normal after leaving full-time education.* The symptoms of under-employment are high rates of youth unemployment; high proportions of employment in part-time, temporary and otherwise marginal jobs; and over-qualification relative to the jobs that young people obtain. All these symptoms are evident nowadays in most parts of the world. In the west they are often viewed as indicating weakness, backwardness, in the economies. Not so; the symptoms are products of normal 21st century global market conditions and these conditions are currently more pronounced in Eastern Europe than in the west.

(iii) *The normalisation of a life stage variously labelled post-adolescence, post-youth, or (currently popular) emergent adulthood* (see Arnett, 2005, 2006). This life stage is marked most conspicuously by a lengthened period between completing full-time education on the one side, and, on the other, settling in an adult occupation with a salary that will support an adult lifestyle and marriage and parenthood. Young people have some control over this: some have decided to push full adulthood into their futures. This life stage now exists (and is normal) in most parts of Eastern Europe and in the west, but in the east it has some distinctive features.

- Levels of consumer spending are much lower than in the west.
- A common use of the life stage by East European youth is to travel, partly for the experience, but also to earn money in countries where pay levels are higher than at home. In the first instance most of this migration is the pendulum variety; those concerned intend to return home when they have earned enough to buy a flat, start a business or start a family, whatever their objectives.
- Most young people in the new east continue to depend on their families for housing. Their own life stage housing transitions are typically deferred up to or even beyond the beginning of full adulthood (if marriage and parenthood are treated as crucial markers). In this respect young people in Eastern Europe resemble their counterparts in the Mediterranean countries of the west rather than those in northern Europe and North America. We shall see in later chapters that there are additional senses in which the new east's integration into an enlarged Europe (as a political and economic entity) is more likely to mean Mediterraneanisation than convergence with patterns and standards of living in northern Europe. Young Bulgarians may regard Germany, France or the Scandinavian countries as exemplars, but the older EU country that they are most likely to resemble as a full member is their adjacent state, Greece.

(iv) Biographies have been individualised, self-awareness has been heightened, young people recognise that they need to be more active than their parents were and take charge of their own life courses. Research evidence shows that all groups of young people do this albeit within limits, within constraints that differ according to whether they are female or male, their educational achievements, their family backgrounds and other 'connections', and often most of all according to where they happen to live. However, while aware of differences, young people do not usually perceive these as divisions. They are less conscious of and responsive to constraints and opportunities that are shared with members of any social category than the scope that they as individuals possess to forge their own futures.

(v) Access to global consumer cultures. All over the world today young people listen to some similar kinds of music and some of the same performers, follow the same global top sports, and wear the same fashions. The global is always interwoven with local features thus producing myriad examples of 'glolocalisation'.

(vi) Post-communist generations of young people are mostly non-ideological. Few have become highly religious (see Need and Evans, 2001). Few are attracted by nationalist appeals. They tend to reject all total ideologies. Most are pragmatists who prioritise making the best of the world as they find it (Mitev, 2004).

Studying youth

This book examines youth in Eastern Europe, and makes cross-national comparisons, in particular sociological ways. These are not the only ways – they are not even the sole sociological ways – in which young people can be studied, but they have particular merits.

(i) Contextualising youth. First, this book sets young people in their social contexts. In a sense, the book decentres young people themselves. The initial focus is not upon young people's minds or the details of their own lives but on how their circumstances are socially structured by labour market contexts, the organisation of education, family patterns and practices, and consumer industries and marketing. The justification is that starting with the contexts (indicated by this book's chapter headings) enables us eventually to best understand young people's minds and lives.

(ii) Youth as a transitional life stage. In this book 'transition' has a dual meaning. It refers to the countries that have been regarded, and which have regarded themselves, as in historical transition since the end of communism. It also refers to the transitional character of the youth life stage, between childhood and adulthood. Youth is not defined as a particular age group. The chronological ages when youth begins and ends have varied greatly by time and place, and both the beginnings and the ends are 'fuzzy' in all modern societies. The virtue of a transitional view of youth is that it reflects the reality of young people's lives – forever changing. Cross-sectional snapshots inevitably distort reality. Understanding youth is always well-served through a longitudinal, biographical perspective.

(iii) Holism. This book's approach to youth is holistic: we examine all aspects of young people's lives. During the youth life stage, young people experience multiple transitions – from education to employment, in family relationships and housing, from having things bought for them to becoming independent consumers, from benefiting from much state welfare via their parents or guardians to becoming eligible for full welfare rights as full citizens, becoming subject to full adult justice, and becoming fully enfranchised political actors (if they wish). The justification for viewing young people's lives 'in the round' is that their experiences in different domains are interconnected. What is happening in any part of young people's lives becomes easier to understand when experiences elsewhere are brought into view. Influence runs in all directions, but the order of chapters in this book indicates which domains are considered particularly important. Education to work, and family and housing life stage transitions, do not directly determine what happens to young people in other parts of their lives, but these are crucial contexts in which other things are experienced and within which other life stage transitions are made. Furthermore, it is during young people's education to work and family/housing transitions that social class and gender differences widen and harden, usually with long-term consequences.

(iv) Social divisions. Finally, throughout the book we pay attention to differences among young people. The concept of social class summarises a number of these differences. Then there are gender and ethnic divisions, and differences by place. Class, gender and place have basically the same meanings and significance in Eastern Europe and the west, and indeed throughout the rest of the world. Ethnicity is rather different. The main ethnic relations in Eastern Europe are not between white hosts and people of colour from former colonies. This is just one variant of ethnic relations. A global perspective demonstrates the need to treat all ethnic relations with full regard for their specificities. Many young people from Eastern Europe have become migrants in other East European countries and in Western Europe. Throughout the former Soviet Union new ethnic minorities have been created, including Russian minorities in all the ex-Soviet republics except Russia itself. New titular ethnic nationalities and minorities have been created in the 15 new independent states of the former USSR. Georgians, Uzbeks, etc. who continue to work and live in Russia have become foreigners. There are ethnic divisions everywhere, and their significance always lies in the specificities.

Issues in youth studies

This book engages with, or presents evidence that is relevant to, a series of live issues in youth studies, but without attempting to settle any of the debates or even, in some cases, adopting a definite position.

(i) Globalisation. There is now general agreement among social scientists in all disciplines that:

- During the closing decades of the 20th century globalisation intensified due to developments in electronic communications, the globalisation of the market economy following the collapse of communism, the rise of trans-national businesses and financial institutions, and the creation or enlarged role of international organisations such as the World Trade Organisation, The World Bank, the International Monetary Fund, the European Union, NATO, etc.
- Increased inter-dependence does not necessarily lead to homogenisation – everywhere becoming more similar. Youth researchers seem agreed on this: the outcome of globalisation is a variety of examples of glolocalisation – mixtures of the global and the local (see Nilan and Feixa, 2006).

The issue then becomes: exactly what are the global similarities and what are the differences as regards the situations, outlooks and behaviour of young people? The material in this book is relevant, but inevitably inconclusive.

(ii) Structure and agency. This is a long-running debate among youth researchers. The arguments are about the relative importance of:

- Structure, young people's situations, in determining their experiences and life courses.
- Agency, that is, individuals' ability to reflect upon their circumstances, to appraise their own capabilities and inclinations, and then to act purposively and take charge of their own biographies.

There is now agreement that this is not an either/or issue and, indeed, that structure and agency are always implicated in one another. The current argument is about whether late-20th century developments (post-industrialism and associated trends in the west) have amplified the role of agency at the expense of structure, as suggested by Beck (1992) and vigorously contested by Furlong and

Cartmel (2007). As regards the effects of the post-communist transition in Eastern Europe, this book echoes Furlong and Cartmel's position.

(iii) Unitary or divided life stage? Once again, there is broad agreement among youth researchers that in most countries all over the world new life space has been created between young people completing full-time education on the one side, and entering full adulthood on the other indicated by the character of their jobs, marriage and parenthood. The issue is whether this requires us to recognise a new post-adolescent, post-youth life stage, termed 'emerging adulthood' by Arnett (2005, 2006). This book's position in respect of Eastern Europe is that the balance of advantage lies in retaining a unitary view of youth.

(iv) The scarred cohorts hypothesis. The argument here is that the labour market conditions awaiting young people in recent times are leaving them scarred for life. Charvel (2006), using data from France, argues that the baby boomers (the products of the high birth rates that followed the Second World War) were a lucky generation. They experienced childhood and youth supported by strong welfare states, entered full employment labour markets in which middle class jobs were increasing rapidly, and when the gap between youth and adult earnings was narrowing. In contrast, school and college leavers since the 1970s in most western countries (and in East European countries since the 1980s) have experienced weaker welfare states, have entered labour markets with higher rates of unemployment, and in some places have faced a slowdown in the pace of increase in middle class jobs and a widening gap between youth and adult earnings. In real terms (after taking inflation into account), Charvel shows that in France recent cohorts of school-leavers have earned no more than their parents did when they were young. Charvel also shows that in France, up to now, the occupational positions and earnings that individuals have achieved by age 30 have had long-term implications for their lifetime career prospects. Hence the argument that recent and current cohorts of young people are likely to remain scarred for life.

This argument can be nuanced. There have been differences between countries and between regions within countries. In Eastern Europe young people who tried to start their working lives in the early 1990s were confronted by economies and labour markets that were sinking into deep recession. On the other hand, especially when the economies started to recover, there were opportunities to enter virgin space – to set up businesses in markets where there were no established competitors, and to take jobs in new private sector businesses, including international businesses that were investing in the new market economies. More recent cohorts of school-leavers have entered labour markets where labour demand is stronger, but have been confronted by in-post managers and professionals, and proprietors of small businesses, little older then themselves (Marada, 2004).

There are two criticisms of the scarring hypothesis. One is that we simply cannot know, because what happens to recent cohorts of school-leavers in the future is bound to depend partly on what happens in the relevant labour markets. Most children of the Great Depression in the USA were saved from scarring by the Second World War and the full employment conditions that were established and maintained afterwards (see Elder, 1974).

The second and most basic criticism of the scarring thesis is that it misleadingly treats the experiences of the baby boomers as normative (the benchmark of how things ought to be). This book agrees with Wyn and Woodman (2006) who argue that current cohorts of young people treat current conditions as normal, and that viewing their transitions as flawed is an adult perspective that has inappropriately been incorporated into a great deal of youth research. Wyn and Woodman argue that young people today do not expect jobs for life: in fact they accept that it can be difficult to obtain any decent job. On the other hand, they have new options. For example, in the west heterosexual marriage is no longer regarded as an inevitable destiny. Wyn and Woodman urge youth researchers to stop bemoaning how things have changed and recognise that today's young people are devising new ways of working, living, and balancing work and the rest of their lives in ways suited to 21st century contexts. The details are certainly different, but the evidence in later chapters shows that Wyn and Woodman's basic points apply equally in Eastern Europe.

(v) New political generations? Can the 'changed expectations' position be broadened to argue that new political generations are being formed, maybe a single global generation whose concerns and priorities reflect global current youth issues such as under-employment, and 21st century issues such as climate change and international terrorism?

'Political generation' is a concept first used by Karl Mannheim (1952). These generations are formed among the first cohorts to experience historically new conditions; who form new outlooks on life that set them apart from and often in opposition to older generations; who bring new issues onto political agendas; and who form new political movements or transform old ones and thereby transform their countries. The new political generations that were formed in Europe following the First World War were responsible for the rise of the communist and fascist movements of that era. After the Second World War a new post-scarcity generation came into existence in the west. In Eastern Europe new political generations were formed under communism. In the countries into which communism was spread after the Second World War, one generation faction became enthusiasts in building communism. Another faction became dissidents (overt or covert) who eventually challenged and overthrew communism in the 1980s. The post-communist cohorts of young people in Eastern Europe are definitely a wholly new political generation (as the following chapters will show). The position of their western counterparts is less clear-cut.

Book plan and sources of evidence

The order of topics in the following chapters is dictated by which needs to follow which in order to maximise comprehension. Hence, labour markets, education, and family and housing transitions precede the chapters on young people's leisure and political orientations and involvements. There are two chapters which review and anticipate what is to follow. Chapter 4 is about the structure-agency debate. Chapter 7 draws on material in the preceding chapters to identify emergent class divisions among young people in Eastern Europe. This is followed by the chapter on youth and politics. The organisation within the chapters on the various aspects of young people's lives is usually to start in Eastern Europe under communism, then to show how things have changed under post–communism, and then introduce comparisons with youth in the west and the rest of the world. This running order changes only in Chapter 5 on family and housing transitions where the narrative flows most easily by putting the west first.

Labour markets are dealt with first of all in the next chapter. This is despite education coming first in children's and young people's biographies. The justification for promoting labour markets is that changes in education are more often responses to trends in economies and labour markets than vice-versa.

This book is not a monograph which reports the findings from a specific research project or group of projects. The evidence is from a very large number of sources and authors, some based in Eastern Europe and others in the west. However, the book draws liberally from a series of investigations in which the author of this book was involved from the beginning of the 1990s and over the following 20 years. The projects in total have gathered evidence from and about young people in a total of 12 different former communist countries.

These are scattered between Central Europe (Poland, Hungary and Slovakia), south-east Europe (Bulgaria), Russia (specifically Moscow and Vladikavkaz), Donetsk, Dneipropetrovsk and Lviv (all Ukraine), the three South Caucasus countries (Armenia, Azerbaijan and Georgia), and three Central Asia states (Kazakhstan, Kyrgyzstan and Uzbekistan). In some of these places there have been successive projects. All told, these projects make it possible to identify what has been common and what has been different in young people's experiences in different places since the end of communism. We shall see that young people's experiences have been sufficiently similar to vindicate the use of Eastern Europe as a category. The evidence from the successive projects also makes it possible to assess how young people's situations, experiences and responses have changed, and how they have remained constant since the early 1990s.

All the projects gathered evidence from young adults aged 20-something and up to age 30. They all collected combinations of quantitative and qualitative evidence. Both feature in the following chapters. The two kinds of evidence are essentially complementary. Most of the qualitative evidence is from narrative interviews in which young people have described their life stories, which in all cases were shaped, to some extent, by a particular stage in their countries' historical transformations. The quantitative data enable us to see exactly which and how many young people shared particular kinds of life stories. Details of exactly when and where all the material was obtained are given as the evidence features in the following chapters.

Labour Markets

Introduction

Communism was more successful than any capitalist economy has ever been in achieving then maintaining full employment. This was among communism's 'selling points': it removed from workers the insecurity of labour markets. Officially there was no unemployment under communism but in practice there was always some unemployment. There were individuals (including school-leavers) who stayed out of work temporarily in preference to starting in the particular jobs that they were being offered. There were times and places when the local employers could not accommodate all job seekers, but such imbalances were not allowed to persist. Communist planning aimed to match labour supply to jobs. Jobs could be created (even if this meant over-staffing) so that no-one needed to remain idle. Plant managers were usually willing to cooperate. It was in their interests to hoard labour (and stocks of other materials also), 'just in case'. The costs would be covered by 'the plan', and the managers would have the resources at hand if the planners' targets for their organisations were raised.

The next chapter explains how communist education was also planned, and one of the aims was to deliver young people whose education and training matched the requirements of industrial plants, mines, etc., and the state bureaucracies. Young people were able to move smoothly from education into working life, and the 'work collectives' that they joined could become their lifetime places of work and much more besides. It was normally through their jobs that workers gained entitlements to health care, vacations and other leisure facilities, maternity leave, pensions, and sometimes housing also. Workers were not legally tied to their jobs, and school-leavers, in most cases, could arrange employment informally if they wished.

Otherwise they could simply comply with the system's plans for them. Young people who were approaching the end of their education in 1989 or 1991 (when communism ended outside then in the Soviet Union) had jobs and futures mapped before them, and the jobs offered the salaries and benefits in kind that would support the 'way of life' that was normal, under communism, for people such as themselves. These futures evaporated the moment that communism ended.

This chapter proceeds by describing what followed the end of communism. In most of the countries this was shock therapy market reforms, and in most places the results were devastating. We then see how a period of under-employment became, and has remained, normal following young people's entry to post-communist labour markets. A response of some young people has been to migrate, and some of these have joined the workforces in western countries. However, some of those who have stayed at home – always small proportions of all young people – have succeeded in the new market economies either by creating their own businesses or by obtaining employment with salaries that will support western-type lifestyles.

Shock therapy

The labour markets that confront school-leavers in Eastern Europe today are outcomes of the manner in which the countries introduced market reforms. The end of communism unleashed tremors through-out the economies of all the countries that made this break with their recent histories. The first tremors were the result of withdrawing from the system of central economic planning that linked plants throughout the entire Soviet bloc or, in the case of the break-up of the USSR in 1991, the demise of central planning itself (Gros, 1997). Plants lost various combinations of their supplies and customers. Establishments folded or found their throughput and cash incomes shrinking. There were domino-type repercussions. The national economies stuttered. Workers were rarely laid off immediately. They were more likely to be given 'gardening leave' or left hanging around in workless factories. Even when there was work to do plants did not always have the cash to pay salaries, which therefore fell into arrears. Shortages of currency sometimes led to inter-plant debts and salaries being paid in goods, which could then be sold or bartered (see Duffy, 2005). How plants fared depended partly on whether their managers had the flare to be re-born as successful entrepreneurs. Local and regional governments were sometimes the entrepreneurs who saved local enterprises (Michailova and Mills, 1998). As overall output and earnings fell, governments' incomes shrivelled. An outcome was that public sector salaries shrank and/or went into arrears. Wholesale economic melt-down could be avoided only by the governments printing money which led to bouts of hyper-inflation which eliminated people's savings unless these were held in hard currency, typically 'under the bed' because at that time few ordinary citizens had hard currency bank accounts.

The west (represented mainly by the World Bank and the International Monetary Fund) offered assistance but with strings attached. During the collapse of communism a 'Washington Consensus' was established whose prescription for the transition countries' difficulties was shock therapy (as it became known). The prescription was for 'big bang' rapid transitions to be triggered by price liberalisation, the end of state subsidies to loss-making plants, rapid privatisation, and governments balancing their own books. It was recognised that, in the very short term, these measures would intensify the pain of transition, but the pain itself was supposed to stimulate therapeutic market forces. People were to be forced to become entrepreneurial. They would have no alternative. Thus private enterprise and market forces would revive the economies, and levels of output and households' living standards would soon surpass anything achieved under communism. This was the theory which was endorsed by radical 'monetarist' and 'neo-liberal' western economists. They would never have been allowed to experiment in their own countries but Eastern Europe was different. In the event, the theories proved part right. There was plenty of shock. Unfortunately, the theories proved part wrong: the therapy was slow (if ever) to materialise (Gerber and Hout, 1998).

There was an ulterior motive in the west's advocacy of shock therapy. This was to destroy the old system rapidly, beyond repair. This worked. Thus the Cold War came to an abrupt end, the west reaped a peace dividend and world power became uni-polar. Capitalism and the market were globalised. Henceforth there was no (full employment) working alternative. As the old system collapsed, groups with vested interests based in that system fell apart – politicians, public officials, and the intelligentsia. Organised opposition to 'the reforms' evaporated. Communists who wanted to remain in politics transformed themselves into ex-communists (social democrats, in practice, in most cases). It was believed that stabilising the reforms depended on creating groups who would be staunch supporters: a new capitalist class and a new middle class. Here there was a serious problem: the countries were to become capitalist but no-one in the countries owned substantial capital. This situation had to be remedied. The only solution (apart from selling the countries' assets to foreigners which could have created opposition to the reforms) was to virtually give away assets in 'honest robbery' privatisations. Thus the 'new rich', new classes of so-called oligarchs, had been brought into existence by the mid-1990s (see Hoffman, 2002). Simultaneously, in ways that are described below, new middle classes of private sector managers, the self-employed, proprietors of small businesses, new professionals and new state bureaucrats were created.

It must be said that the first governments to be voted into power in the former communist countries did not resist shock therapy. They were typically enthusiastic. They were anti-communists (albeit some-times very recent converts) who wanted the old system gone for good. They were attracted by neo-liberal economic theory. Markets were believed to be good. As for government, the less the better. Their polit-ical heroes were Ronald Reagan and Margaret Thatcher, both vocal Cold War warriors in the 1980s who had been strident in their denun-ciations of the 'evil empire' of communism, and in their advocacy of private enterprise.

Some countries did not accept shock therapy. The arch-refuseniks, still unreformed in western eyes in the 21st century, have been Belarus, Turkmenistan and Uzbekistan. Other countries that initially opted for or stumbled into shock therapy have subsequently pulled back. Russia under Putin re-asserted state control over basic, strategic industries such as oil and gas. In Russia, and in all five Central Asian 'stans', presidential power has been consolidated and political opposition stifled. The countries that have pressed ahead with 'reform' despite the pain (elaborated below) have been tempted by glittering rewards – full membership of the European Union, NATO and other interna-tional (western) institutions. These prizes have not been on offer to Russia or the Central Asian republics. Belarus has declined all offers. The South Caucasian countries (Armenia, Azerbaijan, Georgia), and Moldova and Ukraine have all been given signals that the prizes could be available for them. In all these countries, key public issues/political questions have included, and still are: whether the prizes really will be delivered; whether the prizes will be worth having; and whether there is a more attractive alternative which would probably be an economic/security zone with Russia at its core.

Where the medicine was applied, the immediate effects of shock therapy were usually devastating. Up to 50% was ripped from output and people's living standards. The impact was comparable to a major war. Unemployment rose steeply, though official unemployment often remained extremely low. At this point it is necessary to issue a hazard warning. All official statistics, in all countries, are imperfect measures, and up to and including the present day, official statistics in the new market economies have needed to be treated with wide allowances for error. Much unemployment is unregistered (the reasons are explained below). All the new market economies have shadow economies of unknown size but with most estimates in the range of 20% to 40%. Small and large businesses conduct part of their operations 'in the shade'. Ordinary workers and the unemployed do odd jobs for cash. Public officials collect unofficial payments (gifts or bribes). However, in the early 1990s nearly every household experienced a serious shrinkage in its income, and people got by as best they could. The value of state welfare payments shrank. Pensioners were made destitute or forced to depend on their children, which they usually found degrading. Older workers had their careers terminated prematurely. The system in which some citizens had earned status (star athletes included) collapsed, and so did their status. Those whose life's work had contributed to building communism experienced the denigration of all their efforts (see Box 2.1).

Some young adults (like Ludmila's children, see Box 2.1) found themselves in a moral dilemma. They wanted to live their own lives but they knew that if they left home their parents would be destitute. There was intense and widespread anger. However, as explained in the previous chapter, small countries situated on the EU's borders

---

Box 2.1

Older lives in transition

Ludmila was born in 1944 in Belarus. Shortly afterwards her father, who had been injured in the war, was moved to Lviv (in west Ukraine), where Ludmila then spent all her life (and where she was interviewed in 1999). She had been a volleyball player for the Ukraine national team, and a sports/physical education teacher at the local university. Her husband had also been an athlete – a member of the national army basketball team. Because of their sporting success Ludmila and her husband had qualified for a flat early in their married life, and later they were able to move into a larger three room flat. Ludmila believed that the old system had given her family a good life and regretted the changes since 1991. *'When we were young we could buy fridges, TVs etc. Now it's almost impossible for our children and we, the older generation, can't help them. We have very little money.'* Ludmila had retired at the normal age for women in Ukraine, 55, and her pension had shrunk to just $13 a month. *'The system has changed. We couldn't avoid it because the Soviet Union collapsed. Life is not good. In fact it's painful* (begins to cry). *Our governments have never cared about the people. Child benefit payments are ridiculous – trivial. I'm very worried about what will happen to the children. The government care only about their own pockets. They're all corrupt. We vote, and we hope that they'll do what they promise, but once they're elected they act just like all politicians.'*

suffered less seriously (if at all) than others, and anger was never mobilised into effective opposition to the reforms (except possibly in Russia in 1996 when it was only during the presidential election campaign that Yeltsin, with cash from Russia's new super-rich and western advice on electioneering, overturned what had been a massive communist lead in opinion polls).

Since the mid-1990s all the transition economies have recovered, to varying extents. Some have recorded economic growth rates year-on-successive-year of around 10%. In 2005 Azerbaijan's economy grew by a massive 40% (thanks to oil and gas exports). By the turn of the millennium GDP in some of the transition countries was recovering to or even surpassing its levels in the 1980s. Some of this growth could be illusory – a product of economic activity switching from the unofficial into the official economies, or an appearance created by the devaluation of the USA $ in the early 21st century. Equally to the point, while the pain of reform was widespread, the benefits have been concentrated. Income inequalities have widened everywhere (Domanski, 2000). Most people, in most of the transition countries, are still no better off than in the 1980s. Improvement is most visible in country capitals and other major cities. In stark contrast, there are many towns whose only major employers closed at the beginning of the 1990s and where the economies have still not restarted (see Tarkhnishvili *et al.*, 2005). There has been a debate within the transition countries on whether the cohorts who were completing their education in 1989 and the early 1990s, or those who followed, have been the more advantaged/disadvantaged (see Marada, 2004). On the one hand, those who entered the labour market during or soon after 1989 faced no established competitors in small businesses, or in private sector management, or in post in the international organisations that quickly established themselves in Eastern Europe. On the other hand, in most places the economies have been stronger since 1995 than during the previous 5 years. The juries are still out on exactly which of the younger age cohorts have fared best and worst, but there is general agreement that the big losers have been people in late-career or retired in 1989 who lost their positions (or saw their state benefits devalued) and have had no opportunity to recover.

Youth under-employment

Social scientists and other commentators in western countries have coined various terms to describe what is happening in a new life space between completion of compulsory education and settling in an adult occupation. Germans have spoken of a 'moratorium' in which social expectations are placed on hold, when young people are allowed to experiment, to take stock of themselves, and change course if they wish (Zinneker, 1990). Americans have written about beginning workers 'floundering', moving between a series of jobs, though it is likely that, rather than standing still, the young people move into progressively better jobs, and enlarge their skills and experience (Bills, 2004). Recently American social scientists have identified an 'emergent adulthood' life stage created by young people pausing their development in order to enjoy a prolonged youth (Arnett, 2005, 2006). In the UK some of the young people concerned are portrayed more negatively in official discourses; they are the NEET group (not in employment, education or training) who need to be pulled up, given a helping hand and set on progressive career tracks. Eastern Europe has not yet coined anything more original than unemployment.

I propose 'under-employment', a condition that has been normalised (come to be regarded as normal by all those concerned) throughout the new market economies, and which seems preferable to, in being more comprehensive than, the alternative labels that are in use in various parts of the world. Youth under-employment has the following defining characteristics:

- High rates of unemployment (sometimes, but not usually, long-term).
- Employment in less than permanent, regular (official), full-time, fully-paid jobs. What remains? Jobs that are temporary, part-time, casual and low-paid.
- Employment in jobs that fall well short of young people's qualifications and ambitions.

Under-employment has become a common, indeed normal, condition of youth in the labour markets throughout Eastern Europe. It is not confined to particularly depressed regions or particularly disadvantaged young people. In Moscow in 1999 around 30% of 25–26 year olds were either unemployed, in part-time jobs, or were working no more than 20 hours per week in nominally full-time jobs and/or were earning no more than $50 per month (Roberts *et al.*, 2002). The proportions who are under-employed vary from place to place and are highest where the economies are most depressed, but even where the labour markets are expanding and where there is otherwise full employment (as conventionally measured), large numbers of out-of-school youth are under-employed. In Eastern Europe these young people's labour market problems are invariably attributed to 'the transition' being incomplete – to the market economies still needing to expand to absorb all the labour that was shaken out from the old public sectors. However, the global evidence suggests that this is wrong. The evidence indicates that youth under-employment is a normal product of the operation of global markets in 21st century conditions, and this is most easily recognised in the newest (hyper-modern) market economies.

The International Labour Office (2002) has drawn attention to the fact that nowadays youth unemployment is a global problem, and that all over the world an increasing proportion of the jobs that young people obtain are low-skilled, part-time, and non-permanent. In 2006 the International Labour Office estimated that globally the unem-ployed, discouraged workers (sheltering from the labour market by remaining in education), and the working poor amounted to 35 percent of the total youth population: *'today's youth are faced with a growing deficit of decent work opportunities and high levels of economic and social uncertainty'* (International Labour Office, 2006, p. 1). In 2007 the United Nations reported that across all the ex-communist transition countries around a third of out-of-school youth were unemployed (and more would have been under-employed). In Japan, a glittering economic success story in the 1970s and 80s, youth unemployment has risen, and the support formerly offered by schools and families has become less reliable (Inui, 2003; Nagasawa, 2004). Bae (2006) reports rising levels of youth unemployment and part-time jobs in South Korea. In the Netherlands non-standard youth jobs have been replacing standard (full-time, permanent) employment (de Vries and Wolbers, 2005). In Spain nowadays three-quarters of the jobs held by 16–25 year olds are insecure (Ivacovou and Berthoud, 2001). In Sweden, once renowned for its commitment to full employment and strong social protection, by 2005 the youth unemployment rate exceeded 20% and 50% of the jobs held by young people were temporary positions (Quintini and Martin, 2006). In Britain, since the 1960s, despite young people becoming much better qualified, beginning workers have faced greater uncertainty and have been experiencing more frequent changes of status (between jobs, and from unemployment to jobs, then sometimes back to unemploy-ment, for example) (Pollock, 1997). Nowadays most of the jobs held by Britain's out-of-school 16 and 17 year olds are low skilled and low paid (Hayward *et al.*, 2005).

Louis Charvel (2006) has systematically charted the deterioration in young people's position in France's labour markets. The baby boomers (born during the two decades following the Second World War) entered the workforce when unemployment was low and during a period when middle class employment was expanding. As a result, they derived good returns from their educational qualifications, and youth wages converged with adult pay. Cohorts entering France's youth labour markets since the 1970s have faced higher levels of unemployment, the earlier expansion of higher-level jobs has slowed, and youth wages in France have stagnated. In 1977 the earnings gap between 30–35 and 50–55 year olds was just 15%; by the early 21st century it had widened to 40%. Chauvel predicts that recent cohorts of school leavers will experience long-term 'scarring' from their inability to establish themselves in decently paid jobs during young adulthood.

What kinds of jobs are entered by under-employed youth in Eastern Europe? There are two broad types. First, there are 'bitty jobs' created by *de novo* private businesses. The private sectors in the new market economies have so far proved far more energetic in opening bars, restaurants and shops than in taking-over and expanding employment in coal mines and steel mills. Most of the new jobs are in consumer services ('McJobs', as they have been described in the west). These jobs are often part-time, seasonal, otherwise temporary, often casual (shadow, off-the-record), and invariably low-paid. The jobs require no particular qualifications and can be done with minimal training. The young people who take these jobs are usually massively over-qualified. In Eastern Europe a second group of 'bitty jobs' is in the remaining public sectors or privatised companies which are still over-staffed, where lay-offs are always possible, where salaries are low, and sometimes in arrears. Few school and college leavers want to take such jobs. The prevalent view is that these kinds of employment have no future.

There are high levels of youth unemployment throughout Eastern Europe: the unemployed are the reserve army from which 'bitty jobs' can be filled. The numbers of young people registered as unemployed at state Labour Offices are usually low – sometimes extremely low. Young people do not bother to register for a combination of reasons:

- They will not be eligible for benefits.
- The benefits to which they are entitled are pathetically low.
- They know that the Labour Offices will have no jobs.
- They do not want to be pressured into 'bitty jobs' or, worse still, training schemes that amount to 'slave labour' and lead nowhere.
- They prefer not to expose themselves to situations in which their past or current unofficial earnings might be revealed.

Labour Force Surveys in all parts of present-day Europe usually record youth (16–25 year olds) unemployment rates of 20% or higher, but even these rates are under-estimates. In order to be counted as unemployed rather than economically inactive in these surveys one needs to be actively seeking work (which the unemployed may regard as pointless) and prepared to start more or less immediately if offered any job. There is endless scope for debating which groups of out-of-(official)-work youth are *really* unemployed. Research suggests that East Europe's young unemployed can be divided into six lifestyle groups (see Jung, 1997):

- *De facto* full-time housewives who are willing to accept, and who would ideally prefer to be in, jobs compatible with their domestic responsibilities (they would have occupied such jobs under communism).
- Active job-seekers, usually in the early stages of spells of unemployment, who make an occupation out of job hunting.
- Hobbyists, who have a pastime – maybe a sport or music making – that fills the slot in their lives that would be taken by paid work.
- Students who are taking part-time courses, engaging in qualification accumulation.
- Workers who have unofficial economy jobs, or who are working abroad intermittently.
- The long-term unemployed who are psychologically devastated and socially isolated, and appear destined for long-term welfare dependency. These are the most serious casualties of the new labour markets, but they amount to only a small minority of all the young people who experience unemployment.

Although East Europe's young unemployed are more likely than other young people to have elementary education only, and are less likely to have been through higher education, most of the young unemployed (just like most young people in general) are from 'intermediate' educational backgrounds. There is little difference between the 'specialties' – the vocationally relevant subjects (if any) – that unemployed and employed young people have studied. In terms of family backgrounds, although the unemployed are more likely than other young people to have parents whose jobs were unskilled, most of the unemployed, again just like most young people at large, have parents who are or were 'workers' in white-collar or blue-collar jobs (see Machacek and Roberts, 1997). Most of the young unemployed in Eastern Europe have some experience of employment in the new market economies, and have not been impressed. Box 2.2 presents two cases of unemployed young people who were interviewed in Plovdiv (Bulgaria) in 1996. Both had experience in employment, and both were under-employed rather than totally unemployed when interviewed.

Box 2.2
Youth under-employment

Jovko had held several jobs. He was aged 23 when interviewed, and was qualified in electrical engineering which he had studied at a professional secondary school. On graduating at age 17 Jovko had been unable to find a job so his parents had paid for him to take a 9 month course in radio and television work. This course had led to a job with a private radio station but Jovko had been laid off after just four weeks when the business shrank. His next job was selling audio-visual equipment in a shop which closed after three months. His subsequent job, installing and repairing electronic games machines, might have become more permanent but Jovko had been conscripted into the army. On completing military service Jovko had been employed by a company that installed cable television but left of his own accord after five months because the pay was irregular, and extremely low. When interviewed he had been registered unemployed for 18 months, ineligible for benefit because he had left his previous job voluntarily. He was not interested in another similar job because he was in fact earning money by repairing audio-visual equipment in people's homes. Jovko definitely wanted a proper job but saw little point in repeating his earlier experiences.

Paul, a registered unemployed 22 year old, also in Plovdiv, had graduated from a professional secondary school in 1994 having specialised in mechanical engineering. *'But there was no future in that field at the time. All the factories were closing.'* Paul had then spent one-and-a-half years doing army service. *'It was depressing. Conditions were difficult. I became ill in the army but no-one paid any attention. But a person gets used to it.'* On leaving the army Paul had registered as unemployed basically because he needed to be registered to qualify for free medical treatment for the illness that he had picked up while doing army service. *'But in practice it's impossible to obtain the free medicines. My medicines cost a dollar a day and I can't afford that so at the moment I'm doing without.'* On leaving the army Paul had applied to a university and had been accepted at a medical school. *'I was pleased about that. It was a very prestigious school but the university was in another town and I had to turn down the place because I wouldn't have been able to afford the living costs. I didn't tell my parents. It would have upset them.'* Paul's father had spent 32 years in a state factory where he had been an active communist party member. *'So he was among the first to be dismissed, but at the moment the entire factory is being liquidated.'* At the time of his interview, having been registered unemployed for 18 months, Paul was on a programme for the long-term unemployed. His 'active measure' was a temporary job guarding a local school for which he was being paid $2 a month. Paul was scathing about the programme. *'It's been devised by bureaucrats. They want to give the impression that they're finding work for people.'* Although registered unemployed Paul was in fact in the second year of a two-year part-time course in management at a local college. Management was the field in which he had decided to seek a career. While at secondary school he had held a part-time job with a stockbroker at the Plovdiv stock exchange. *'That closed two years ago. Privatisation was not*

working out very well. But the exchange will open again when privatisation is completed.' Paul really wanted to study management at a university which he believed would be necessary if he was to embark on a career in stockbroking or something similar. *'You really need a university qualification nowadays to get a job with a firm that attracts support from western companies. In any case, a qualification in management or finance is always useful. You can work independently, as an accountant for example, or use the knowledge in any other business.'* Paul did not expect to achieve this aim. Since leaving school his only job, apart from military service and the 'active measure', had been at a seaside resort (in the second economy) during the previous summer. Paul was still living on the savings from that job when interviewed. His short-term intention was to go abroad. He had a friend in Chicago who had done well, and Paul would have liked to follow in this friend's footsteps, *'But for that I need to raise $2000. That is very unlikely. It's more likely that I will go to Hungary or the Czech Republic.'* Paul was one of many young people who, despite a record of continuous unemployment officially broken only by army service and his current temporary 'job', had been doing other things as well, and was able to feel that he was making some progress. He also felt that he had reasonable prospects. These were to involve emigration in the short-term, but in the longer run Paul expected to return to Bulgaria, to what he hoped would be a more favourable labour market. In any case, he intended to return with some capital and useful experience.

It will be clear from the above that East Europe's young unemployed are not all suffering grievously. Few regard themselves as floundering hopelessly or as losers from the reforms. They do not blame themselves for their lack of proper jobs. In their view, the job situation is the problem, and this view is usually echoed by their families, neighbours and friends. The young unemployed are not blamed for their predicament. No-one expects them to settle for less attractive jobs than they would have obtained under communism. East Europe's young unemployed cannot be likened to an underclass. They are from all kinds of family and educational backgrounds. It is true, of course, that some groups are more at risk than others, but no social category is immune. They are not isolated or pushed into deviant social networks. Their levels of spending and leisure participation do not set them apart from the majority in their own age group who are in regular jobs (see Roberts, 2001a). The explanation of the extremely loose relationship between labour market status and income levels among young people in Eastern Europe is that, on the one hand, a lot of jobs are very low paid, and, on the other hand, some of the unemployed (without proper jobs) have sources of income, sometimes from their families, but also from various types of work in the second/grey/unofficial economies.

Globally, the details of out-of-school youth's labour market experiences differ from country to country, and between regions within countries. They vary depending on the character of the education system (see next chapter), family patterns and practices, economic conditions, and upon the national cultures and their conceptions and explanations of what is happening among young people. In the west, 21st century adverse youth labour market conditions are often regarded as outcomes of de-industrialisation (the decline of employment in older 'smokestack' or 'rust bucket' industries), and the economic restructuring that has created new jobs in high-tech service sectors, and young people's qualifications and skills lagging behind the demands of a 'knowledge economy'. An outcome of restructuring everywhere is that there are fewer lower-level jobs than in the past, and the overall quality of lower-level jobs has deteriorated. Fewer of these jobs are skilled occupations in manufacturing or extractive industries. New technology and the reorganisation of the labour process have reduced these industries' need for operatives. This has also happened in Eastern Europe where labour is relatively cheap, but even there the restructuring of manufacturing and extractive companies has invariably led to downsizing at the operative levels. The new low-levels jobs that have been created in the west (as in Eastern Europe) are nearly all in consumer services. Students take these jobs to help to pay for their studies and maintenance. After completing their courses they often find themselves doing the same jobs as stop-gaps. Meanwhile, alongside de-industrialisation, education systems have expanded and young people are generally better-qualified and more ambitious than ever before. The sense in which these young people 'choose' to defer full adulthood is debatable. We know that young people (and adults) have a tendency to tailor their ambitions and expectations into line with their opportunities (Roberts, 1968). In Eastern Europe the situation is more clear-cut: it is not that young people do not want to establish themselves in long-term careers but rather that they do not intend to settle in the kinds of employment to which they find themselves currently confined.

In the developing world, for well over a generation, young people have been fleeing from under-employment in rural villages. They have been aiming for the cities, where many have then found themselves unemployed or under-employed, often for life. There are similarities in the labour market predicaments of youth throughout the present-day world, and my contention is that the prototypical examples and some of the clearest, starkest illustrations are in Eastern Europe. The under-employment of their young people is a product of 21st century modernisation rather than the countries' failure, so far, to catch up (see Kornai, 2006). Ever since the industrial revolution the normal condition of youth in the labour market has been marginality. The 30 glorious post-Second World War years in the west were exceptional, not normal. Centrally planned economies constructed young people's routes to adulthood and integrated them into the workforces more smoothly than markets have ever accomplished. These countries, and the west, are now experiencing 21st century normality.

Youth on the move

All over the world young people are travelling as never before. In the rich global north, the wealth of the populations and low airfares have made international leisure travel a normal experience. Every year, young backpackers set off around the world, often intending to earn their maintenance while en route. It is important to bear in mind that over 90% of the global population does not travel internationally in any year. Opportunities to travel, and the reasons why people travel, have varied historically and they still vary from place to place. Higher education students often move away from home to a major university in a major city. In Europe, the SOCRATES programme enables students to spend a semester or two at a university in a second EU country. The LEONARDO programme offers similar opportunities to young people in vocational training. However, the labour markets that young (and older) workers in West Europe and North America explore rarely extend beyond their own countries. In every EU country except Luxembourg, prior to EU enlargement in 2004, over 89% of the workforces were nationals, and most of the non-nationals were from outside the EU (European Commission, 2006), but this is changing.

In Eastern Europe young people have been taking advantage of their new opportunities to travel. In the early 1990s a series of changes set these young people free (this was their experience at the time). Internal passports in which authorisation had been required if one wished to move to live and work in another part of one's own country were scrapped. Exit visas for international travel were also abolished. Then the EU made it possible for citizens from the candidate countries to visit without entry visas. To go west all that was needed was to board a bus, pay the fare and show one's passport at the border. By 1992 most young people in Czechoslovakia had visited Germany (Dubsky, 1995). However, for young people in Eastern Europe some opportunities to travel have diminished. There are no longer state organisations offering low cost vacations in other socialist countries (as the communist party youth organisations did). Students throughout the USSR used to enter Russia, and head for Moscow if they could, for their university studies. In the new independent states other than Russia, this has now become too expensive for all but a few. On the other hand, young people now have more freedom, and have become more likely to migrate in search of work. Some arrive in West Europe, but they are not typical migrants from most of their home countries.

Young people who leave their home places for work or study are most likely to move only within their own countries. This is as true in Eastern Europe as it is in western countries. They often move to capitals and other major cities, though in parts of Eastern Europe there has been a counter-movement – re-ruralisation – as impoverished city folk have returned to families in the countryside where they know that they will be fed and housed (for example, see Khmelko, 2002; Vincze, 2003). Young people in Eastern Europe who move to another country in search of work are most likely to head for an adjacent territory. A typical destination for young migrants from all other ex-Soviet republics, except the Baltic states, is Russia. Young and older workers from the other 'stans' head for resource-rich Kazakhstan where typical earnings are four times as high. Young people from west and central Ukraine head for south-east Europe. Those from south-east Europe aim for Greece or central Europe – a common stopping-off point before moving further west (see Bagatelas and Kubicova, 2004).

Since 1989 these population movements have had sharp demographic impacts in some countries. In the early 1990s Armenia and Georgia both lost around a fifth of their populations due to out-migration, mainly by young people. They were escaping from the harsh economic conditions and, in the case of some males, the prospect of military service and the risk of action in the local wars (Roberts *et al.*, 2000). Also, at that time, there was widespread pessimism about the countries' futures. Migration has made some countries more multicultural – the typical experience in Western Europe. However, in Eastern Europe most countries have become more mono-ethnic: minorities have been the most likely to move and have often returned to what they regard as their real homelands (Gachechiladze, 1997).

It is always important to see migration from both sides. Net receiving countries in the west debate how to control the inflows and how to integrate those who are admitted: how to curb xenophobic or racist elements among the hosts, and how to assist the migrants to settle. From the migrants' perspectives, the problems are rather different. One is how to get in. Once 'in' they rarely intend to settle, at least on first arrival. Youth migration is mostly the pendulum variety. The migrants intend to earn some money and save enough to purchase a dwelling or start a business on returning home, or simply contribute to their households' living costs. Globally, remittances from abroad amount to three times the total of all governments' combined international aid budgets (Orozco, 2006). In poorer countries these remittances can be an important source of income for households, and in the countries' trade balances. Family members are sometimes far more valuable to their households when they are away than when they are at home (Dikici, 2003; Khachatrian, 2002). In Armenia in 2005–06 the total value of remittances from abroad exceeded the national government's total budget. Roughly three-quarters of all remittances into Armenia were from Russia, and 37% of Armenian households were benefiting from remittances (Khachatrian, 2006). Young migrants may make several 'to and fro' movements. Whether they eventually settle as immigrants will depend on the kinds of employment and quality of life that they are able to achieve, and whether they form a romantic attachment. It will also depend on whether conditions improve in their countries of origin. Regardless of all this, throughout their own lives they are most likely to feel that their places of origin are their true homelands.

The receiving countries are usually the net beneficiaries from youth migration. They can obtain ready-skilled labour – doctors, dentists and plumbers as well as unskilled agricultural workers and hotel staff. The countries of origin bear the costs of child-rearing, education and training. Fair trade? In 2006 the European Commission reported that migrants from the new (in 2004) EU member countries who had migrated to work in the older EU states tended to have intermediate rather than especially high or low educational qualifications, and that overall there were more women than men among the migrants. Young migrants in West Europe's labour markets experience higher unemployment than local youth, and when unemployed the migrants tend to remain out of work for longer. Also, due to the absence of social networks (families in particular) to which unemployed locals may turn for support, unemployed migrants tend to suffer more financially and in terms of mental health (see Malmberg-Heimonen and Julkunen, 2006). By 2006 Britain alone had an estimated 700,000 migrant workers from the new EU countries. Their typical age was 27. On average they had received 13 years education. They were working longer hours on average, for less money on average, than the native population, and the migrants were generally over-skilled and over-qualified for the jobs that they had managed to obtain (Anderson *et al.*, 2006). The people exporting countries lose (albeit only temporarily in many cases) the people who would be among the most valuable members of the workforces – typically decently educated, fitter and more ambitious than their elders. The problems associated with ageing populations are exacerbated in the migrants' countries of departure.

Nowadays global migration flows are mostly from poorer to richer countries. Every movement tends to generate further waves. People then have contacts in the receiving countries who can assist them in finding jobs and places to live. There is always a counter-wave – back home – because, as explained above, when they initially move the migrants usually expect to return, and some trips end in disappointment and net financial loss rather than gain. Migrants who are seeking work always benefit if they can obtain assistance from a relative, a friend, or a friend of a friend who has already been or, better still, who is already at the destination and will welcome them and help them to settle.

Some migrants need more tricky forms of assistance – obtaining a visa, working illegally (either because of the nature of the work, or because the visa excludes employment). When does assistance become trafficking? Possibly when money changes hands. Trafficking has become an emotive topic. The word conjures images of young women being kidnapped or lured with false promises, sold to middlemen, then passed to brothel owners as sex slaves. Maybe this sometimes happens, but grapevines usually provide fairly reliable information about the types of work that migrants can expect at the end of their journeys. A problem faced by all migrants, especially by those who need to be assisted – which is usually by someone in the family or known to the family, even when money is paid out – is that they may be unable to find the kind of jobs and earn the sums of money that they expected (see International Organisation for Migration – Azerbaijan, 2002). The streets of western cities are not paved with gold – not for most migrants. Illegal workers cannot command high wages. Living costs in the west are much, much higher than in Eastern Europe. No-one likes returning home having lost money on a trip, but this does happen. In 2006 British voluntary associations requested help from the Barka Foundation, a Poland-based charity. The UK agencies did not have staff or volunteers who spoke East European languages, and needed assistance in their work with destitute Polish immigrants in London. It was estimated at that time that at least 30% of the people sleeping rough in London were from the new (post-2004) EU member countries (McLaughlin, 2006). They were free to enter and work in Britain, but were not eligible for any state welfare benefits until they had worked and paid National Insurance contributions for 16 months.

Winners

Under-employment and migration do not account for all young people in Eastern Europe. Some have stayed at home and succeeded in the new labour markets. There are two principal ways in which young people have been able to do this: by succeeding in business, or obtaining a middle class job with a salary that will support a western-type standard of living and style of life. The proportions of winners vary from place to place. They are always the most strongly pro-reform sections of their age group. The larger the proportions who are winners, the larger are the proportions of countries' populations that support the reforms (Adamski *et al.*, 2001; Tilkidjiev, 2004). However, among young people the winners are always a small minority.

Business became Eastern Europe's glamour career in the early-1990s. This was a completely new opportunity – to start your own business, to work for yourself, and to become rich. Thousands upon thousands of new businesses were registered, most of which, it appears, never began trading. However, at that time most young people (especially the males) appear to have made some attempt to do business. This usually meant buying and selling – anything, maybe cigarettes, alcohol, clothing or any other consumer goods. Trading soon became, and still is, a common route into business. In the early 1990s individuals who had accumulated only modest capital could make 'shopping trips' to countries where goods were slightly cheaper than at home, or purchase at home and travel to sell in a country where prices were higher. Successful shuttle traders were then able to branch into other lines of business – a kiosk, a shop, a restaurant, a hotel, a nightclub, a taxi/minibus service, or even a bank (exchanging currencies). In the central European countries with Germanic histories and business cultures that could be recovered after 1989, young people have been likely to start a business in the occupations for which they have been trained – motor repairs, building etc. Elsewhere the typical young entrepreneur has been a generic 'biznessman' whose aim is simply to make money. The term biznessman (incorporated into all the local languages throughout Eastern Europe) is gender neutral in these countries, but most of those concerned are males. Women in business are likely to need a male sponsor or protector (see Roberts *et al.*, 1998).

In the early 1990s there was a window of opportunity in virgin markets where there were no established competitors. It was possible for individuals to 'come from nowhere' and quickly become successful and rich (by local standards). However, most of the businesses that were created at that time were 'basic' and vulnerable as soon as 'quality' western firms (such as McDonald's) moved in.

Box 2.3 describes a young entrepreneur who was succeeding in business in Poland in 1993. As in this example, emergent micro-businesses in Eastern Europe in the early 1990s were most likely to be operating at least partly in the shade. Commercial laws were unclear at that time.

> **Box 2.3**
> **Youth doing business (1)**
>
> Maciek, aged 24, who lived in Suwalki in north-east Poland had been unemployed for two years since finishing a professional secondary school course in economics. He was still registered as unemployed when interviewed though he was no longer eligible for benefit and was earning quite a good living through cross-border trading. Maciek was travelling a lot in his BMW, buying in the East and selling in the West, and had been to most West European countries for this purpose. For six months he had worked in a restaurant in Belgium, the type of job in which many young Poles had endeavoured to acquire some capital. Subsequently Maciek's trading had been so successful that he was no longer interested in obtaining an orthodox job. Rather, he hoped that his enterprise would grow and, at some future time, become a legitimate business.

It then became standard practice to pay state officials to expedite any certificate or permission that was required, or to settle a tax account. Knowing how to do this was, and still is, a desirable business skill. In the early-1990s it was possible, though exceptional even then, for 'biznessmen' to be sufficiently successful to use the capital that they had accumulated to bid for companies that were being privatised. Thus some became 'oligarchs', fabulously wealthy. That window of opportunity soon closed. It was a once in a lifetime chance. Interviews conducted with young business people in Tbilisi (Georgia) and Yerevan (Armenia) in 1996 (see Box 2.4) illustrate how by that time, some (though certainly not all) had 'come from nowhere' to be proprietors of successful businesses that set them (not necessarily securely) in their countries' new middle classes.

The examples of young entrepreneurs in Box 2.5 are from interviews with self-employed young people who were running officially registered businesses in Hungary and Slovakia in 1996. Note how they were both doing business in the occupations for which they had been trained. Hungary and Slovakia were once part of the Hapsburg Empire in which they acquired Germanic business cultures which could be resurrected as soon as communism ended.

Vladimir (see Box 2.6) was more typical of the generic 'biznessmen', some of whom, by the beginning of the 21st century, were prospering across the eastern borders of Hungary and Slovakia, in Ukraine.

In most parts of Eastern Europe, between 7% and 9% of young people manage to establish themselves in business as a main occupation on a continuing basis. This proportion is unlikely to rise. As the threshold for market entry has risen, self-employment has become more suited to adults with experience as employees in the kinds of

---

Box 2.4
Youth doing business (2)

Mikhail had graduated as a historian from Tbilisi State University at age 22, then worked for one year for a 'financial house' where his brother was a co-owner. *'After graduating I faced the dilemma of either retiring from my specialty (historian) or living in permanent poverty. I chose the former. The owners of the finance house had decided to open a computer/business centre, and I became one of the co-owners. After 6 months we had made enough money to privatise a meat factory in Telavi.'* When interviewed in 1996 Mikhail had a personal income of $1000 a month (which made him very well-off) from the two businesses in which he was a partner.

Levon, aged 28 and based in Yerevan, had studied history and archaeology in Moscow. He had graduated in 1991, worked briefly as a labourer in a state factory, then served in the Armenian army in Karabakh. Subsequently he had become involved in a Yerevan-based NGO which assisted families in Karabakh. Based partly on the experience obtained with this NGO, together with a partner Levon had created a tourism company which was organising archeology-oriented visits to Armenia and related seminars and lectures. They had 3 permanent employees and another 30 who could be called on to take excursions. The business had an annual turnover of $40,000 and Levon himself was earning $6,000 a year from the business.

---

businesses into which they then branch out, as is the case in the west. In some parts of Eastern Europe – those with the highest levels of unemployment – there are considerably higher rates of youth self-employment, but in most cases this is 'survival self-employment' and those concerned would take jobs with employers if any were available.

The second way, a wider route, to success in the new market economies is to obtain a middle class job with a salary that will support a western-type lifestyle – new(ish) car, smart city centre flat,

---

Box 2.5
Youth doing business (3)

'I was a skilled worker in a state firm but the salary was too low. So I went to another state firm where the job was better paid but then the business went into decline. So I began doing odd jobs on my own account. I realised that I was doing everything and that it would be sensible to start my own business. I'm much better off than I was before' (carpenter, Vas, Hungary).

'I spent three years in a private firm. Then I realised that I could earn much more working for myself. I earn three times as much as when I was an employee' (metal goods producer, Trencin, Slovakia).

Box 2.6
Youth doing business (4)

Vladimir, aged 28, was a fairly typical example of a successful young businessman in west-central Ukraine in 2002. Vladimir lived in Sharovechka, a village with a Polish population. The ethnically Polish inhabitants had begun to describe themselves as Polish-speaking Ukrainians. Under communism only a minority of the village's population had worked in agriculture. Most had worked in factories in a nearby town. Most of the factories had closed and many families in the village had turned to 'trade'. These included Vladimir's father. Vladimir had left school at age 16 in 1992 and did two years military service. On returning to the village from the army he borrowed $200 from his father and started trading. At first he bought clothes and shoes in Odessa (a Black Sea port) and sold them in Khmelnitskiy, a city in his home region. Vladimir's trade had subsequently taken him to Poland, Hungary and Germany. With the capital generated by this business he had bought a bus and employed drivers while he himself continued to trade. He also built a large house for himself (with assistance – practical rather than financial – from other family members). He also owned a prestige car – a Volkswagen.

---

visits to restaurants and nightclubs (for those so inclined), Mediterranean holidays, etc. Who offers such jobs?

- First, international organisations – government missions, international NGOs and commercial businesses. These all need local managers and professionals.
- Second, local organisations that become linked to international circuits of money by providing services (legal, accounting, marketing, consumer surveys, construction, anything) for international clients; or public sector organisations whose assistance can facilitate imports and exports, solutions to taxation problems, and the negotiation of the various local regulations with which the international clients need to comply.
- Third, very successful and profitable local businesses which can afford to offer good salaries to their top managers and professional staff – a telephone company, a broadcaster, a beer or vodka manufacturer, a cigarette factory.

Who gets these jobs? You need luck and connections, probably a university education, familiarity with ICT and western ways of working, and foreign languages, but most young people who can tick all the boxes are disappointed. Once in one of these jobs, it is relatively easy to move on to another. The jobs, and the people who fill them, form a separate labour market segment (see Lepper and Schule, 1999).

As noted above, the proportion of all jobs that pay attractive salaries varies from place to place. It is always highest in capital cities, but even in these places there are far more well-equipped young people competing for the jobs than vacancies.

In 2002 a discussion group was held at the Moscow (now Russian) State Social University with 9 young adults who had graduated 2–4 years previously and who had subsequently been reasonably successful in the Moscow labour market. These were not typical members of their age group in Moscow, even of social science graduates – they were from among those who had succeeded in obtaining reasonably good jobs. They all earned at least $200 a month in 2002 and usually much more than this. Their jobs were junior and middle management positions in local private companies – a firm that manufactured and sold paint, a book publisher, a chain of supermarkets, a firm that mined minerals, another that sold and installed air conditioning systems, another that marketed CDs. Some members of this group had more than one job, and there was general agreement that to achieve a really good income you needed more than one source. A popular combination among the females in the group was a job in the state sector which was secure, stable, and compatible with future motherhood, and another much better paid private sector post. One extreme example was a young woman from Dagestan who was employed in the local (in Dagestan) migration department but actually lived and worked primarily in Moscow and paid occasional visits to her workplace (which was continuing to pay a salary) and family in Dagestan.

How did this group obtain their jobs in Moscow? In a variety of ways – *'It is my father's firm . . . I was invited to join . . . I just sent my CV . . . I replied to an advert.'* These young people had not found it difficult to obtain their jobs. Most were into their second, third or fourth jobs since graduating. They had the combination of qualities that employers sought – higher education, computing, foreign languages, and (since graduating) experience in commercial environments. Most of their contemporaries in Moscow would have regarded all the members of this group as doing rather well for themselves, but the group was not sure that they were successful. None of them regarded themselves as 'well-off'. Being well-off was always seen as needing an income somewhat higher than the speaker's own – $1000, maybe $5000 a month. The group stressed that even this was different from being truly rich. Being rich meant having savings, owning a company, being able to give to charity. *'There are just about 100 truly rich people in Russia, and we can all name them.'* Another point on which the group agreed was that they would not consider living and working anywhere other than in Moscow if they stayed within Russia. Most saw no advantages in emigration to anywhere. They argued that there were just as good opportunities in Moscow. *'Other regions of Russia are 5 years behind. There are many more companies in Moscow. It's far easier to get a job. There's more entertainment and things like that. Moscow is a state within a state.'*

In Moscow higher education had become a requirement to be considered for a management or professional post, but a university qualification did not guarantee that one would be offered well-paid employment. In this and other respects, things are not very different nowadays in the west. Self-employment, growing one's own business, is not a realistic option for most young people in western countries. Dotcom millionaires notwithstanding, fresh school and college leavers are less likely to succeed in business than older entrepreneurs with relevant experience. So ambitious young people usually seek salaried positions with prospects of advancement to the upper levels of the occupational structure. Who is allowed to climb these career ladders? Entry to the careers is rarely possible today without higher education, but there are far too few top jobs to absorb all university graduates. So everyone who wants to succeed must try to gain an edge. Ambitious parents will ensure that their children attend good schools that will give them the qualifications demanded by the top universities. Students try to gain relevant experience, sometimes as unpaid interns. CVs are rewritten constantly into congruence with job specifications (see Brown and Hesketh, 2004). Whatever young people do, the fact remains that there are just not enough good jobs to accommodate them all.

There is a further way in which Eastern Europe is prototypical, an extreme case: the rewards for success and the penalties of failure – the gap in incomes, living standards and styles of life between the winners and the rest – is now much, much wider than in the past. In the west in many countries, in recent years the gap has been growing wider than formerly. The gulf between winners and losers has widened globally, and there are no longer any types of education or training that offer reliable routes to the really good jobs.

Summary and conclusions

This chapter has explained what the end of communism has meant for school and college leavers in the relevant countries. They have been given new options. Migration is one. There has also been the chance to succeed in business. Also on the plus side there are new jobs paying salaries that will support western-type lifestyles. However, for most young people entering the labour markets in Eastern Europe today, the main outcome of the transition from communism has been under-employment (a mixture of unemployment, temporary, part-time and casual jobs, and employment for which they are vastly over-qualified). Having first converged with the west, there are senses in which Eastern Europe has developed extreme examples of features characteristic of global youth labour markets in the 21st century: namely, the normalisation of under-employment, and excessive numbers of well-qualified young people competing for far, far fewer quality jobs.

Further reading

Bagatelas, W. and Kubicova, J. (2004), 'Bulgarian emigration – a closer look', *South-East Europe Review*, 6, 4, 27–35.

Charvel, L. (2006), 'Social generations, life chances and welfare regime stability', in P. D. Culpepper, P. A. Hall and B. Palier, eds, *Changing France: The Politics that Markets Make*, Palgrave Macmillan, Basingstoke.

Gerber, T. and Hout, M. (1998), 'More shock than therapy: market transition, employment and income in Russia, 1991–1995', *American Journal of Sociology*, 104, 1–50.

Kornai, J. (2006), 'The great transformation of Central Eastern Europe: success and disappointment', *Economics of Transition*, 14, 207–244.

Malmberg-Heimonen, I. and Julkunen, I. (2006), 'Out of employment? A comparative analysis of the risks and opportunities longer term unemployed immigrant youth face when entering the labour market', *Journal of Youth Studies*, 9, 575–592.

Roberts, K., Adibekian, A., Nemiria, G., Tarkhnishvili, L. and Tholen, J. (1998), 'Traders and Mafiosi: the young self-employed in Armenia, Georgia and Ukraine', *Journal of Youth Studies*, 1, 259–278.

Tarkhnishvili, L., Voskanyan, A., Tholen, J. and Roberts, K. (2005), 'Waiting for the market: young adults in Telavi and Vanadzor', *Journal of Youth Studies*, 8, 313–330.

Education

Introduction

The condition of youth and the condition of education are always closely entwined, more so than ever nowadays because all over the world young people are remaining in education for longer than ever before. One reason for this – not the sole reason, but an important reason – is that they are sheltering from under-employment. They also know that to maximise their chances of obtaining really good jobs they need to become as well-qualified as possible before seeking full-time, permanent employment.

Sociologists have always been fascinated by education because it offers clear and powerful illustrations of a basic sociological premise – that the different parts of any society are inter-related and, therefore, that societies need to be examined as wholes. The kinds of schooling that young people receive, and their levels of attainment, have always been related to their family origins, in particular their families' social class locations. This applies in all present-day European countries, and indeed everywhere else in the world where the relevant information is available (see Zaidi and Zolyomi, 2007). There are many other determinants of educational attainment (including gender and ethnicity in most societies) but the influence of family social class has been especially strong and persistent over time, and across countries. Simultaneously, in all modern societies the types of schooling that young people receive, and the levels to which they progress, are important determinants, usually by far the most important determinants, of the types of jobs that they subsequently obtain, and the levels at which they enter the occupational structure. All these relationships preceded communism, endured under communism (see Gerber and Hout, 1995), and are continuing under post-communism. Eastern Europe offers no surprises here.

The sociology of education has identified important historical and inter-country constants (as noted above), and these constants must be considered remarkable since there are as many education systems as there are countries. Each educates in its own language, teaches its own history, introduces students to its own literature, and has its own examinations and qualifications. These differences are responsible for producing different kinds of young adults – young Germans, young Russians, young men and young women rather than just people. The organisation of education, and the kinds of teaching that children experience, make powerful impressions on their self-concepts (who they feel they are) and the groups with which they identify – regional, national, religious, social strata, etc. – as well as on their personal hopes and expectations for the future. The USA adopted the comprehensive high school as standard between the world wars largely because the country wanted a common school to blend children from different immigrant communities into a single American nation, and this worked! As explained below, communism made comparable use of education.

This chapter opens with an account of education under communism, which was actually a variant of an existing European model in separating young people into those who received a full academic secondary schooling with the prospect of higher education to follow, from others who were tracked onto vocational programmes. We then see how some ex-communist countries have modernised this model, usually to create closer resemblances with West European practices, and how, in doing this, they have encountered problems that are increasingly serious in all parts of present-day Europe. The chapter then presents the rather different ways of organising education that were developed in the USA in the mid-20th century. We then see how and why education in much of Eastern Europe (everywhere that the governments have not retained tight central control) has become more American-like. The chapter concludes by identifying likely features and problems of global education in the 21st century in so far as Eastern Europe and America (rather than Western Europe) signpost the future.

Communist education

All (a big all) that was distinctive about education under communism, what made it different from every education system in the west, and manifestly communist, was the ideology. Marxism was a compulsory subject at all levels. In fact it penetrated the entire curriculum much like the faiths in some religious schools. Also, the communist party youth organisations operated within and alongside all schools, offering daily extra-curricular activities and holiday programmes plus, of course, political education. However, in structural terms the communist school system was generically European in that after a common curriculum up to age 14/15 pupils were divided into academic and other tracks (for descriptions and discussions of communist education see Bronfenbrenner, 1971; Grant, 1968; Jacoby, 1975; Shimoniak, 1970; Smith, 1976; Zajda, 1980). This division is characteristically European. In Europe it is generally regarded as the obvious, normal, even natural way to organise education, but we shall see below that the practice is not universal. In some West European countries nowadays the critical division is delayed until age 16. In Germany the division begins at age 10. The modal age across Western Europe is currently 14.

Why European countries organise their education in this way requires a historical explanation. All the countries have schools and universities that were created before the continent became industrial, urban and mainly democratic. Italy has Europe's oldest university – Bologna – where teaching has been offered continuously since the early 11th century. Austria has the oldest still surviving secondary school with a continuous teaching history – a *gymnasium* that began teaching early in the 12th century. When Europe modernised, these ancient institutions (which then existed across the continent) were not abolished. Rather, they were embraced and incorporated as the prestige institutions in mass, generally state-funded education. Existing schools and universities were enlarged, and new institutions of the same type were created. Entry was made meritocratic – open to all children with the necessary talent. However, these kinds of education were not offered to all children. New, different kinds of elementary, vocational and technical schools were created for the remainder. This way of organising education has its origins in Europe but has become global, mainly through the imperial powers transplanting their practices to colonies, where they have sometimes survived independence and other decolonisation measures.

In 1917 the bulk of Russia's population was illiterate. The Czars had not provided schools for ordinary Russians (who were mostly peasants). By 1939 all this had changed as a result of crash programmes of adult education and school building, and the rapid training of teachers. During this era teacher training became part of all higher education programmes. All specialists were required to learn how to teach their subjects. This continued in some places until the end of communism, and is sometimes still the rule under post-communism. It is not an unreasonable idea. The German master craftsman qualification (the *meister*) has always, among other things, been a licence to instruct.

The Russian Bolsheviks developed their own variant of European education, which was imposed throughout the communist bloc (which was enlarged after 1945). Up to age 14/15 children received a common elementary (polytechnic, general, comprehensive) education. The initial drive everywhere the communists gained power was to make full elementary education universal and by the 1960s this had been achieved. The drive then was to provide secondary education for all, but after age 15 it ceased to be a common education. Young people could continue their general (academic) education and this was the normal route to higher education. Entry to these schools was competitive, on the basis of exams set by the schools (the same system governed admission to higher education). There was also a limited number of academically specialised schools (usually in maths and science or foreign languages). These were not designed to produce the future economic or political elites. They were educating specialists who were likely to become research scientists and translators (see Dunstan, 1978). The route to the top was via activity in the communist party youth organisations, leading to full party membership, possibly appointment as a full-time cadre, and eventual membership of the *nomenklatura* (the named ones) for whom top positions in all institutions were reserved. Between a third and a half of all young people joined the Komsomol: the exact proportion varied according to time and place, but they always included well over half of those who entered higher education (Bronfenbrenner, 1971; Matthews, 1972).

Around three-quarters of young people (the exact proportions varied from country to country and between regions within countries) finished their general education at age 15 and proceeded to a vocational, technical or professional school. These institutions were always linked to state departments or plants, and work experience was always part of the curriculum. Sometimes the schools were sited inside industrial plants. Hosting such schools was a way in which establishments recruited the labour that they required. The normal expectation was that pupils would progress into employment in the occupations (and often in the same plants) where they had been trained, and then remain throughout their working lives. Vocational-type schools differed in the length of their programmes and the proportions that were classroom-based, and some of the courses culminated in the award of both a professional credential and the qualification needed to enter higher education. It was possible to enrol in a vocational school (to take a shortened course) after completing general (academic) upper secondary education. This was an alternative to progressing into university: train immediately for a specific occupation.

Work establishments (collectives) resembled mini-societies. As the previous chapter explained, it was through membership that workers gained access to health care, daily recreation, vacations, childcare, pensions and sometimes housing. This was one sense in which work was central in people's lives (see Stenning, 2005a). So much else followed from one's job, and so much of this 'else' was shared with other members of the work 'collective'. Communist party cells (branches) were usually based on workplaces. The wide role that work collectives played in people's lives was intended to foster, and it appears that it really did foster, solidaristic, communal attachments. Communist societies really were more communal than countries with market economies. Under communism transitions from education to working life could be smoother than in any other kind of modern society. Young people (and their parents) had some choice over which school to attend, and for which industry and which occupation to train, though in many places there was just one major employer. It was always possible for a young person to break out, to change track and seek employment in another establishment and in a different occupation. Labour shortages were endemic, so this right was not purely nominal. Most young people heard about their first jobs from their families or other informal 'grapevines', and found work without assistance from the official agencies (see Reiter, 2006). There were always drives to recruit labour to regions where the authorities were keen to develop the economies. Labour was attracted (not coerced, unless they were prisoners or, in some instances, recent higher education graduates – see below), sometimes with the prospect of slightly higher earnings, but more often with the promise of new housing (housing shortages, like labour shortages, were endemic). It was always easiest for an individual to flow with the system. Young people could exercise initiative, but they did not need to display any.

Communist higher education produced specialists. There were general universities but most students attended mono-technical institutions, and the typical subject studied was some branch of engineering. Like vocational-type secondary schools, programmes in higher education were always linked to government departments or sectors of the economy, and for the first three years after graduation young adults could be directed into specified jobs. This was a way in which the authorities ensured that key industries (those that were military-linked, for instance) obtained the specialists that they needed, and likewise plants in regions to which it was difficult to tempt well-educated young people who were likely to have become attached to big city life while studying at university. Accepting direction, if necessary, was said to be the graduates' obligation to the societies that had conferred their educational opportunities. Needless to say, graduates who were able to do so used informal contacts and 'influence' in order to obtain employment in the places and occupations of their choice. For their part, plant managers often preferred a recruit who was recommended by someone they trusted, or who could be asked for a reciprocal favour, and they could decline to hire 'directed' graduates.

This was the education that all the post-communist countries inherited, and at least traces are still evident everywhere. Education systems, like much else, are path dependent. The 'slate' can never be wiped completely clean. Whatever laws are passed, on the morning after there are still the same buildings, teachers and textbooks.

That said, there have been major changes in education in every country of Eastern Europe. As soon as communism ended, Marxism disappeared from the curriculum, the communist party youth organisations just faded away, and uniforms were replaced by free dressing. All the countries have 'nationalised' their education, albeit to different extents. They have all decided to make the national language the normal language of instruction while permitting schooling in other languages in regions and districts populated by minority groups. In the teaching of history, geography and literature, music and art there is always more emphasis than formerly on the particular nation's history and culture. These changes have proved controversial and difficult to implement in some places, especially in former Soviet republics such as Kazakhstan where there are substantial ethnic Russian minorities and where, when communism ended, there were no or few textbooks and teachers of some specialist subjects who used the new official Kazakh language, and where Russian language schools remain the best equipped and are popular among ambitious parents whatever their ethnicity (see Fierman, n.d.).

There have always been some additional changes. Curricula have been modernised. New vocational programmes reflecting new patterns of employment have been introduced. In the countries that now regard themselves as belonging to mainstream Europe, syllabuses have become less Russian and more western, and Russian has usually ceased to be taught in schools as a main foreign language the preference being for West European languages, especially English.

Euro-modernisation

When, in addition to the above changes, post-communist governments have decided to embark on wholesale modernisation of school education, this has always meant modernising the communist system, maybe tinkering with the age at which young people are split into different tracks, and always re-labelling schools to make them appear less communist and more European (even in Central Asia). General/academic secondary schools have typically become *gymnasiums* and *lycées*. Non-academic schools have become technical and professional colleges. Poland has a new modernised school system. Romania has introduced similar reforms, as have most countries that have joined the EU. In Romania primary education has been separated from lower secondary schooling, and the division of young people into academic and other tracks now occurs at age 14 (the modal age across the present-day EU) (see Agabrian, 2006). Similar 'Europeanising' reforms have been introduced in some post-Soviet republics. Uzbekistan now has academic lyceums and professional colleges for the upper secondary age group (15–18). The former German Democratic Republic, of course, was to be given the Federal German system (tripartite lower secondary schooling, followed by a range of *gymnasiums*, higher education, technical and vocational schools, and employer-based apprentice training).

Countries that have opted for modernised European school systems have all encountered problems which illustrate, in prototypical fashion, problems that all European countries, east and west, are now confronting. One such problem is whether central or regional governments are well-advised to try and, if they do, whether they are currently able to impose 'master plans' on education in 21st century conditions. The governments of former communist countries have all been short of money. They are rather poor tax gatherers. Businesses and citizens dislike paying taxes. Under communism governments raised money less visibly (mainly from enterprises). Such private business as was undertaken (mostly illegal) was untaxed. People have believed that under post-communism there should be less government, not more government than there was under communism. Hence the rapid normalisation of tax avoidance. Post-communist governments are still struggling to become effective tax gatherers. In western countries most governments raise (through various taxes) and spend around 40% of the countries' incomes (sometimes more). The average in former Soviet republics in 2002 was just 24.8%. In Armenia it was a pathetic 14.6% and in Georgia 14.5% (Igityan, 2003). One outcome has been that the governments have been unable to maintain the comprehensive welfare systems that they inherited from communism. They have all devised ways of transferring some costs to users: in transport, housing, pensions and health care as well as education (see Watson, 2006). Schools throughout Eastern Europe have often introduced 'voluntary levies' on parents in order to pay for repairs, heating, new textbooks and other equipment. Also, new private schools have opened, often affiliated to churches (see Dronkers and Robert, 2004; Milenkova and Molhov, 2002;Tomusk, 2000). These independent schools may not see any reason to fit in with any government plan. Another fact of post-communist life is that, in the (at best) very loosely regulated new market economies, it is impossible to require firms to provide work experience for pupils on vocational courses, or to recruit from these courses. West European experience shows that maintaining robust vocational tracks in education depends on employers being willing to partner schools by offering on-the-job training and protecting these routes into the relevant occupations, meaning that the routes become the only ways in for beginning workers, and young people from academic courses (or without any occupation-specific training) are not allowed to compete for the jobs. This requires corporatist planning involving governments, employer federations, and probably trade unions and professional associations (see Shavit and Muller, 2000). None of the new market economies have trade unions or employer federations that are strong enough to take on this task. The ex-communist countries that have been best placed to create modernised versions of European education are those that have been slowest to reform. In Belarus and Uzbekistan even privatised firms remain under administrative state control, and in these countries educational policies are unlikely to be derailed by changes of government.

A further problem with the European model is that parents are increasingly reluctant to accept second best for their children. Every generation of parents is better educated than its predecessor, and wants its own children to do at least as well, preferably better, than they themselves. The former German Democratic Republic illustrates all the problems of trying to maintain European traditions in education. The *hauptschule* (the third and lowest tier in Federal German secondary education, behind the *realschule* and the *gymnasium*) has proved completely unacceptable in the new eastern German states (see Evans *et al.*, 2000). The *hauptschule* has run into serious trouble in West Germany, but more gradually. In the 1950s it educated the majority of children and turned them into Germany's skilled workforce. Today it educates only a fifth of the age group and has in reality become a residual school (see Solga, 2002). East Germany's young people and their parents have also been reluctant to accept apprentice training. They prefer academic courses which promise far better long-term prospects. In any case, businesses in East Germany have been reluctant both to bear the costs of training apprentices and restricting employment in officially skilled occupations to workers who have been through the prescribed training (see Evans *et al.*, 2000). Many prefer cheaper immigrant labour from Poland and countries further to the east. Furthermore, corporatist planning proves slow and cumbersome, and its rules often prove too expensive in an age of rapid technological change, and when businesses need to respond quickly to compete in forever changing global market conditions (see Kohler, 1999; Kuda, 1998).

However, the European Union (the Brussels bureaucracy) remains wedded to European educational traditions. Its standard medicine for youth unemployment is vocational education and training, or remedial courses in basic skills (literacy and maths). The presumption is that the young unemployed are deficient and need to be brought up to market standards. In 2006 the youth (16–25 year olds) unemployment rate across the enlarged (25 countries) European Union was 18%, roughly twice the rate for the European working population as a whole. The EU's current answer to persistent youth unemployment is a so-called 'flexicurity-oriented approach'. This means combining weak employment protection (protection from dismissal, for example) with proactive training and education measures so as to shorten periods between jobs (*Social Agenda*, 2006). Funding has been made available to the new member states to tackle their youth unemployment with such measures. In these countries it is obvious to one and all that youth unemployment is not due to those concerned needing remedial classes or basic vocational training. They know full well that much of the training is really just 'warehousing' young people before returning them to unemployment (see Tomev and Dashkalova, 2004). However, the countries have learnt quickly that they need to present applications for funds in the way that Brussels expects in order to receive the money, and scheme organisers know that their own jobs depend on producing evidence of 'positive outcomes', as defined bureaucratically, which they are usually able to do.

European educational traditions are weakening throughout the continent. Countries have been raising the ages at which children are split into different tracks. This is now 16 in Ireland, the UK, and all four Scandinavian countries (it used to be earlier in all of them). These countries have also closed the 'space' between the different tracks that young people can take after age 16. They all offer academic and vocational courses in the same schools and colleges, and nowadays they all stress the equivalence of the different tracks, especially how they can all lead into higher education, instead of emphasising, and basing the appeal of each track, on the particular destinations (occupations) to which it leads.

Euro-convergence

European countries are seeking to converge their education systems. The European Union does not have competence over education: this is the responsibility of national governments. However, a single market, including a single labour market, requires that qualifications are transportable. In academic school education equivalence is established in terms of the ages at which qualifications are normally obtained: 16 for the completion of lower secondary education, and 18 for upper secondary education. In vocational education there are efforts to benchmark qualifications with lists of skills. In higher education the Bologna Declaration (see Box 3.1) is a non-binding statement of intent. Its non-binding character could be why it has proved popular; most countries of the former Soviet Union have now joined.

Convergence is likely to prove difficult even within the old (pre-2004) European Union countries. As seen in Table 3.1, there are currently enormous variations in how long it takes to gain a first degree. The UK and Ireland have Europe's shortest first degree courses (typically three years full-time study). The modal length in western Europe is five years, and it was five years in communist countries. Bologna proposes that countries converge on a 3 + 2 system, BA followed by MA. The three year BA has some appeal everywhere, especially to governments, because it will be shorter and therefore cheaper than five year programmes. However, where five years has been the norm, anything less than a post-Bologna MA is unlikely to gain easy acceptance as a full higher education.

Box 3.1
The Bologna Declaration

This agreement was signed in 1999 in Bologna by the Ministers of Education from 31 European Union, accession and candidate countries. Subsequently additional countries have 'signed up' for Bologna, including most countries of the former Soviet Union.

The main points in the Bologna Declaration are that by 2010 the countries will have established:

• Comparable higher education degrees.
• A three year BA followed by a two year MA cycle.
• The promotion of student mobility and free movement.
• Cooperation in quality assurance.
• Promotion of the European dimension through curricula, institutional cooperation, staff exchanges, and student mobility.

Table 3.1 *Average years spent studying for a first degree in various European countries*

Germany	6.8
Austria	6.7
Portugal	6.0
Finland	6.0
Spain	5.5
Netherlands	5.2
Ireland	3.6
England and Wales	3.4

Source: Sastry and Bekhradnia (2007).

There are also substantial inter-country variations in the number of hours per week in term time that full-time students typically devote to their studies. The figures in Table 3.2 are from time-diary research, and the hours spent studying include both hours in classrooms and those spent in private study. The UK has not only the shortest first degree courses, but its students spend fewer hours studying per week than anywhere else in Europe. The UK also has Europe's most expensive higher education for students and their families. Students incur substantial debts. In this respect the UK resembles the USA (see below) rather than continental Europe. It has become the norm for UK students to hold part-time paid jobs during term times as well as during vacations. This could be part of the explanation for the limited number of hours that they spend actually studying. Proposing to extend standard higher education in the UK to five years would be resisted by all parties (certainly by students and their families, and the government). Meanwhile, students insist that they need to earn while they are studying: whether or not this is desirable is less urgent for

Table 3.2 *Average hours per week spent studying by full-time higher education students*

Portugal	41
France	35
Germany	34
Netherlands	32
Austria	31
Ireland	30
Spain	29
England and Wales	26

Source: Sastry and Bekhradnia (2007).

them. Attempts to increase students' academic workloads would be resisted. As noted above, Bologna is just a declaration!

The American alternative

There is an alternative to the European way of organising a modern education system – the American way. Education in North America followed European practices until the 20th century: the settlers were mostly from Europe and brought with them that continent's ideas about what universities and secondary schools should be like, and who they were for. Education in the USA became decisively and distinctively American between the First World War and the 1960s. What happened?

First, formerly separate academic and vocational high schools were merged into comprehensives. There remained (and there still are) distinctions between academic (college preparatory) and vocational modules in the senior grades, but all lead to the same major goal, high school graduation, and completing high school became the norm across America during the 1930s, the years of recession when school-leavers faced serious difficulty in finding any employment (see Osterman, 1980). During this same period most of the employers (and there were never many of them) who had formerly done so ceased offering apprenticeships to teenagers, thereby eliminating the only serious competitor to the high school. Thus America created a single broad educational highway for all young people up to age 18/19. Why did this happen? First, as mentioned earlier, America wanted to use common elementary and secondary schools as melting pots, to create a nation of Americans. Second, there was a reluctance in much of America to accept the European idea that classics were better, higher, than motor mechanics. Third, Americans regarded their country as a land of opportunity, and maintaining this view seemed to require keeping all young people in the contest for the highest honours at least until they were on the threshold of adulthood. Fourth, across most of North America there were no long-established prestige secondary schools and universities around which the remainder of a mass education system could be built.

The second big reform that Americanised USA education was widening access to the college system, which was and still is a mixture of state and private (not for profit) institutions. This was done by making state college systems accessible to all high school graduates. Enrolments rose steeply after the Second World War and by the end of the 1960s around half of young Americans were enrolling in college (it is now around two-thirds) (Duncan and Goddard, 2005). College is the sole desirable goal that America's high schools can set before their students. This is a feature of their education that some American commentators deplore and wish to change (see, for example, Rosenbaum, 2001; and also see Box 3.2).

During the last 50 years there have been no momentous structural changes in American education. There are always campaigns and policies to address some endemic problems (see below) and to generally raise standards, but there have been no serious, widely supported proposals to 'Europeanise'. The American education system works in America to most Americans' satisfaction. It has helped to create a nation of loyal Americans. It has helped to sustain the American view

---

Box 3.2

Apprentice training in Germany and Canada

For many, many years, North Americans have gazed with admiration at Germany's system of apprentice training. Visitors have seen, and journalists and academics have reported German apprentices working seriously towards vocational qualifications and being taught useful skills. They have compared this German industriousness with the aimlessness and modest efforts of American high school students, and the large numbers of non-college bound youth who become disengaged and sometimes drop-out of school altogether. There have been numerous attempts to introduce a vocational alternative to high school in North America, but none have succeeded.

Wolfgang Lehmann (2004, 2005) has described one such recent attempt in Edmonton, Canada. He compared apprentices in Bremen (Germany) matched for trades with young people in Edmonton who were on a high school based apprenticeship programme that was introduced in the 1990s. There were huge inter-country differences in the apprentices' experiences.

- The German apprentices knew where they were heading. Their apprenticeships were regarded as reliable paths to skilled occupations. The Canadians, in contrast, were unsure about their futures.
- At work the German apprentices were taken seriously, and were treated as on the first rungs towards entering the skilled workforce. The Canadian apprentices were more likely to feel that they were being used as temporary unskilled labour.
- In Germany there was close integration between classroom instruction and on-the-job learning.

Experience in Europe shows that vocational routes work properly only if employers are involved in their design and operation, and if the routes really do lead to good jobs. North American employers have never been willing to cooperate to the degree that would be necessary for vocational routes to bed in.

that theirs is an exemplary open society of opportunity. Also, arguably, America's schools and colleges educate one of the world's most productive workforces whose members enjoy one of the world's best standards of living. Given all this, and that during the 20th century America became the world's premier super-power – politically, economically, militarily and culturally – it is no surprise that its educational practices served as a model for other countries, especially in the Pacific Rim region, who wanted to modernise their own education systems.

At this point it may be useful to note a series of contextual features that allow its education to work to the satisfaction of most concerned parties in America, and some systemic problems with which they cope. First, around 15% of young Americans do not graduate high school, and despite a wide-ranging and persistent search for solutions this proportion has not declined since the 1960s (Schupp *et al.*, 1994). The drop-outs tend to be from lower-class, ethnic minority families who make slow progress and become disaffected with high school. In the USA, being a high school drop-out is a stigma. High school graduation is the starting line for competing for all decent jobs. The drop-outs have high rates of unemployment when young, and bleak long-term prospects. As noted above, this has been the case ever since the 1960s (see Conant, 1965). Every conceivable measure has been tried in attempts to reduce the number of drop-outs and to improve the labour market prospects of early school-leavers, but nothing has worked (see Box 3.2). European systems, which create curricula tailored to the abilities, interests and future employment of less academic young people, seem more successful at retaining the upper secondary age group (16–18/19 year olds) in education or training.

Table 3.3 describes how, since the 1970s, there has been a substantial increase in the number of young black males in America who are enrolled in college. However, the table also shows that there has been a steeper increase in the number of black American males in prison. By

Table 3.3 *Numbers of US black males in colleges and prisons*

	Colleges and universities	Prisons
1980	463,700	143,000
2000	603,032	791,600

Source: Burkeman (2002).

2000 America has more black males in prison than in college. The populations from which the college and prison populations are drawn are not identical. College students are mostly aged 18–25 whereas prisoners can be any age. However, young males are most likely to start long-term careers of intermittent or unbroken judicial incarceration at the same age as when others are preparing for or enrolling in college. As transitions into the labour market have lengthened (a worldwide trend, as we saw in Chapter 2), young people have been remaining 'at risk' of trouble for more years than formerly. Young people who do not progress through higher education are less likely than formerly to be absorbed quickly into stable employment (and into stable marriages and parenthood), which have always reduced risks of offending. All over Europe the size of the 'at risk' group has expanded as transitions from school to work have lengthened, and those concerned are now more mobile, liable to create or encounter trouble in countries other than their own. We saw in chapter 2 that not all young migrants in Europe find jobs in the countries to which they travel.

Second, standards of attainment in America's high schools are modest by global yardsticks. A price for keeping nearly all young people in 'the contest' is that standards need to be realistic for nearly all young people. The 'brightest and best' can forge ahead later on, and early loss of talent is minimised.

Third, most young Americans complete their education with high but imprecise ambitions, and no specific vocational skills (Schneider and Stevenson, 1999). For a time they flounder (are under-employed) in the labour market. It takes quite a long time before they reap financial returns on their 'investments in human capital' (Gangl, 2001; Szdlik, 2002). Over-education is a long-standing issue in the USA (see Freeman, 1976; Rumberger, 1981). Americans appear to find this acceptable. They will incur what appear, to Europeans, huge debts as they progress through college, sustained by confidence, or at least hope, that in the long run their education will pay off.

Fourth, employers need to provide initial vocational training for most recruits, whatever their levels of attainment in education. The employer-based training tends to be firm specific. Firms then develop internal labour markets within which employees (but only the firm's own employees) can compete for higher level jobs within the companies. This is unlike in Europe where many (most in some countries) beginning workers already have 'specialties' and where labour markets tend to be structured occupationally. In Europe careers are at risk if demand for a particular occupation contracts. In the USA there are equivalent risks if a firm downsizes or closes (Gangl, 2001; Szdlik, 2002).

Fifth, European education segments young people into a series of groups, with different specialties, who seek different kinds of jobs. American education arranges young people in a single metaphorical queue. Those at the head of the queue get the best jobs and the employers who are offering the best jobs get the best young recruits. 'Best jobs' means those offering the best short-term and long-term rewards in the form of pay, other benefits, security and prospects for career progression. 'Best young people' means those who have progressed furthest, and developed the strongest CVs during their progress through education. It is easy for American employers to judge this. Young people can be ranked according to whether they have graduated high school, done some college, gained BAs, and been to post-graduate school. Colleges can also be ranked. Some are considered better than others and it is easy to discover any college's ranking. College entrants sit national examinations (the SATs, Scholastic Attainment Tests) and different colleges require different scores in order to gain admission.

The Americanisation of education in Eastern Europe

It is best, for analytical purposes, to treat the European and American models of education as (Weberian) ideal types, each of which has numerous variants – by countries, maybe by regions and even localities, with none of the variants being as pure as the ideal models. American-type broad educational highways always contain some internal differentiations, and some young people are prepared for specific occupations (teachers and medics, for example). In Europe university students who read sociology do not all become professional sociologists. The types are best used analytically, to compare education in different countries, with each country being situated somewhere between the two ideal poles, and to gauge how any country's education has changed over time. We can then see how, since the end of communism, the education systems in much of Eastern Europe have become less European and more American. This has happened everywhere the government has not tried to maintain or impose a masterplan, and these places include Russia. Under these conditions, 'Americanisation' has been an outcome of a number of developments.

(i) The closure or downsizing of vocational secondary schools as the state firms to which they were linked have closed or downsized, and have therefore been unable to offer employment, and/or have seen no point in continuing to offer training (Grunert and Lutz, 1996; Kogan and Unt, 2005; Markowitz, 2000; Meshkova, 1998; Saar, 2005; Sattarov and Lemberanskaya, 1999).

(ii) New private businesses have often been reluctant to accept the expense and 'hassle' of offering work experience and partnering schools (Evans *et al.*, 2000).

(iii) In order to remain in operation, many former vocational schools have needed to 'generalise' their curricula and to offer the leaving qualifications required for higher education (Roberts and Szumlicz, 1995).

(iv) Competition for (the best) pupils between public and private schools has led to many branding themselves as *lycées*, *gymnasiums*, academies and so on, thus creating a hierarchy of institutions rather than parallel schools offering different specialties (Meshkova, 1998; Saar, 2005). However, it is rarely possible to make an objective judgement as to where schools stand in the rank order when (as is the norm) they all set their own entrance tests.

(v) Enrolments in academic upper secondary and higher education have risen. Demand for places (shelters) has risen as labour markets have become harsher, and there has been a widespread belief throughout Eastern Europe that, eventually, the new market economies will demand higher standards and therefore that higher education will pay off (Grunert and Lutz, 1996; Kogan and Unt, 2005; Mirzakhanyan *et al.*, 2002; Saar, 2005; Simonova, 2003; Vaitkas, 2006). Simultaneously, as their incomes from governments have fallen in real terms (the typical experience), higher education institutions have sought to boost their incomes by offering more paid-for places (Meshkova, 1998). New private sector colleges and universities have added to the supply of places for secondary school-leavers. In some countries, particularly in Central Asia where in former times many students used to go to Russia for their higher education (which was encouraged by Moscow as likely to nurture identification with the Soviet system), it has been necessary to create new universities, sometimes by upgrading former upper secondary schools. Russia has become far too expensive for most young people from the Central Asian states, which, in any case, want to produce their own university graduates.

By 2005 Kazakhstan had 50 state universities (mostly post-1991 creations) and 114 private universities (all established since 1991) (Tursunkulova, 2005). In 1999 Kazakhstan introduced a national examination for university entrance and 23% of secondary school-leavers sat this exam. By 2002 89% were taking the examination (Zhakenov, n.d.) and there were university places for all of them if they wanted to enter and could afford the fees (usually under $1000 per year, and slightly lower in private universities than in state institutions). This pace of expansion raises questions about the quality of the new higher education. How were the additional staff trained? How were university libraries created? The rate of increase in the number of university teachers has lagged well behind the expansion of university places: teachers 'moonlight'. Private university teachers typically have their main employment in state universities. Library facilities (like the supply of computers and internet access) are usually meagre. Students are taught in classrooms mornings and afternoons throughout the week. Teachers dictate and students take notes. This was normal university education in Soviet times. Reading matter is usually *the* course text. Much testing has always been oral. Corruption is rumoured to be widespread. Gift-giving (customary in Central Asia) easily becomes bribery. In a national survey in Kazakhstan a quarter of the households with students at university said that they had paid bribes, usually to gain admission (Rumyanyseva, 2004). These problems are acknowledged by the Kazakhstan government. Employers complain that the system tests just knowledge and does not nurture critical thinking. The Kazakhstan government aims, or hopes, to strengthen the assessment of teaching quality and its system of accrediting universities (Lillis, 2007).

It is not just western commentators but also local employers and the national governments in the new market economies who believe that teaching needs to become more interactive and less dogmatic, and that students need to learn to listen, read and think critically. Path dependence is a serious obstacle. How can teachers *en masse* be expected to adopt methods entirely different to what they experienced as students and to what they have used hitherto? A response of many governments has been to expand opportunities for students to study at western universities. Students from countries that are now in the EU are able to spend a semester in Western Europe under the ERASMUS programme. In other countries this is very expensive either for the governments or for the students and their families, and it also depends on the students being competent and feeling competent in the foreign language (see Asmailzade, 2007). Western languages, especially English, are now taught in nearly all secondary schools across Eastern Europe. However, becoming proficient is likely to require more than secondary school offers. Private coaching, preferably by a native English speaker, is really necessary. A semester or a summer abroad can make a huge difference. These are ways in which East European families with the inclination and resources can ensure that their children 'gain an edge' (see Box 3.3).

Where education in Eastern Europe has been 'Americanised' it has become normal for young people from all kinds of social backgrounds to complete upper secondary education, and higher education has

---

Box 3.3
English language

Twenty-four young employees (aged up to 30) who were interviewed in Almaty (Kazakhstan), Bishkek (Kyrgyzstan) and Samarkand (Uzbekistan) in 2006 were asked for their views on the value of English language. All those who were proficient in English felt that their careers (and often their lives outside employment as well) were benefiting.

Knowledge of English is extremely important nowadays. My English language has been more important than my specialty in my career.

English is an inseparable part of my life and career. I have contact with foreigners at work and correspond with them regularly.

English language is a very important skill to have today. In my career it has played an important role. I started here as a secretary but then we began to have foreign clients. My English language began to help me then. At present I participate in all negotiations with these clients. In other words, English has got me a promotion.

Without English there are few possibilities for career growth, to learn about new accounting methods for example.

It is necessary in order to answer letters. I must speak English language.

I need English in my work, for the Internet, and to communicate with partners and customers.

English becomes more and more important every year. It helps one to find a high paid prestige job.

English is the language of international communication. So of course it's useful to me. I can speak with people from Europe, America, all over the world. Also, I need to be able to read specialist technical literature.

Some of the young people who could not communicate in English did not regard this as a handicap

English is not required in my work.

➡

Knowledge is never useless but it is useless in my work (construction). *With whom would I speak English?*

English! How would it help me? (construction worker).

For me, I don't see any benefits.

I don't need English so not knowing it does not disturb me.

However, there were more young people who felt disadvantaged by their lack of English.

Not knowing English does not affect my job, but it's useful whenever you apply for a job.

I am attending private classes in English language, and I have saved some money to attend a course in England. After I return home many gates will open for me.

Knowledge of English is not important in my job but I would love to know foreign languages, to talk freely with foreigners and understand their cultures.

Of course it's useful. Many foreigners come here and our citizens go abroad. If I knew English language I wouldn't be working here (in a sewing shop).

I have never needed foreign languages at work but they would be useful in life, for communication.

Nowadays English is in demand everywhere. Computer literacy requires English.

I haven't yet been faced with situations where I needed foreign languages, but of course they're useful. They are useful at work and to speak to Americans and other people.

I used to work in a sanatorium. There were always foreign guests. I found it difficult to communicate with them. I felt ashamed, uneasy and uneducated.

At present I have to pass documents to a translator. It's a waste of time, a drawback. Also, the translator's job status is lower than mine but he gets paid as much as me.

become the first stage at which social class inequalities become glaring. In many countries in Eastern Europe, and likewise in the west where overall participation rates in higher education have reached 50% or above, participation has become near universal for young people from families in the top socio-economic groups. Young people from other backgrounds become divided into those who progress through university and those who never enter.

(vi) Engineering has become unfashionable. It is also an expensive subject to teach. The new prestige higher education subjects are law, economics, business, management, banking and accountancy (Vaitkas, 2006). In the early 1990s there were shortages of graduates with these qualifications. Before long this situation had been transformed into grotesque over-supply.

(vii) At all levels more of the costs of education have been shifted from governments to 'consumers'. This has always been an important way in which college studies have been financed (and rationed) in North America where all colleges charge fees, the amounts depending on the college, and the cheapest education is in the lowest ranking junior/community colleges. The European tradition has been to ration higher education to the numbers of highly educated worker-citizens that the countries were believed to need, to identify the young people considered the most worthy, then to provide higher education as a gift in return for which the highly educated were expected to use their skills and knowledge for the benefit of their societies. The American way is to treat higher education as a private investment in human capital from which the recipients expect private returns (and gains).

There are still at least traces of the old education everywhere in Eastern Europe, even where change has been most thorough. There are still free places at state universities, and maintenance grants for the top performing students. There are still some vocational secondary schools everywhere. Some have been maintained by state departments and firms, or by privatised companies. A few have been created along-side new businesses. Some are popular because they provide training in skills with which a business (a bakery, or a construction firm, for example) might be established (see Roberts and Szumlicz, 1995). Some now operate as residual schools, taking pupils who fail to gain admission elsewhere (Markowitz, 2000). However, as explained above, some countries have retained a full set of vocational tracks, but also as explained above, when they have done this the tracks are no longer functioning in the old Soviet way. Walker (2007) has described how in Ul'ianovsk (Russia) in 2004 vocational schools were still operating formally as if communism had never ended. They were still producing graduates for state and privatised plants to which the young people could progress even when the plants had no work for these young employees or cash to pay salaries. Vocational schooling had become a 'zombie' (living dead) system. However, the young people were not complying in zombie-like fashion. Around two-thirds of those inter-viewed by Walker had entered or were planning to enter higher education, usually as part-time or distance learning students at new private universities. Some, described by Walker as 'pragmatists', were working towards higher qualifications in the professions for which they had already been trained. They knew that such qualifications would lead to higher grade jobs and rates of pay (though the plants would not necessarily be able to supply regular work or salaries). Other young people, described by Walker as 'aspirational', were seeking qualifications in different fields such as finance and management in the hope that they would be able to obtain good jobs in expanding sectors of the economy. Whether this strategy would work for the young people was very uncertain.

Wherever there has been a trend towards Americanisation, certain problems have arisen at the education–labour market interface, and these problems are likely to spread across all parts of Europe if, as regards education, America is the future.

(i) East European firms that are unaccustomed to training raw recruits, and which have never needed to develop internal labour markets, have either avoided beginning workers, preferring to hoard older experienced staff even during periods of slack demand, and recruiting other such staff who have been off-loaded or attracted from other companies (see Schwartz, 2003), and sometimes from abroad. Or they have taken on unskilled youth labour while opting for low-skill, low-wage, low-cost production and marketing strategies. However, throughout Eastern Europe there are now foreign-based or linked enterprises that are demonstrating 'best western' practices, and local firms in entirely new business sectors (IT companies, for example) have had no choice but to train up initially skill-less staff.

(ii) Many young people in Eastern Europe have continued to expect to work according to their specialties. They have not learnt to regard their education in international marketing or European business as just a means of acquiring generic transferable skills – absorbing information, processing information, sifting and organising evidence to address a set problem, and communicating ideas and evidence to different audiences.

(iii) Eastern Europe's education systems are not yet arranging students in a clear hierarchy which can send clear signals to employers about individuals' employability. When communism ended there were no national examinations, and today there is rarely a clear rank order among secondary schools or higher education providers (see Box 3.4). However, since the early 1990s country after country has been introducing national secondary school-leaving or university entrance examinations (see Saar, 2005; Vaitkas, 2006). In some countries proposals to introduce such examinations (in Georgia for instance) have encountered stiff resistance. Students have believed that entry to their preferred universities will be made more difficult because they will no longer be able to use gifts/bribes or family connections (Kandelaki, 2005). The absence throughout the 1990s of reliable signals of young people's value will be one reason why so many employers in Eastern Europe have placed so much emphasis on personal recommendations and why, therefore, so many young people have felt that it is 'who you know' rather than 'what you know and what you can do' that really count in the new labour markets (Clarke, 2000; Yakubovich and Kozina, 2000).

Box 3.4
Which university, which subject?

The twelve out of the 24 young employees who were interviewed in Almaty, Bishkek and Samarkand in 2006 who had been to university were asked whether it was better to study at some universities, and to take some subjects, rather than others. It was only in Bishkek that anyone mentioned a private university or universities as being superior, and in Bishkek this was always the American university.

Graduates of the American university have better prospects but not everyone can study there. It is necessary to be able to afford to go and to speak English.

It's worthwhile to choose a better university, like the American university. They deliver more knowledge.

Everything depends on the teaching staff and the facilities. At the American university there is a very good library. Everything is on the premises.

However, there was some dissent about the value of attending the American university.

Those who study at the American university have rich parents and some English but they are such goofs. No matter how much you invest in them – no sense.

The sole Samarkand respondent who felt that it was possible to distinguish between universities argued that it was the location – capital city – that made the real difference.

I attended the Tashkent Polytechnic Institute. At the time, in the 1990s, it was prestigious to obtain a technical specialty. I think that universities in the capital are better

➡️

equipped with up-to-date computer facilities, libraries and teaching staff. In any case, at that time there were no higher education institutes in Samarkand where you could specialise in my area of interest.

All the other respondents, and they included every single respondent in Almaty, said that which university was best depended on the subject that was studied.

I chose my university because it was the best place to study telecommunications. Overall some universities are probably better. It depends on the personnel and the university's financial base.

One needs to pay attention to the teaching personnel, their length of service, and the programmes.

I think they are all the same. The only difference is the teachers. I had good teachers.

If you have brains the name of the university doesn't matter much.

I think that if you have a head on your shoulders and a goal, then anyone can get the education he or she wants at any university.

I know some graduates of prestigious institutions and their parents are still making decisions for them. Their qualifications don't mean much. They cannot achieve anything by themselves, and their knowledge is at the bottom level. Who comes in to teach in the auditorium is not all that matters – so is who is sitting at the tables, what they know and how they work together.

As regards disciplines, in Almaty none of the respondents made any distinction, whereas in Bishkek and Samarkand there was a broad consensus as the following quotations make clear.

Some faculties at Samarkand State University – foreign languages and economics – are considered the most prestigious.

Which university is best depends on the specialisations that they offer. Economics, law, foreign languages and banking are considered better than other specialties.

All universities are state universities (in Uzbekistan) so it is difficult for one to be better than another. However, studying in the law faculty is more prestigious than studying geography.

I studied social work because there was little competition to enter and the fees were low. I found that I was not interested and I also realised that the salary and prestige of social work were low. So I quit.

One of America's persistent problems – the stigmatisation of high school drop-outs – has not yet surfaced in Eastern Europe (Roberts, 2001a). Maybe it never will. The situation in the USA could owe more to the ethnic composition of the stigmatised group rather than their mere failure to complete high school. In Mediterranean Europe the earliest school-leavers (often before age 16) do not have especially high rates of unemployment because they are willing to accept low-level jobs in agriculture and consumer services. The beginning workers in some Mediterranean countries who run the highest risks of unemployment are those who quit education at age 17–19 with inter-mediate (secondary school) academic qualifications (see, for example, Bernadi, 2003). Returns on academic credentials appear to accrue only to those who progress beyond secondary school into higher education, and this could become the case in Eastern Europe where most coun-tries, like the Mediterranean states, have large agricultural sectors and plenty of new private sector consumer services which generate lots of low-level entry jobs.

Gender in education and the labour market

During the closing decades of the 20th century, all over the world girls first caught up with then overtook boys in terms of levels of educa-tional attainment. In the 21st century most countries where boys still out-perform girls are devoutly Muslim (these countries do not include any of the ex-Soviet 'stans' where Islam is the main religion). Improved performances by girls have been part of a broader set of changes in gender roles. Rates of labour market participation by women have risen. Recent cohorts of young women have had mothers who held paid jobs while their daughters were children. Today's young women have been brought up expecting to be in employment throughout their adult lives. Their parents and teachers realise that education is just as important for girls as for boys. A problem group in many countries today is composed of under-achieving males.

The Soviet Union led the west in the above respects. Women were expected to work full-time and continuously except for short periods of maternity leave because free nursery and kindergarten places were available (or were supposed to be available) everywhere. During the rise of second wave feminism in the west (from the 1960s onwards) Soviet women were told (and they appear to have believed) that they already enjoyed the rights that western women were claiming. In principle, under communism, all education programmes and all occupations were open to men and women, and equal pay for the same work was the rule.

Although modern feminist thought can be traced back for over two centuries, and although there was a first wave feminist movement at the end of the 19th and the beginning of the 20th century which demanded votes for women, better opportunities in education and employment, divorce on the same grounds as men, and the right of married women to own property, the view that males were naturally masculine and females feminine was not challenged until the 1960s. Sociologists, and feminists more generally, then distinguished sex differences (with a biological basis) from gender roles (which are learnt). It was argued, and became a domain assumption in sociology and among most feminists, that by nature males and females were equally suited to all kinds of education and employment, equally capable of undertaking all political roles, and that men were no less inclined (by nature) to fathering than mothers to mothering. These are all hypotheses, very difficult to prove or disprove, but it has become taken for granted that different outcomes in education and employment require a socio-cultural explanation and indicate that one or both sexes are victims of injustice. The communist authorities never budged from the view that men were naturally masculine and females feminine, and women's natural role as mothers had to be 'understood' by employers who would be compliant when women needed time off to care for sick children, and even to queue for provisions (shopping was a time-consuming chore). The fact that males and females tended to opt for different programmes in education, and entered different occupations, was not regarded as a problem to be addressed. Rather, the differences in education and employment were treated as outcomes of the natural differences between the sexes. In western countries it is equally (neither more nor less) the case that boys and girls tend to opt for different subjects in education, especially in post-compulsory education, and enter rather different occupations. The difference is that in the west these different outcomes are likely to be attributed to socio-cultural stereotyping.

The different kinds of subjects in education that males and females tend to study are basically the same all over the world. Males are the majority on courses in science and engineering, females on courses in the social sciences, humanities and languages. These curricular choices should not damage young women's labour market prospects. In Eastern Europe and the west alike, employment in manufacturing has declined. Girls' overall higher educational attainments, and especially their preference for learning languages, should be advantages in the new service-oriented labour markets of Eastern Europe.

The evidence from Eastern Europe shows that in the labour market the situation is not one of unmitigated female disadvantage.

Table 3.4 *Gender in the labour markets in the South Caucasus (in percentages)*

	Males	Females
Unemployment	24	41
Self-employment	22	8
Non-active	6	14
Higher-grade jobs	21	28
Other jobs	17	7
Other	10	3
N =	510	659

Source: see below.

Table 3.4 is derived from a survey in 2007 among representative samples from the capital cities and a contrasting region in each of the three South Caucasus countries – Yerevan and Kotayk in Armenia, Baku and Aran-Mugan in Azerbaijan, and Tbilisi and Shida Kartli in Georgia. The respondents had all been born between 1970 and 1976, and supplied detailed information about how their lives had developed since age 16. Table 3.4 divides them into career groups according to their overall labour market experiences (not their positions at the particular time of the survey). Those described as unemployed, self-employed, non-active (in the labour market), and in higher-grade (non-manual) jobs had been in such positions for at least 50% of their time since leaving full-time education. The 'other jobs' group had been in jobs for at least 50% of their time, but not in the kind of jobs that would have placed them in the higher grade employment category. Over 90% of the respondents fell into one or another of these five career groups.

Females had been more successful than males in obtaining higher grade jobs. These jobs tended to be public service professions (in education, health care, and social services for example). Most of the higher-grade jobs in all three countries were still public sector jobs in 2007. Females were also more likely than males to be in the unemployment and non-active groups, and were far less likely to have become successfully self-employed.

Motherhood is the sole plausible explanation of females' higher risk of unemployment as well as being non-active in the labour market. Countries that have joined the European Union have been required to outlaw sex discrimination in the labour market. This has not been a major issue anywhere because, as explained above, under communism all courses in education and all occupations were open to men and women, and people were paid according to their jobs rather than according to whether they were male or female. However, there is abundant evidence from across the whole of Eastern Europe that since the end of communism women have been more vulnerable than men to unemployment, and have been paid less than men (typically around 70% of male earnings in the case of young employees despite the females being better qualified than males).

Motherhood creates labour market difficulties because child care in all the ex-communist countries has become expensive, and private sector employers do not wish to be left with the expense and inconvenience of accommodating maternity leave. Thirty-five percent of the respondents in the 2007 survey had become parents by age 23. Motherhood rarely prompts young East European women to quit the labour market. They want and expect jobs that are compatible with motherhood. Such jobs would have been available under communism but have become scarcer since 'the reforms'. We shall return to gender in later chapters, especially Chapter 5 (on family and housing transitions) and Chapter 7 (on class divisions).

Summary and conclusions: education and global youth in the 21st century

Having reviewed how education in different groups of East European countries has changed since the end of communism, this chapter must conclude that America to the west of the Atlantic, and Eastern Europe, may well signpost the future for education and global youth. If this is so, education in the 21st century will have the following features:

- Rising percentages of young people completing full secondary academic education.
- Likewise the proportions of each age group progressing into higher education. Globally the number of higher education students rose from 13 million in 1960 to 82 million in 1995 then 132 million in 2004 (Morley, 2007).
- Declining proportions taking courses that confer occupation-specific skills and identities.
- One outcome will be cohorts of young adults with high but imprecise job aspirations.
- Young people will need somehow to 'pay their way' through post-compulsory education, and they will do this with support from

their families, some support from governments (though rather less than in the past), and through earnings from the part-time and temporary jobs that are being created in consumer services.

- They will encounter heavy congestion at the ports of entry to attractive careers. In Britain in 2004 over 300,000 new university graduates competed for around 15,000 elite jobs (Morley, 2007).
- Most will face a period of under-employment, during which high ambitions and hopes may be cooled out (replaced by more modest ambitions), or they may be retained, prior to each cohort settling (if individuals ever settle) at different levels of employment.

Further reading

Evans, K., Behrens, M. and Kaluza, J. (2000), *Learning and Work in the Risk Society: Lessons for the Labour Markets of Europe from Eastern Germany*, Macmillan, Basingstoke.

Markowitz, F. (2000), *Coming of Age in Post-Soviet Russia*, University of Illinois Press, Urbana and Chicago.

Shavit, Y. and Muller, W. (2000), 'Vocational education: where diversion and where safety net?' *European Societies*, 2, 29–50.

Walker, C. (2007), 'Navigating a "zombie" system: youth transitions from vocational education in post-Soviet Russia', *International Journal of Lifelong Education*, 26, 513–31.

Individualisation and the reflexive self

4

Introduction

This chapter applies a body of western theory to East European realities. The theories are relevant in all areas of young people's lives – their leisure, education, political engagements, work, housing and family relationships. Therefore the theories will re-appear throughout this book. We shall see that in many respects the marriage between the theories and the situations of young people in Eastern Europe works well. Eastern Europe needs the theories to make sense of the changes in its young people's situations since the end of communism. Simultaneously, experience in Eastern Europe exposes limitations of the theories. Eastern Europe can be regarded as an almost perfect test case. If the theories apply anywhere, then it can be argued that they should definitely work well in the transition countries. We shall see that the theories do indeed work reasonably well and thereby highlight the theories' strengths, while exposing limitations.

The theories with which we deal in this chapter have been formulated in response to changes that have taken place in western countries over the last 30 years. The catalysts and symptoms include de-industrialisation, the associated economic and occupational restructuring, higher unemployment than in the 1950s and 60s, ICT, globalisation, and the development of so-called knowledge economies. The outcome, it is said, is 'new times' variously labelled post-modern, late-modern, high modernity, plastic modernity, liquid modernity, and modernity II. These 'new times' are said to differ from an earlier modern age in life being more fluid and flexible, and less solid. Social structures are said to have weakened. Culture is now said to be playing a larger and stronger role in social affairs. Hence the so-called 'cultural turn' that has swept through the social sciences. The outcomes with which we are particularly concerned here are an alleged spread of individualisation and the growth in importance of the reflexive self. In any country – in Eastern Europe or in the west – if these developments really have occurred this should be most apparent among their young people.

This chapter begins by defining its keywords, individualisation and reflexivity. Both concepts gained a high profile in sociology following the publication of Ulrich Beck's *Risk Society* (see Box 4.1). The chapter then explains the value of these concepts in analysing how the transition from communism has transformed the situations of young people in Eastern Europe: they have become more self-aware, and are not just able but obliged to make more choices than in the communist past. However, the chapter then explains how major systemic inequalities have been maintained. These include links between young people's social class origins and their educational attainments, between the latter and the occupations that they enter, by labour market segments and by place. The chapter concludes by arguing that the individualisation that has spread in Eastern Europe and the west is a structured variety of individualisation.

Box 4.1
Ulrich Beck (1944–   ) and the Risk Society

Many of the concepts used regularly by present-day youth researchers were invented, or first became well-known, following the appearance of *Risk Society*, a book written by the German sociologist Ulrich Beck, first published in Germany (in German language) in 1986, and translated and published in English in 1992. These dates are important because the book was responding to trends up to, not since the 1980s.

Youth researchers were already studying young people's risk-taking behaviour, meaning behaviour that was liable to damage the actors – binge drinking, drug use, unprotected promiscuous sex, dangerous sports and delinquency. They were also studying 'at risk' youth, that is, young people whose family circumstances, conduct in school and beyond suggested that they were heading for trouble. These were not the kinds of risks that Ulrich Beck highlighted. His book was about a new kind of risk. The Chernobyl disaster occurred in 1986. In 1985 the Three Mile Island (in the USA) nuclear power plant re-opened following its closure upon a leakage of lethal gases in 1979. Since the 1970s there had been alarm about impending limits to growth, the depletion of fossil fuels, and various potential ecological calamities. Beck's new risks were products of science and modern life more generally. They were new in the sense of being global, affecting everyone, and in being uncontrollable and uninsurable.

The equivalent new risks in young people's lives are said (by youth researchers, not Ulrich Beck) to be situations and steps in life where the outcomes have become less predictable than in the past. For example:

- The kind of employment (if any) that can be expected to follow higher education or a training programme
- How long a job, an occupation or a career will last
- Whether a marriage will be for life

Risk Society also introduced the concept of individualisation. In Beck's book individualisation was due to a weakening of traditions and modern institutions such as nuclear families, and neighbourhood and religious communities. It was also said to be the result of the welfare state, especially meritocratic education that made young people's life chances independent of their sex and social origins. A consequence was said to be that individuals were obliged to become reflexive, that is, to reflect upon their abilities, inclinations and opportunities, and to plan their own futures.

Sociologists have been quick to point out that links between social class origins and destinations remain as tight as ever, and life courses remain gendered. Beck has been criticised harshly on these grounds (see Atkinson, 2007; Mythen, 2004, 2005). However, the point that subsequent youth researchers have seized on is that young people may feel empowered to take charge of their own lives, and that if class origins and sex continue to govern life chances, the relevant processes may well be rather different than in the past.

Individualisation

Western youth researchers are unanimous that individualisation has indeed occurred. They are also agreed on the processes that have been responsible, and how individualisation can be recognised in young people's lives. Basically, individualisation refers to the uniqueness of each individual's biography. When individualisation is low, every person should share major life experiences, their timing and sequencing, with most other members of a social category (those living in a particular town or village, of the same sex and social class, or working in the same industry). When individualisation is high, the common patterns fragment, each individual's life becomes a unique story, and it is expected that people will be more sensitive to their individuality than to experiences and interests that they share with others. Every experience of every individual will very likely still be shared by many other people – a programme in education, losing a job, getting married, etc. Individualisation does not mean that specific experiences are unique to a particular person but that each individual's chain of experiences is a unique series. The uniqueness lies in the ordering, the sequencing, and the particular combinations of experiences that constitute a life. Individualisation is a matter of degree rather than an either/or absolute state. Once grasped, which is not difficult because the idea is quite simple, it seems strange that the word has not been used until recently. Once equipped with the concept we begin to see individualisation everywhere. Up to now no-one has measured individualisation, but the condition, or trend, is not immeasurable. There is no reason, in principle, why the concept cannot be operationalised (see below) and the degrees of individualisation compared between different social categories, and at different times and in different places.

It is important to distinguish individualisation from terms used in earlier times to analyse what were then new social conditions. Individualisation is different from individualism. The individualist is or was inner-directed as opposed to other-directed or tradition-directed, to use David Riesman's (1952) terminology. The individualist is/was a strong character, with clear personal goals and convictions, expressed in deeds and words whatever other people's opinions. The individualist is/was never afraid to be in a minority of one. He or she does/did not bow to circumstances even if all others around acquiesced. The individualist struggled to change the circumstances, or ignored or escaped from them. These were the self-made men (rather fewer women in the historical record) who ignored traditions, built successful businesses, and created modern industrial societies. It is easiest, maybe only possible, to be an individualist when individualisation is low, when there are settled ways of thinking and doing things from which one can deviate. When individualisation is high, individualism becomes difficult, maybe impossible, because living one's own life becomes a necessity rather than dependent on special strength of character.

Individualisation must also be distinguished from privatism, a social condition which some sociologists identified as epitomising the 1950s and 60s (Goldthorpe *et al.*, 1969). Actually, at that time they wrote about 'privatisation' but this term has subsequently been used, and is now best known, for describing the transfer of economic assets from state to private ownership and control. So we now use 'privatism' to describe lifestyles that are home and family centred, and when there is little engagement, physical or psychological, with the wider world, when extended families are weak, and likewise relationships with work colleagues and neighbours, and when any attachments to organisations such as trade unions, professional associations and political

parties are calculative and for private betterment rather than solidaristic and emotional. Individualisation is different from privatism.
Individualised lifestyles can involve frequent interaction and engagement across wide-ranging social networks. Gregariousness and individualisation are fully compatible. However, when individualisation
is high, every person will have his or her own personal social network,
and these networks will be fluid, forever changing throughout the life
course. This is in contrast to all members of a family belonging to the
same neighbourhood, whose members all attend the same church,
whose children go to the same local school, then work in the same
industry; that is, when social relationships are super-imposed and
reinforcing and one could go through life without leaving the same
social circle (as opposed to an evolving network).

In recent times western youth (and other) researchers have found
individualisation an extremely useful concept in comparing the
present with the past. It was never quite this neat, but in the past in
Britain all children from a working class neighbourhood would often
attend the same local elementary school. Most of the boys would then
go to work in a major local industry – the coalmine, the steel mill, or
the shipyard. In some places most of the girls went into the cotton mill.
All the boys would have expected to stay in their industries and occupations for life. Boys who learnt a trade expected to be skilled for life
(though this was not necessarily how things worked out). The young
men and young women who had grown up together and who went to
school together would later on marry one another then settle down in
the same neighbourhoods where they grew up, have children at
roughly the same time, take holidays at the same regional resorts, and
travel the entire life course together sharing common experiences
including all major life events (marriage, parenthood, etc.) at roughly
the same times, and they would celebrate these events with one
another. It was as if they had boarded a public transport vehicle when
young, then journeyed on it together for the remainder of their lives.

Life is no longer remotely like this for the majority. Life has become
less predictable. The older 'solid' social formations have decomposed.
Families are less stable. People move about more. They move from
neighbourhood to neighbourhood during housing careers. Large firms
have downsized. Jobs are no longer expected to last for life. More
young people attend non-local secondary schools and universities.
Nothing seems to be for keeps any longer – jobs or personal relationships. ICT has enlarged and accelerated cultural flows. People can pick
up ideas and tastes from all parts of the world. The globalisation of
markets has made it more difficult for countries, and the communities
within them, to retain control over their fates. People are more mobile

– necessarily so in some cases and by choice in others. The motor car has made it easier for people to live at some distance from their workplaces. In any neighbourhood nowadays, at the beginning of the workday, residents disperse in many directions to practise many different occupations in different industries. At the end of a workday, colleagues disperse in all directions. The class structure has changed in shape. The middle classes have expanded and the working class has shrunk. One outcome is better chances for working class children to move up. Meanwhile the middle classes have become more diverse, riven by positional competition and inequalities.

Educational careers have been individualised. Young people study different combinations of modules in secondary and higher education. They need to maintain personal CVs in order to record their personal accomplishments. While still in education they gain particular bundles of experience in part-time jobs, then later in full-time jobs, and update their portfolios of experience and skills in lengthening CVs. The proportion of a population that maintains CVs could be used as one (preferably among several others) measurable indicator of individualisation. Consumer markets give everyone access to a wide range of goods and services. Individuals may make purchases in order to align with and signal their membership of a particular sub-culture (of which there are many nowadays – see Chapter 6), or more typically today, through their combinations of purchases they can express their individuality.

Social origins have not become irrelevant to life chances. Far from it! Families with the relevant financial, social and cultural resources can still give their children good starts in life. Success in education is, if anything, more vital than ever before. However, the procedure nowadays is not metaphorically to purchase tickets to board particular public transport vehicles (those reserved for the privileged) but to set up individuals in their own private vehicles, with differently powered engines, in which they then embark on personal journeys towards then into and through adult life.

Reflexivity

Individualisation is an objective trend or state, but can be expected to make a huge difference to how people feel and think about themselves and their circumstances. The subjective counterpart is said to be reflexivity. Individualisation should make every person more aware of and sensitive to how he or she is different from rather than what is shared in common with others, whether the others are the population of an entire country or a particular sub-category. Their individualised circumstances are expected to make people think about, to reflect upon, their personal biographies; how they reached their current situations, their particular assets (physical, mental, qualifications, financial etc) and how they might plan and purposively build preferred futures. This paradigm (definition of the situation to be studied) has become popular among western youth researchers (for example, see Cohen and Ainley, 2000; European Group for Integrated Social Research, 2001; Pais, 2003). They argue that concepts such as career routes, pathways and trajectories, however useful in the past, now obstruct rather than serve as aids to understanding young people's lives. They argue that young people's experiences are now fragmented and disjointed, and that order can be introduced into their lives only through biographies that are self-chosen, and which become personal projects rather than shaped by wider and powerful social forces and thereby laid out in advance. In other words, coherence in people's lives is constructed by the actors rather than imposed by recognisable external structures. Even if their lives do not unfold according to preconceived personal plans, coherence can be constructed by the actors after the events (see Devadason, 2007). Individuals' life stories about what has happened to them will then not only account for their current positions but also act as baselines from which they can plan their futures. In the past young people could look ahead at the adult lives of older cohorts from the same social categories as themselves, and thereby glimpse their own futures. It is argued that lives are no longer patterned in this way, that there has been a general destandardisation of the life course and the processes of making all life stage transitions, and that the scope for 'agency', that is, for individual 'agents' to reflect upon, plan and fulfil their plans, has been enlarged. This way of interpreting the lives and thoughts of present-day youth has been taken up by youth researchers throughout the western world, including Australia (see Box 4.2).

Young people today are certainly encouraged to think in the above terms. The 'entrepreneurial self', to use Kelly's (2006) description, has become hegemonic throughout the western world (treated as a fact of life that all must accept as such and come to terms with rather than just one of many possible ways of thinking about life). Careers advice is no longer as simple as presenting stark and limited options – shop or factory, apprenticeship or unskilled work (all for life). Young people are encouraged to diagnose their own talents and preferences. Computer packages can aid this, together with web searches for courses and jobs that are available all over Europe (if the young people live in the EU). Careers advice and guidance can no longer be once and

---

Box 4.2
Youth transitions in Australia

Johanna Wyn and various co-authors have reported the findings from the Life Patterns Project, which has tracked the lives of around 2000 young Australians from 1991 onwards. The Australian researchers claim that post-1970s cohorts of young people are a new generation, different from their predecessors in numerous ways:

• There are no longer any clear pathways into employment (or adulthood more generally) along which young people can travel.
• Life course transitions are now non-linear: young people often study and work simultaneously, and may leave then return to education.

Wyn and her colleagues argue that today's young people embrace the new uncertainties. They argue that adults (parents and governments) are misguided by old thinking if and when they try to repair young people's broken routes. They insist that today's young people:

• Do not want to settle immediately in stable adult roles.
• Are aware of and enthusiastic about their scope for choice.
• Are optimistic, have high aspirations, and really do self-determine their own biographies.

See Dwyer and Wyn, 1998, 2001; Stokes and Wyn, 2007; Wyn and Dwyer, 1999; Wyn and White, 1997; Wyn and Woodman, 2006.

---

for all time events. Individuals can and do re-assess themselves constantly, and re-assess their opportunities as their biographies unfold. It is said to have become much more difficult to simply stay with one's own crowd. These formations have disintegrated, or form and reform constantly. Pressures to simply conform have therefore lessened. The pressure is now said to be to develop personal initiative and resourcefulness, and to take responsibility for one's own life. Young people themselves usually interpret their biographies in this way. They blame themselves for 'messing around' at school, or for leaving school too soon. Then they typically go on to explain how they have 'got themselves together' and, however difficult their situations appear, they insist that they are 'in control' and accept responsibility for getting out (and up). There is certainly plenty of evidence of young people trying to plan their lives and futures, as best they can (see Anderson *et al.*, 2005). Manuela Du Bois-Reymond and her colleagues have assembled impressive evidence from the Netherlands (see Box 4.3).

Box 4.3
Youth transitions in the Netherlands

Manuela Du Bois-Reymond has studied 120 initially, declining to 85 young people in the Netherlands over a nine year period from 1988 until 1997. Henk Vinken has provided supportive evidence from a survey of 961 Dutch 16–40 year olds.

The evidence from these studies suggests that, just as in Australia (see Box 4.2), young people's life courses have been destandardised (transitions today are often non-linear, and are often reversed – back into education, for example). Youth life courses are said to have been biographised and dynamised. Today in the Netherlands young people are said, first of all, to decide who they are and what they want to become, and then to set about creating the lives that they want through choice biographies. While in life stage transition they typically prefer not to commit themselves but rather to keep options open.

This is said to apply in education, employment and sexual relationships. In the 1950s young people in the Netherlands typically postponed sex until marriage or at least until they were in stable relationships. Today's young people know that they have choices. They know about and have access to contraceptives. That said, the nine year longitudinal study has revealed some continuities across the generations. Most teenage girls still prefer sex to be within a steady relationship, and at age 19 there are still some deliberate postponers, but they are not frustrated – it is their choice.

See Du Bois-Reymond, 1998; Du Bois-Reymond *et al.*, 2001; Ravesloot *et al.*, 1999; Vinken, 2007.

It is necessary to emphasise that we are identifying trends. There are still young people who progress through upper secondary education then into universities, who had always assumed that this was what they would do, and explain their behaviour 'because it is what everyone else is doing' and what their parents expected. There was never a golden age when everything was mapped out and all school-leavers made smooth and rapid transitions into employment. In the 1950s and 60s many boys' hopes of apprenticeships were dashed (see Goodwin and O'Connor, 2005; Vickerstaff, 2003). Some young people did not settle quickly in employment but hopped from job to job. 'The lads' in Paul Willis's (1977) *Learning to Labour* felt that they were making their own career choices and were successfully wresting control of their biographies away from teachers and careers advisers. However, Paul Willis's lads did this as a group. Their response was sub-cultural rather than individual. In the past, when ambitions were thwarted at the time of school-leaving, achieved jobs were rarely very different from young people's hopes in terms of earnings or status, and the job hopping that went on was mostly between broadly similar (unskilled) jobs.

Young people in the past were not completely unreflexive. Nor nowadays are they all unable or unwilling to 'do what everyone else is doing' and to feel no need to provide any further explanation. That said, there is impressive evidence that youth life stage transitions have become much more complicated than in the past, more varied, and that there is simply less scope for drifting along with the crowd (see Bynner *et al.*, 2002). There are more decisions that young people are required to take: which courses in education, exactly when to leave, whether a particular job is worth taking, whether a training scheme will be helpful, and whether to remain home-based or to search more widely. Western youth researchers all agree that young lives have ceased to unfold in linear sequences, and that there is now more zig-zagging or yo-yoing – into the labour market then back into education, from unemployment into a job or training then back to unemployment, and also out of then back into the parental home following the break-up of a marriage or cohabitation (see European Group for Integrated Social Research, 2001; Pais, 2003). Few young people now marry their first serious boy/girlfriends. Most experience multiple sexually active relationships prior to living together, which in some countries is now most likely to be cohabitation which may, but does not necessarily, lead to marriage (see Chapter 5). It is claimed that these seemingly haphazard movements cannot be explained in terms of young people following pre-set routes, and that the only plausible explanations are in terms of their own reflexivity, plans and choices.

There is a huge western sociological literature on how adults' lives have been damaged by the economic and occupational restructuring, and by the so-called flexiblisation of labour markets and employment that have occurred during the last 30 years or so. This is a common discourse, not just applied to but also adopted by adults, not only in the west but also in Eastern Europe, when careers and expectations of orderly ends to their working lives, followed by secure retirement, were shattered when communism ended. A now widespread view in western sociology is that people need stable roles, jobs in particular, in order to maintain a sense of, and respect for, who they are and what they do. Insecurity is said to be corrosive of character (see Sennett, 1998). Today, the identities that people construct are always liable to be undermined. Hence, it is claimed, people live with perpetual anxiety about the state of their 'selves' (see Elliott and Lemert, 2006; Furedi, 2004).

In contrast, youth researchers have been virtually unanimous in claiming that today's young people are generally comfortable about handling uncertainty (see, for example, Wyn and Woodman, 2006). Youth's new condition allows young people to feel that they can become whoever they want to be irrespective of sex, race, religion, nationality or social class origins. 'Emerging adults' are said to be content, for the time being, to remain in a life stage where the future is full of possibilities (see Arnett, 2005). We shall see below that young people in Eastern Europe, unlike their elders, are mostly enthusiastic about the new possibilities and would not exchange these for the certainties of the past. Most of today's young people in East and West Europe appear to be competent in taking charge of and constructing their own lives, forming a sense of who they are and where they are heading, and building social capital (useful connections) rather than just receiving these from their families, neighbourhoods and education (see Holland *et al.*, 2007). It appears that how people in both Eastern Europe and the west have responded to macro-changes in their countries since the 1970s or 80s varies by life stage, which is not at all unusual but presents two future possibilities. Today's young people could grow disillusioned and frustrated as they become adults, still unable to establish themselves securely in jobs and lives of their choice. Alternatively, the adults of the future could be more comfortable living in present 'flexible' conditions than the adult cohorts whom they replace. Needless to say, outcomes may well differ from country to country, and also between socio-demographic groups within countries.

Post-communism

My experience is that with a few exceptions (see below) wherever and whenever ideas about individualisation and reflexivity are presented in Eastern Europe, the ideas are embraced enthusiastically. Local social scientists seem to realise that they need the concepts in order to grasp how things have changed in their countries: not the macro-economic and political changes themselves, but how these have transformed the lives of ordinary people, especially young people. The ideas accord with the view of the vast majority of young people in Eastern Europe who feel that they have been liberated from former constraints. Today's young people have no personal experience of life under communism, except possibly when they were young children, and this depends on how young they still are. Even so, they know about communism. They are told constantly about what it was like, just as young people in the west learn from parents and teachers how much more straightforward things were when they left school. Today's youth in Eastern Europe know that under communism their lives would have been planned for them. They know that they would have had little choice over which school to attend or when to leave. Their studies would have led directly to corresponding types of employment. They know that they would not have needed to worry about finding a job because the system always delivered, and they could have expected their jobs to last indefinitely. They know that their leisure time would have been catered for by the communist party youth organisations. They would not have been required, or able, to make major consumer choices. Young people under communism had some scope to manage their own time. There was private life when one was at home and among friends who, if they wished, could entertain themselves with pirated western music and dress in western fashions. Inside the communist party and its youth organisations there was scope for ambitious young people to display drive and initiative, but this had to be within strict limits. Today's youth in Eastern Europe are aware, because they are made aware of the past, that things are very different today. They are usually capable of and confident about making comparisons between the past and the present. Most say that life has become more difficult since the reforms. Most still say this even though communism is becoming ever more distant history. They know that there is now more poverty, that it is more difficult to obtain jobs, that in many places supplies of electricity and water are still unreliable, that savings have been wiped out by inflation (and this could happen again). Despite this, very few young people feel that the reforms were a mistake. They want their countries to press ahead, not to turn back. They know that they have lost the old security but they prefer the new uncertainties in which very little is guaranteed but so much is possible (see Chapter 8).

With the end of communism everything changed abruptly and dramatically for young people. Those who were approaching the end of their education saw the futures that were mapped out suddenly snatched away. Soon these same young people needed to make decisions. They (and their families) had to decide for how long to continue in education, which courses to apply for, and how to finance their studies. There was no longer a system which delivered job offers. Young people have needed to find jobs by asking family members and friends, approaching employers, scanning newspaper adverts and, increasingly, the internet. They have needed to learn how to present themselves and how to sell themselves to employers. Students have needed to decide whether to seek part-time jobs while studying, and if so they have needed to plan their timetables. Youth in the labour markets (employed and unemployed) who have been dissatisfied with their positions have needed to be constantly alert to new opportunities. Young people have been able to decide whether or not to leave home and search for work elsewhere. Internal passports have been scrapped and so have exit visas. Labour markets have widened. Whether to seek work away from home and, if so, exactly where, is up to young people; the system no longer has an answer. As soon as communism ended western consumer goods and advertising swept across Eastern Europe. Consumers had real choices. They had to make choices because there was always a choice of brands or genres – of music, clothing etc. Even if young people could not afford to purchase they could dream about the goods and lifestyles that they would buy if they could.

A highly significant change in all the former communist countries derives from a very basic difference between command and market economies. In a command economy it is possible (and this actually happened) that when a national economy expands virtually all sections of a population can share the benefits. People who are old enough usually recall the 1970s as the high point of communism. The economies were growing, targets had been met in successive 5-year plans, and consumer goods (televisions, washing machines, etc.) became more plentiful. All grades of workers in all industries benefited from this. When the economies ran into trouble in the 1980s (the reasons are irrelevant here) virtually everyone felt the pain. The West European social democratic regimes (which had tripartite economic planning and strong welfare states), which probably had their heyday between the 1950s and the 1970s, were pale imitations in this respect. The communist authorities tried to ensure that all sections of the populations benefited from growth and that, when necessary, all belts were tightened. In contrast, in any market economy it is possible for a particular business to prosper even if a national economy is depressed. Likewise an individual's career can progress even if a firm is downsizing and when most people are experiencing hard times. Conversely, some businesses and some careers flounder even in the best of times. The links between individuals', firms' and countries' fortunes are loosened. This decoupling means that, since the end of communism, young people's life chances have not been wholly dependent on the success of their countries' transitions. Individuals have been able to maintain personal optimism even when they have been pessimistic about their countries' prospects. In the dark days of the early 1990s there was widespread pessimism about some of the post-communist states' prospects. In some countries surveys found large proportions of young people planning to leave or at least thinking about leaving (not as many in recent years as in the early 1990s) (see Marasovic, 2004; Pejic, 2004). Subsequently young people have become more optimistic about their countries' futures, but most have been even more optimistic about their own. In a market economy it is possible to believe that your future depends mainly on you yourself – your choices, your determination, your ambition, your skills and your potential.

Individualisation and reflexivity are western concepts. East European researchers and young people have talked about the heightened importance of 'the self', especially the 'active self'. Young adults who succeed usually attribute their success to themselves (see Roberts *et al.*, 2002). Other young adults may disagree (in fact most disagree), while insisting that their own futures are in their own hands.

Tomanovic and Ignjatovic (2006), using Serbia as a case study, have disputed the applicability of the concept of individualisation to the lives of young people in Eastern Europe. They argue that individualisation is inhibited by structural constraints – the shortage of jobs, the shortage of housing, and pathetically low incomes. Indeed, they argue that rather than the progressive de-traditionalisation about which some western sociologists write (see Giddens, 1991), in Eastern Europe under post-communism there has been a contrary process of re-traditionalisation. It is not difficult to find evidence of re-traditionalisation in Eastern Europe – extended families being forced again into interdependence, peasants cultivating fields by hand, people 'making and mending', and urban dwellers resorting to growing their own food. However, life is not really reverting to how it was in pre-modern times. Eastern Europe is not losing its education systems and other modern services. Nowadays people have TV and radio which provide news, entertainment and role models. Tomanovic and Ignjatovic are certainly correct about young people in Serbia (and elsewhere in Eastern Europe) being denied access to the particular kinds of individualised lives led by young people in the west. They are right to point to the limits, the parameters set by structural constraints, on young people's agency. However, within these parameters, however wide or narrow, young people's biographies – their careers in education and the labour market, and their behaviour as consumers – can still be more individualised than was the case in the past, whether under communism or in an earlier period of capitalism. Moreover, in the face of whatever structural constraints apply, instead of relying on and waiting for a collective solution which lifts the constraints, young people can feel and decide that they need to find their own ways of building the lives and the futures that they want. As explained below, the real limitations of the concepts of individualisation and reflexivity – the gaps between the ideas and the realities – are just as serious in the west as in Eastern Europe, and the possibilities for individualisation and reflexivity are not tied closely to countries' levels of economic development and the prosperity of their populations.

Persistent systemic inequalities

Eastern Europe offers some clear examples of greater individualisation and a heightened role for personal reflexivity and agency during youth transitions, but it is equally clear, startlingly clear, that some older systemic inequalities have survived the major transformation that has occurred in these countries, and some new systemic inequalities have been created during the transformation. In all cases, these are exactly the same systemic inequalities that continue to pattern the life chances of young people in the present-day west just as fiercely as they did in the past. North American youth researchers have emphasised these continuities (see Box 4.4).

Box 4.4
Youth transitions in North America

North American youth researchers have played little part in an otherwise global debate about individualisation and reflexivity. Why have they stood on the sidelines? In North America there have been some similar recent trends to those in west Europe and Australia:

- Economic restructuring, with run-downs in employment in older 'smoke-stack' industries.
- Higher levels of youth unemployment.
- Later marriage and child-bearing.

These trends will have caused less shock (among young people and their investigators) because by the 1960s not only had completion of full secondary education (at age 18/19) become normal across North America; by then the USA and Canada also had mass systems of higher education, student fees, student debt, students combining learning with earning, and drop-outs returning to education. Also, a post-school period of under-employment (often called floundering) was already normal.

Since the 1980s North American youth researchers have stressed that:

- Young people overall have become even more highly educated, and even more ambitious (Lowe and Krahn, 2000).
- Different outcomes from youth transitions according to family class, gender,

and between rural and urban youth, have remained as wide as ever (Andres *et al.*, 1999).
- But the influence of parental class operates increasingly via educational attainments, and in this sense the processes have become more meritocratic (Bills, 2004; Andres and Grayson, 2003).
- Agency (personality factors, choice) operates only within structurally defined groups (Cote, 2002).

Conceptual innovation among American youth researchers has been mainly in response to:

(i) The spread and strengthening of consumer culture and values, delaying young people's development into responsible adults (Cote, 2000).
(ii) The consolidation of a post-youth, emergent adulthood life stage among 18–25 year olds (Arnett, 2005, 2006). During this life stage young adults:

- Feel in between youth and adulthood.
- Engage in identity exploration.
- See the future in terms of possibilities.

This life stage is said to have become normal among young adults from all social classes, and only those who become parents early are excluded.

In Europe and Australia the creation (not consolidation) of this life stage has provoked the debates about individualisation and reflexivity.

(i) Education and social class. It is as true in Eastern Europe as throughout the western world that connections between family social class and young people's attainments in education remain as strong today as ever (see chapter 3 for evidence from Eastern Europe). In the UK nowadays, around 80% of young people with parents in higher-level management and professional occupations go to university whereas less than a fifth from the non-skilled strata do so. In this respect, the UK is not an exceptional western country, and the relationship is equally strong throughout Eastern Europe (Roberts *et al.*, 2000). Lay people are usually surprised when they see these figures. They say that they had expected there to be a relationship, but not such a strong one. The character of the new class divisions that have arisen in Eastern Europe is discussed in chapter 7. In surveys up to now, investigators have used indicators of class such as income or parents' occupations and education. Young people from 'solid' middle class families (both parents with higher education and high-level jobs) have always, in the relevant investigations in Eastern Europe, stood a better

than evens chance of entering higher education (the exact figures have varied from country to country, and between regions). In all the lower class groups the percentages have always been far, far lower (see Roberts *et al.*, 2000).

This is not the place to debate the mechanisms whereby social class positions are transmitted inter-generationally (but see Box 4.5). Experts debate the relative importance of inherited ability, financial resources, and social and cultural capital. We know from surveys that were conducted during communism (see Gerber and Hout, 1995) and since the system ended that parents who themselves went to university have always been especially keen for their children to do well at school. We also know that young university graduates educated since the end of communism have been determined, and calculative, in planning their own children's educational success (Roberts *et al.*, 2002). They decide

---

Box 4.5
Pierre Bourdieu (1930–2002)

In addition to, or instead of, the ideas of Ulrich Beck, French and UK youth researchers have often turned to Pierre Bourdieu, the French sociologist, for concepts that aid our understanding of changes and continuities in youth life stage transitions. Bourdieu is best known for producing concepts which clarify how social inequalities are maintained and reproduced over time.

(i) Habitus. A habitus is a metaphorical dwelling in which we live, but it is in our minds rather than outside ourselves. The habitus is formed during childhood socialisation and is composed of perceptions, understandings and predispositions to action. A habitus can change, but only by building on what is already there. Bourdieu contended that different social classes develop and transmit different and distinctive habituses which contain accumulated class experience.

(ii) Social, cultural and symbolic capital. These operate like economic capital in so far as they can be invested and expanded, and produce returns. Depending on their social class locations, people are said to acquire different kinds and amounts of social capital (trusted relationships) and cultural capital (tastes and knowledge), which enable them to recognise people like themselves. Bourdieu also argued that persons with similar habituses will interact most easily.

These concepts suggest ways in which class inequalities can be perpetuated over time and passed on inter-generationally throughout major structural changes.

See Bourdieu, 1984; Bourdieu and Passeron, 1977.

at which stages they will use state schools, and exactly when they will intervene with private resources. Under communism, and subsequently, ambitious parents have paid for private coaching to prepare their children for the entrance exams at prestige secondary schools and universities. Nowadays some use private schools and pay for places at prestigious (rather than just 'ordinary') private universities (usually far more expensive than less prestigious private universities and state institutions). Many ensure that their children learn English. The particular ways in which advantaged parents transmit advantages may differ between countries, and may have changed over time, but the family background–educational attainment relationship has proved to be among the strongest and most persistent relationships discovered by modern sociology. If the relationship is suppressed at one level (during elementary schooling for example) it invariably pops up somewhere else (in secondary or higher education).

The relationship between education and social class origins may be less obvious today to western young people and their parents than was the case in the past. It would have been clearer when all secondary and higher education was paid for, and when few working class children received more than elementary schooling. Nowadays there is considerable upward mobility out of the working class (much more than in the past in absolute, though not in relative terms). Young people from working class homes and their parents may well feel that how pupils fare at school nowadays is basically due to their own ability and efforts. Higher education students know that collectively they are drawn from all kinds of social backgrounds, as are the occupants of higher-level jobs. The numbers and proportions of jobs at these levels have increased substantially in recent decades in all the advanced economies, creating extra room that could only be filled by promotions from beneath. Lay people will be most conscious of and sensitive to absolute chances of social ascent and descent: only sociologists measure relative rates of social mobility, which indicate how fluid or open a class system is, and these calculations always show that inequalities have not diminished over time. It may be the case that social class no longer directly 'causes' educational attainment but is mediated through students' own abilities and efforts. Even so, the fact is that these efforts and abilities are not pure personal characteristics, products of internally-generated reflexivity and agency, but are shaped by wider social forces.

(ii) Education and employment. Throughout Eastern Europe educational attainments have continued to be related to the kinds of occupations that young adults enter. This, like the relationship between family

backgrounds and educational attainments, is equally the case throughout the western world. In Eastern Europe higher education graduates
usually move into management and professional-grade or, if necessary, other non-manual jobs. They will rarely accept anything inferior
except as stopgaps. In this respect they are more like their
Mediterranean counterparts than young adults in Northern Europe
and North America who are quicker to move down the labour market
and accept the best that is offered (Roberts, 2001a). East Europe's
university graduates are more likely to prevaricate, to remain unemployed if necessary, or to enrol for more education if they cannot
obtain commensurate employment. Young people without higher
education are unlikely to be offered any non-manual positions. They
may move up to these levels during their adult careers, but they are
unlikely to be able to start in such positions.

During the 1990s the normal (in all modern societies) relationship
between grades of employment and pay levels became 'fuzzy'
throughout Eastern Europe. This was because public sector salaries
shrank alarmingly, including the salaries of university professors. It
became a matter for debate whether an academic really had a better
job than a taxi driver or hotel waiter both of whom were likely to be
earning much more when their official and unofficial incomes were
totalled. University education has not guaranteed immediate labour
market success (measured in terms of earnings) in post-communist
Eastern Europe. Rates of unemployment and under-employment have
been and remain high even among the best educated. In the short-term
there has often been scant if any reward in terms of remuneration.
However, as East Europe's economies have recovered from the initial
shock of reform, the normal relationship between occupations and
incomes has been re-established, most emphatically in the Central
European countries where recovery has been strongest (Domanski,
2000, 2001). Financial returns to education have risen in these countries, though they generally remain inferior to the returns that have
been normal in the west. Whether the east will catch up, or whether
the west will be easternised in this respect, is still unclear. However,
beneath the uncertainties and fuzziness, the normal relationship
between educational attainment and types of occupations has proved
enduring because of the expectations of the well-educated on the one
hand, and employers' requirements and preferences on the other.

(iii) Labour market segments. Once in the labour market the development of individuals' careers becomes subject to powerful labour
market processes. The positions that individuals achieve in the early
stages of their labour market careers exert a powerful influence over

their futures. This has been the case in the west for as long as information has been collected (a very long time). It applied under communism and in this respect nothing has changed in Eastern Europe.
Young adults who obtain full-time permanent jobs early on are most
likely to remain in such employment, even if they change jobs, for year
after year after year. Those who are mainly unemployed during their
first year in the labour market run high risks of remaining unemployed year after year. Those who become successfully self-employed
early on are most likely to remain so for many years.

These continuities are displayed in Table 4.1, which is based on the
education and labour market careers of samples totalling 1,800 25–29
year olds from selected regions in Ukraine, Georgia and Armenia who
were interviewed in 2002 (see Roberts, 2006a). The table gives the
proportions of all those in a given position during each year, who were
still in the same position during the following year. The table shows a
steady outflow from education, then indicates how those young
people who found full-time jobs soon after leaving school or college
were most likely to remain in full-time employment for year after year
after year. It also shows how those who experienced persistent unemployment during their first year in the labour market stood high risks
of remaining out-of-work for year after year after year. There are other
strong continuities in youth labour market careers in Eastern Europe:
by occupational levels – management, professional, other non-manual
etc – and also in employees tending to stick within either the public or
the private sector (Roberts, 2006a). The explanation of these continuities is straightforward and well known in western labour market sociology. Successful experience in a particular kind of employment
makes the individual attractive to employers who want to fill similar
jobs. A record of unemployment has the opposite effect. Individuals
look most attractive to any future employer if they can demonstrate

Table 4.1 *Percentages who remained in the same main labour market positions between consecutive years*

	1993/ 94	1994/ 95	1995/ 96	1996/ 97	1997/ 98	1998/ 99	1999/ 00	2000/ 01	2001/ 02
Education	86	80	80	76	73	62	63	72	69
Full-time job	89	82	88	92	88	92	95	93	92
Self-employed	100	82	81	92	82	96	93	93	87
Unemployed	87	82	86	89	89	92	84	89	93

Source: Roberts (2006a).

successful experience in a similar occupation. Many private sector employers in Eastern Europe prefer to avoid staff who are accustomed to public sector routines (which are more indulgent). The manner in which young employees who gain experience with international organisations become a distinct career group is just one example of more general processes (Lepper and Schule, 1999). These processes may not be as visible as the rules of a command economy but they are extremely powerful. Job changing tends to occur within labour market segments. The boundaries are not built with the same materials as brick walls but they can be just as hard to break through.

We know from western experience of youth transitions that apparently haphazard movements usually take place within limits (MacDonald *et al.*, 2001). Individuals rarely yo-yo from a steady professional job into unskilled work, or *vice versa*. Yo-yoing back to full-time education tends to be confined to a small number of young people and they are usually pushed back by labour market difficulties. So-called non-linear careers are usually symptoms of disadvantage rather than a new general pattern (Furlong *et al.*, 2005).

The normalisation of a period of youth under-employment (see chapter 2) could be due to young people wanting to keep their options open and wanting to delay becoming tied down by adult responsibilities (Arnett, 2005), but these preferences (if indeed these are the preferences of those concerned) have developed in contexts where many young adults are unable to enter occupations in which they want to settle. In Eastern Europe most young adults seem to know what they really want. They want to work according to their specialties – to use and to be respected for their special qualifications and skills – in jobs that will enable them to access the western way of life. They grasp such jobs and settle when the chance arises.

(iv) Place. This tends to be overlooked by researchers who portray young people constructing choice biographies. How young adults' lives unfold depends hugely on where they happen to live: place is one of the 21st century's great dividers. Inequalities between countries, between the global north and south, for example, widened during the second half of the 20th century. There are also huge inequalities in life chances that depend on whether a person is born and reared in east or west Europe. Place is also a major source of inequalities within countries (see Roberts *et al.*, 2002). The labour markets in country and regional capitals always offer wider options, and more top-level jobs, than the labour markets in smaller towns and rural areas. Regions that were once close to the iron curtain (on the eastern side), which tended to be economic backwaters in communist

times, have often become boom areas under post-communism. Regions on the new eastern border of the EU, which could have been on major trade routes pre-1989, have been vulnerable to the opposite fate. Some towns and cities in Eastern Europe have been revived by inward investment. Others have become business wastelands. We know that in all western countries risks of unemployment, and likewise chances of obtaining a management or professional level job, vary greatly from place to place even when young people's educational qualifications and family backgrounds are held constant. This applies all over the world. It may be true that migration is an option (a new option, with a much wider range of possible destinations, for young people in Eastern Europe). However, there are always costs (leaving friends, family and home place), and migrants rarely have equal opportunities with locals in the places to which they move.

(v) Gender, race and ethnicity. Gender divisions among youth in Eastern Europe were discussed in Chapter 3 and will be revisited in Chapter 5, but to recap, there are major differences in males' and females' educational careers (the subjects that they study), the kinds of employment that they obtain, and (as will be explained in Chapter 5) their domestic responsibilities. Throughout Eastern Europe the Roma are a seriously disadvantaged ethnic group. Particular countries have other ethnic, racial and national minorities. Is there any country in the world where young people's transitions to adulthood are unaffected by these inequalities? Individualisation and reflexivity have not obliterated these long-standing social divisions.

(vi) Families and housing. These topics are also discussed in detail in the next chapter. The point that needs to be anticipated here is that, in some western countries, new 'emergent adulthood' life space has been created by the normalisation of an interval between young people leaving their parents' dwellings and settling down in marital, child-bearing/rearing relationships. This life space, where it exists, may be a period for self-discovery and self-growth free from the constraints of childhood on the one side and adulthood on the other. However, this life space does not exist for most 21st century youth. It does not exist in most of the developing world, or in Europe's Mediterranean countries, or in Eastern Europe where most young adults remain under daily parental gaze until after they have married and have their own children. In any case, western young people's ability to make successful transitions out of their parents' homes into independent accommodation depends heavily on the support (advice and money) that their families are able and willing to offer (Goldscheider and Goldscheider, 1999).

Summary and conclusion: structured individualisation

We have seen that the concepts of individualisation and reflexivity are of great value for understanding how the end of communism has transformed the situations of young people in Eastern Europe. Their biographies have been individualised. Circumstances today oblige them to be self-aware and reflexive. However, we have also seen that it is a mistake to imagine that these trends have even lessened let alone eliminated long-standing systemic inequalities. Some youth researchers who have highlighted the extent of individualisation and emphasised the importance of the reflexive self in present-day youth transitions have based their conclusions on qualitative studies of necessarily small samples of young people and can be accused of failing to see the 'big picture'. They can also be accused of paying great attention to what young people say and neglecting what is actually happening to them. It is important to bear in mind constantly that individualisation and the enlarged need and scope for reflexivity are just trends.

While acknowledging these trends, some sociologists attempt to take account of persistent systemic inequalities by arguing that individuals' scope for choice is bounded (within limits) and that the breadth of these limits varies between different groups of young people (Evans, 2002). They accept that all young people are decision-takers: they all have some say over when to quit full-time education, and whether to accept a particular job offer, but none have a free choice from all the jobs in an economy. The young people who form ambitions, then gradually bring them to fruition, are mostly from advantaged families, and exceptionally successful in education (Evans and Heinz, 1994). Others change their minds. Courses in education may be chosen 'just in case' a qualification may prove useful, and decisions are often deferred until 'just in time' when few options are open (Vaughan, 2005). Job ambitions often crystallise – firm up – only after a particular type of employment has been entered.

Rather than 'bounded choice' my own terminological preference is 'structured individualisation' (see Roberts *et al.*, 1994; see also Ball *et al.*, 2000). Bounded choice implies that there are boundaries for researchers to identify which circumscribe the life chances of particular groups of young people. This terminology also allows that historical trends may have widened the boundaries and weakened these barriers. My own reading of the evidence is that all the old predictors of life chances, certainly in labour markets (family background, educational attainments, place etc) remain as powerful as ever, and that there has been no widening or weakening. However, the predictors now work in individualised configurations. A person's life chances still depend on his or her particular family background, educational attainments, gender, ethnicity and so on, and these dependences have not lessened in strength, but every individual young person is now less likely than formerly to know many others who share exactly the same configuration of circumstances. The outcome will be that individual young people are more sensitive to how they differ from others, and less aware of opportunities and barriers that they all share in common. Young people themselves (and other lay people) are therefore likely to commit what Furlong and Cartmel (2007) call the 'epistemological fallacy' and fail to recognise the extent to which their own pathways towards adulthood are socially structured. They can be excused. Youth researchers who hear only young people's voices and fail to identify the structures have less excuse.

Further reading

Cohen, P. and Ainley, P. (2000), 'In the country of the blind? Youth studies and cultural studies in Britain', *Journal of Youth Studies*, 3, 79–95.

Du Bois-Reymond, M. (1998), '"I don't want to commit myself yet": young people's life concepts', *Journal of Youth Studies*, 1, 63–79.

Evans, K. (2002), 'Taking control of their lives? Agency in young adults' transitions in England and the new Germany', *Journal of Youth Studies*, 5, 245–69.

Furlong, A. and Cartmel, F. (2007), *Young People and Social Change*, Open University Press, Maidenhead, second edition.

Roberts, K., Clark, S. C. and Wallace, C. (1994), 'Flexibility and individualisation: a comparative study of transitions into employment in England and Germany', *Sociology*, 28, 31–54.

Wyn, J. and Woodman, D. (2006), 'Generation, youth and social change in Australia', *Journal of Youth Studies*, 9, 495–514.

Housing and family transitions and gender divisions

5

Introduction

Eastern Europe is definitely not prototypical in these aspects of young people's lives. Since the end of communism, youth in Eastern Europe have been catching up (very slowly in most places), and, contrary to much opinion in Eastern Europe, some of the problems about which young people and their families currently complain are consequences of this catching-up rather than continuing to lag.

This chapter opens with a brief history of changes in family and household formation among young people in the west, then explains how Eastern Europe ended communism in a time warp, unaffected by post-1950s western trends. Subsequent developments in Eastern Europe including delayed marriages, lower fertility and more unpartnered parents are then shown to be outcomes of modernisation rather than, as generally suspected within the countries, the particularly difficult labour market conditions confronting young people. The chapter then explores gender divisions in family life, and notes and explains the very limited appeal (up to now) of western feminism in Eastern Europe.

A brief history of western practices

The nuclear family has become the normal residential unit whenever and wherever countries have urbanised and industrialised (Shorter, 1976). This has applied irrespective of how common the nuclear family household was in pre-modern times. Nuclearisation makes it possible for young people to move in search of jobs. Modern employment provides individuals with their own wages or salaries and thereby releases them from dependency on their families. The resultant modernisation of family life always poses problems. One is the control of children assuming that they are excluded from employment while both of their parents may be employed, and when care and control by extended families cannot be relied on. Another problem is the care of elders. The child problem has been addressed by various combinations of the domestication of women and compulsory schooling. The elder problem has usually been addressed by providing pensions and other forms of state welfare.

Young people need a supply of affordable and accessible housing if they are to establish their own nuclear families. In the earliest industrial societies, the normal practice was for them to rent lodgings or dwellings from a private landlord. These rentable provisions were subsequently complemented by housing which was owned and managed by charitable associations and public authorities. Young people enrolling in higher education, if they have not remained home-based, have usually been able to expect housing in student accommodation, or to be offered sheltered transitions into the private rented sector (see Rugg *et al.*, 2004). Young people have also been able to purchase their own properties on the housing market, and in the advanced economies the proportions of dwellings that are owner-occupied have risen and renting has declined, though it is still a very common first step after young people leave their parents' homes. Long-term loans (mortgages secured by the value of the dwelling) have been made available, and have become the normal way in which entrants step onto the house ownership 'ladder'.

It has always been possible for young people to leave the parental home to live singly, but in western countries there has been no general social expectation or associated pressure on singles to leave. In contrast, if and when they have wished to marry or to live with a partner, young people have usually been expected to leave the parental home. Starting married life in the home of one set of parents has been considered unsatisfactory. When they can afford their own place, it is said that a couple are able to marry. If they lack the means, they are expected to wait.

When responsibility for setting up and maintaining a new nuclear household passes to a young couple, their feelings towards each other, and these feelings alone, dictate whether or not they are suited. Families' views become irrelevant unless a couple care to take them into account. No permission to leave home and marry is required. When this happens traditional rules disappear – the contributions to the home-making couple that are expected from the man's and the woman's family, and even who should pay for a wedding. These matters are left to negotiation among those concerned.

Another 'grey' area that is left to negotiation at the household level concerns parents' obligations to children of working age who are still living at home, and the contributions that employed young people should make to household expenses. Should parents charge their children for their keep? Are the parents obliged to be supportive? The law may not require, but in all countries government policies assume and expect. Young adults (up to age 25 or so depending on the country) have reduced welfare entitlements (unemployment benefit for example) while living with their parents. Governments usually assume that parents will provide some support for students in post-compulsory education. Government assumptions may not accord with parents' opinions. Parents typically want their governments to do more, not necessarily because they themselves want to offer less but because they feel that whatever support they offer should be manifestly their own choice rather than an obligation (Holdsworth, 2005).

Exactly how western youth make their housing transitions has changed over the last 50 years, not so much because of any changes in the housing regimes but because of changes in how young people form and dissolve relationships with one another, and the uses that they make of the housing stock. Many years ago it was common for marriage to be the outcome of a young couple's first serious heterosexual liaison, and for full sexual intimacy to be deferred until marriage. Before the Second World War it was common for women not only to be virgins when they married but also to remain ignorant about sex and conception: they had been told that their husbands would instruct them. If a couple was seen together regularly it was presumed that they were 'courting' rather than just 'dating', and friends and families would assume that they were en route towards marriage.

After the Second World War it became normal for couples to become sexually intimate prior to marriage (Schofield, 1973). The reasons included the declining influence of religion and respect for traditions more generally, the sexualisation of youth by Hollywood, popular music and the fashion industry, and full employment and higher earnings for young workers which meant that couples could afford to marry if they 'had' to. Pre-marital sex was condoned provided that, in the event of pregnancy, both parties were prepared 'to do the right thing'. Under these circumstances, pre-marital sex could be regarded as home-making (and therefore virtuous) as opposed to home-breaking extra-marital sex (Klein, 1965). In many countries the mean age of first marriages fell during the 1950s. Many of the marriages between teenagers were so-called 'shotgun weddings'.

'Shotguns' became increasingly rare in the 1960s and 70s. The contraceptive pill became available from 1961, and its use by young single women gradually became normal. For the first time in history women had a reliable, aesthetically acceptable form of contraception that they controlled. Sex and conception were henceforth decoupled. Sexual intimacy came to be accepted in relationships that were neither intended nor expected to lead to marriage. Over time what was accepted became expected in anything other than a casual dating relationship. So a series of sexually active affairs became normal prior to settling down. Nowadays in Britain, before first living as a couple, young men and women have typically already had 4–6 sexual partners (National Centre for Social Research, 2003).

Sexual intimacy in private is easiest when young people have moved out of their parents' homes. Many higher education students, those who do not attend a local university, have always begun to live independently ahead of others in their age group (Jones, 1995). Over time, as explained in Chapter 3, more and more young people have been enrolling in higher education. How likely they are to return to their parents' homes depends on whether they need to (for economic reasons as a result of unemployment or low salaries), and it also varies from country to country. In Europe there is a north-south split. Family ideologies in the Mediterranean countries stipulate that children should remain at home until they marry: anything else indicates that something is wrong with the family unless a young person is 'compelled' to move, usually for education or employment (Holdsworth, 2004). In northern Europe and North America during the last 30 years it has become the norm for all groups of young people, irrespective of whether they enter higher education, to leave the parental home prior to marriage. They move out to become independent (Molgat, 2002). They may live singly, share a house or apartment with other young singles (see Heath and Kenyon, 2001), or cohabit with a sexual partner. Cohabitation may, but does not necessarily, lead to marriage, but cohabitation is rarely flippant – the partners usually express a long-term, indefinite commitment to one another (Jamieson *et al.*, 2002). Most first-time marrying couples in Britain have previously cohabited with only one partner (the person they subsequently marry) (Ermisch and Francesconi, 1999). Today, most marrying couples in northern Europe are already living at the same address; in other words, they are cohabiting. Cohabitation has been normalised, meaning that it is now a statistical norm and is considered acceptable. The meaning of marriage is no longer crystal-clear. It is certainly a public declaration of a couple's commitment to one another. However, it may precede or follow parenthood. Some cohabiters simply remain cohabiters. Housing and family life stage transitions are now much more complex and varied than when young people would leave their parents' homes, marry, settle in a new nuclear family household, and lose their virginity all within a single day, which remained common until the 1960s (see Leonard, 1980).

As transitions have become more complicated, no longer governed by any strict rules, new lifestyle options have become available for young people in western countries. Nowadays some live openly as gay, lesbian and bisexual. Single parenthood (nearly always single motherhood) has become more common, and socially acceptable. The number of cohabiting parents has blurred the old divide between single and other mothers. In the past the status of single mother was never sought – it was always an unfortunate consequence of a relationship breakdown. This is no longer always the case. Single women who become pregnant are no longer expected to abort, marry quickly, or have the baby adopted. These are still options, but the mothers can also choose to keep their babies and raise them as single mothers. Earlier on it became possible to have sex free from worries of conception. Nowadays women can conceive without having sex. Some opt for donor insemination. Sex, conception and marriage have been thoroughly divorced.

Eastern Europe

When communism ended the whole of Eastern Europe was locked in a time warp. It was a mixture of pre-modern and early modern practices as regards young people's family and housing transitions. The entire world region had been sealed off from the developments that had taken place in the west from the 1950s onwards. An important set of reasons for this had to do with the system of housing allocation that operated under communism.

The housing stock in Eastern Europe was a mixture of socially-owned (rented) and owner-occupied properties. Communism was against landlordism, but it had no principled objection to people owning objects that they used themselves – television sets, cars and houses. The proportions of dwellings that were privately owned varied from country to country and between rural and urban areas. Most regions in most of the countries that became communist were pre-modern at that point. Most people lived in rural areas and most were peasants. In the countryside, when the communists came to power, peasants kept their own dwellings. If the dwellings had been owned by large landowners, the peasants took possession. These properties were passed on through families. A property could be extended, or with permission (which would usually be granted) a family could build an additional dwelling on its 'own' land. Families that migrated to urban areas often retained a country 'dacha'. Urbanites who wished to do so could build a dacha. The building would usually be on a self-help basis (with assistance from friends and relatives) (see Dingsdale, 1986).

In towns and cities the communist state (the local government and other public agencies) took possession of most properties and was responsible for virtually all new building – typically, in the case of residential building, medium-rise and high-rise apartment blocks of two and three-room units. The construction was often poor quality. Apartments were often over-crowded with three generations living together, and all rooms used for both living and sleeping. This housing stock is a legacy of communism that people will live with for years to come.

Owner-occupation in Eastern Europe was not exactly the same as in the west. The big difference was that in Eastern Europe properties could not normally be sold. There were no housing markets. No-one could (legally) save enough money to purchase. It was impossible for private citizens to obtain bank loans for this (or any other) purpose. People could not construct 'housing careers', buying, occupying then selling, then buying again, moving up-market as their incomes rose. Privately owned dwellings were retained and passed on through families.

Much of the socially-owned stock could also be passed on through families. Usually a co-resident had the right to inherit the tenancy on the death of a tenant. Tenancies were rarely handed back to the authorities, if this could be avoided. Once allocated, if at all possible, a dwelling would be retained by a family. A grandchild would move in with a grandparent, partly to make best use of space, but also so that the grandchild would inherit the right to occupy. It was possible to arrange exchanges of socially-owned properties, usually within a family. For example, a widow or pensioner couple might exchange their larger apartment for a young family's more cramped accommodation.

Families could enlarge their housing assets by extending an existing privately owned property or building a new one, but this was rarely possible in urban areas where they could apply for an allocation from the socially-owned stock. This stock was always being enlarged. Everywhere there were constant building programmes yet supply never seemed to catch up with demand. This is another respect in which communism was an economy of systemic shortages – of housing, labour, consumer goods . . . everything. Planning was less effective than market forces in matching demand and supply. Obtaining a new property was usually by placing a name on a waiting list where it would normally remain for years, and throughout this period someone would have to make down-payments for the awaited apartment. Young people could place their own names on waiting lists. Parents could do this on behalf of their children. This would be in the hope that by the time a young person became a couple with children, they would be in line for a unit. Child-rearing families had priority on housing lists. Young singles had no chance.

An effect of this housing system was that young people usually depended on their families to gain access to their own places. Students who attended a university away from home could expect to be offered student accommodation. Young men had army accommodation while on military service. Afterwards they had to return to family dependence unless:

(i)   It was possible informally to rent a room in someone else's dwelling, but this would be a temporary rather than a life-long arrangement, especially if the lodger planned at some point to marry and become a parent.

(ii) Some jobs offered 'tied accommodation'. State and party bureaucrats, university staff and some cultural workers (actors, musicians, artists) could expect to be allocated city centre apartments. Under communism the middle classes lived in the inner cities while workers were housed on city peripheries (see Szelenyi, 1983). Industrial plants often controlled accommodation that could be allocated to key workers. A new apartment was one of the 'carrots' that induced young people to migrate to Siberia and other regions where the economies were being developed.

If a family owned or occupied a property, it was nearly always in the upcoming generation's interest to keep it in the family. As explained earlier, under communism there were endemic housing shortages. Market economies over-produce. Buyers have choice: it is sellers who are under pressure. In a command economy the producers (workers) are protected: buyers have to queue. An outcome was that it was usually some years after they married and became parents that young couples would obtain their own places. Until then, they would live with one or the other set of parents or grandparents in a three-room apartment (at best) if they were in a town or city.

Young people in Eastern Europe were hardly touched by any of the exciting developments that were happening in the west from the 1950s onwards. This was partly due to the extent to which they remained under parental scrutiny. Housing prospects depended on maintaining good family relationships. It was also due to the extent to which the communist authorities could control young people's lives outside their families. The contraceptive pill did not become generally available in Eastern Europe. Abortion was communism's preferred method of birth control. It was available on demand to delay starting a family, to space out births, and to prevent more arrivals when a woman did not want more children. It has remained a common method of birth control under post-communism. In Karelia, a region of Russia bordering Finland, the number of abortions fell during the 1990s but at the turn of the millennium there were still more abortions than live births in the region (Aksentyeva and Gumenyuk, 2000). In 2005 in Georgia the typical woman was still experiencing 3.1 abortions in her lifetime (equivalent to two-thirds of all pregnancies), 3.2 in Azerbaijan, and between 2 and 3 in different regions of Russia (Corso, 2007). A survey of 16–17 year olds in Brno (Czech Republic) and Yerevan (Armenia) at the turn of the millennium found widespread approval of abortion for single women, but less tolerance in the case of married women (Agadjanian, 2002).

Serial affairs were not normalised under communism. Youth was not sexualised in the way that was happening in commercialised countries (through advertising, films and popular music, for example). In any case, although atheistic, post-1920s communist authorities endorsed traditional family values. Their policies were generally pro-natal. The Soviet Union and its satellites had a continuing need to replenish the populations following the losses during the world wars, plus communism's civil wars and purges. Cohabitation was not an option – especially in the more traditional cultures as in Roman Catholic Poland and the Muslim Central Asian republics. Young people in Eastern Europe never enjoyed the independence that is conferred by markets when young people have their own incomes to spend as they please. In Eastern Europe students who lived in university accommodation were subject to the kind of rules that were abandoned in western countries in the 1960s. The counterparts of western student unions (student palaces under communism) were run by the universities, not by students themselves (see Chapter 6). And in Eastern Europe students did not have the option of moving off campus to use commercial leisure facilities (bars, discos and suchlike); such places did not exist.

Since the end of communism things have changed. Markets have arrived in Eastern Europe. So have western culture and role models, and contraception. Even so, as we have just seen, many young women are still relying on old methods of birth control, and most young people are still relying on old methods to make their housing transitions (see Box 5.1).

Box 5.1

Housing transfers

Tania, a young woman who was interviewed in 1999 in Lviv (western Ukraine), had married at age 20. Tania, her husband and their daughter lived in a two-room flat, which had been inherited from Tania's parents when the latter moved into Tania's grandparents' flat. In time, Tania expected to make an identical move (into her parents' flat) whereupon the flat that she and her husband currently occupied would house Tania's own daughter.

However, for many young people old methods have become even less effective than in the past. This is because waiting lists move forward less rapidly. Socially-owned housing has been privatised, usually at nominal prices to the occupiers. The authorities have wanted to privatise the responsibility for repairs and renovation. Housing markets have developed. It is now possible to buy or rent a property on the market. The barrier, for most young people, is the cost. Loans for house purchase are now offered by some banks in some countries, but are not yet available for most young people in most of Eastern Europe. In order to buy, a purchaser normally has to pay the full price in cash, which, if at all possible, might depend on pooling family resources. Another barrier to young people moving into their own places is that in less secure post-communist times a household's security has usually depended on maintaining several income streams. Young couples may well feel that they could not afford to live as an independent unit. Or they know that, if they leave home, their parents will be destitute. Bornhorst and Commander (2006) argue that, in Poland, the slow development of housing markets inhibits the movement of labour from high unemployment regions to more prosperous parts of the country.

However, there are huge differences in how families have fared under post-communism. Under the old system some families accumulated as much and sometimes more housing than they really needed. Under post-communism such families may have been able to sell a surplus apartment. Or they have controlled sufficient housing units to allow young couples or even singles to have their own places (provided they have been able to afford to live independently). Some young people have earned enough from business, abroad, or a high salary job to purchase their own apartments and even (in a very few cases) to build Dallas-type mansions on city outskirts. In most towns and (non-capital) cities in Eastern Europe it was possible in the 1990s (and sometimes subsequently) to buy a two-room apartment for

$10,000, sometimes less. Young people who have been able to make housing transitions in their early or mid-20s have been emulating North European and North American practices in other ways: living as young singletons, and cohabiting as childless couples (see Roberts *et al.*, 2003). However, up to now in Eastern Europe the majority of young people have continued to rely on old methods which usually means remaining with their parents, marrying and becoming parents themselves in their 20s (sometimes earlier, sometimes later), then waiting until old methods deliver a place of their own, usually following the death of an older family member.

Tables 5.1 and 5.2 present some evidence from surveys conducted in 1999 among a total of 1,300 25–26 year olds in Moscow and Vladikavkaz (both Russia) and Dneipropetrovsk (Ukraine). We can see in Table 5.1 that a half or more of the 25–26 year olds were still living as singles in Moscow and Vladikavkaz; in Dneipropetrovsk the young adults were making more rapid family life stage transitions. It was also the case that in all three locations there were more couples with children than couples-only. The highest proportion of couples-only was in Moscow. In both the other places living together was being followed quickly by parenthood. We can also see in Table 5.1 (bottom half) that very few singles in any of the locations had their own places. In Moscow a bare majority (52%) of the couples with children had moved into their own places. In the other locations most of the 25–26

Table 5.1 *Place and family/housing situations*

	Place		
	Moscow %	*Vladikavkaz* %	*Dneipropetrovsk* %
Family situations			
Single	50	68	37
Couple	21	9	13
Couple and child(ren)	25	16	41
Single parent	4	7	9
Percentages with own places			
Single	6	6	11
Couples	38	33	23
Couple and child(ren)	52	44	34
Single parents	25	14	22
Total	25	15	23
n=	500	500	300

Source: see text.

year old parents were still living with their own families. Table 5.2 lists
the ways in which the samples' current dwellings had been acquired,
and how the respondents intended to acquire their next dwellings if
and when they moved. We can see that reliance on the state (the most
common way in which current dwellings had been acquired) was
expected to play a much reduced role in future moves. Just under a
quarter of the young adults were waiting for and expecting to inherit
a family dwelling. Those who thought that they would purchase
mostly planned to purchase outright or with family help. Only 10%
expected to make their next moves with loans from other sources.

Temporary migration has been a way in which some young people
have accumulated the money to purchase a flat. However, for other
young people migration has aggravated their housing problems. This
applies when families have been displaced by war, as in the Balkans
and Caucasus. In the South Caucasus the war between Armenia and
Azerbaijan between 1988 and 1994, during which Armenia occupied
Nagorno Karabakh and its surrounding territories in Azerbaijan, led
to around 540,000 Armenians fleeing from Azerbaijan, while around
800,000 Azerbaijanis fled from Armenia or were displaced from the
war zones to safer regions of their country. At first these displaced
Azerbaijanis were housed in temporary accommodation, including so-
called tent cities (see Box 5.2), which then became their homes for
many years.

One might wonder why Azerbaijan, with its oil and gas revenues,
was not rehousing its displaced families more quickly and into better
accommodation. The politics were that unless Azerbaijan had people
who remained eager to return to their original homes, the country

Table 5.2 *Methods of acquiring present and future dwellings*

	Current %	Future plans %
State	40	15
Inherit	33	23
Purchase		
Outright	19	32
Family help	6	16
Other loan	2	10
Other	-	5
n=	1175	1085

Source: see text.

Box 5.2

Tent City, Sabirabad, Azerbaijan: the Hasanli family

In 2007 this so-called Tent City was a site on the outskirts of Sabirabad, one of the major towns in the region of Aran-Mugan, where there were hundreds and hundreds of 'tents'. Most of the canvas had disappeared by 2007 or had been supplemented by stone, metal, wood, mud and other such materials. The 'roads', yards and surrounds, and the floors of the dwellings, were bare earth. Water was from standpipes scattered along the roads. There were rows of communal toilets also along the roadways.

Up until 1993 the Hasanli family had lived in a house in the centre of a village in Nagorno Karabakh. The husband and wife were both vocational school graduates. Both had worked for the state, the wife as an economist, and he in a supply department. Their house was large (by local standards) and they also owned a plot of land. *'Our village was being shelled by the Armenians. We didn't dare to switch on any lights. Our own house was not hit, but the Armenians then entered the village and we all had to flee. At that time all 30,000 people who lived in the area were having to flee. At first we went to the next village. Then we had to go across a river. We had to swim. We then took a truck to a village on the border of Nagorno Karabakh. We stayed there for a month. Then the Armenians occupied the whole region and we were brought here* (to Sabirabad). *At first we were all living in a school. Then we were brought to this tent city. There are people here from all over Nagorno Karabakh. When we first left our house we thought that we would be away for just 10–15 days. We miss our land. Our fathers and grandfathers lived there.'*

In 1993, when the family fled, the Hasanlis had two young children, Nijat a son aged 15 in 2007 and Konul a daughter aged 14. They had grown up in Tent City. The Hasanlis knew that houses were being built for them and they would occupy one in 2007 or 2008. Unfortunately it appeared that some of the new accommodation had shared bath and toilet facilities. The family was existing on the standard government grant of 9 manats ($10) per person per month. This was being supplemented modestly by Mr Hasanli gaining some farm work during summer/harvest time.

The Hasanlis did not expect to be able to re-occupy their original house in Nagorno Karabakh. They had no idea what had happened to it. They did not know whether they would ever be able to return to their original village, but they definitely wanted to go back. *'The children would be happy to go back'* (difficult not to believe this, given the conditions in which they were living). *'We all dream about this all the time.'*

would never recover its lost territories. What would happen to the young people in the Hasanli family? By 2008 the family would have been rehoused into a two or three room apartment. When the son married, his wife would move into the apartment. When the daughter married she would move in with her husband. Flats in Sabirabad could be purchased for $4,000 in 2007, but there seemed to be no way in which the Hasanlis could hope to save such an amount. Maybe the son and/or daughter would eventually migrate from Azerbaijan.

Crisis

All across Eastern Europe there is small talk and public debate about the crisis of young people's inability to make satisfactory housing and family transitions. This sociological jargon is not normally used, but the jargon pinpoints the issues. Economic conditions and governments may be (and usually are) regarded as serious problems, but young people being unable to marry and to have children, and to find their own places to live, are the really hot topics. In Eastern Europe this crisis is invariably attributed to the economic conditions that have arisen under post-communism. This is a mistake. The economic conditions are an important part of the context, but the same trends have occurred in many other parts of the world, including most western countries. The trends are simply explained, and worked into public issues, in different ways in different countries and regions thereof.

(i) Unable to marry. One aspect of the crisis in Eastern Europe is said to be that large numbers of young couples are unable to marry. Why? Because they are not only unable to move into their own places at present but can see no way in which this will become possible even in the long-term, or, even if it became possible, they cannot envisage how they would be able to support themselves as child-rearing independent households. It may also be the case that the young people's own parents can see no way in which they would be able to remain self-sufficient if their children left home. The outcome has been an upward movement in the mean ages of first marriages and live births.

Yet these developments are not confined to Eastern Europe. They have occurred in most western countries. The exceptions are those countries (the Mediterranean countries in Europe) where it remained normal throughout the 20th century for young people to continue to reside with their parents until the former married in their late 20s or 30s. This used to be attributed (by north Europeans) to economic backwardness and the persistence of traditions in the south, which was expected to catch up eventually. In the event it is the north Europeans and North Americans who have changed. In Europe in 2004 the lowest marriage rates (per 1000 inhabitants) were in Slovenia (3.3), Belgium (4.1) and Greece (4.2). The highest marriage rates were in Cyprus (7.2),

Denmark (7.0) and Malta (6.0) (Eurostat News Release, 2006). There is no longer a clear north–south divide, and while it is true that no former communist countries are close to the head of the high marriage rate league table, neither are they all clustered at the base.

Why are western young couples delaying marriage and parenthood? Many are in no hurry to embark on these life stage transitions. In the USA, Rainie and Madden (2006) found that only 38% of 18–29 year old singles described themselves as looking for partners. In a sense, young people are voluntarily and consciously delaying their transitions to full adulthood (Arnett, 2005), but this delaying is occurring in specific contexts. Young people in the west often point to the high cost of housing (to buy and to rent), to their own low salaries and unreliable sources of income given their risks of unemployment and under-employment. In some countries, as Molgat (2002) found in Quebec (Canada), they are remaining in their own parents' homes for longer than formerly. One reason is that moving out, even when financially possible, would mean a reduced standard of living (Holdsworth, 2004). They 'negotiate' independence within their parents' homes. The extension of education and the new global conditions in youth labour markets, plus access to effective and acceptable contraception, are responsible for young people's decisions to postpone various combinations of exits from their parents' homes, marriage and fertility. Strengthening the economies in Eastern Europe is unlikely to reverse the trend towards later marriages. Mean ages of marriage have not shifted upwards into young adults' late 20s or 30s in the whole of Eastern Europe. In 2004 in Azerbaijan the mean age of first marriages by women was 23.3 (State Statistical Committee of the Republic of Azerbaijan, 2004). In spite of the country's vast oil and gas reserves and revenues, labour market conditions for most young people in Azerbaijan are just as adverse as in the rest of Eastern Europe, so the persistence of relatively early marriages among young women in Azerbaijan suggests that the marked upward movements that have occurred elsewhere must have owed much to the choices of the young women concerned rather than having been 'forced' by circumstances.

(ii) Low birth rates. Birth rates have fallen sharply in most countries of Eastern Europe, typically to well beneath population replacement levels. Again, in these countries the trend is invariably attributed to the adverse economic conditions. It is said that young couples cannot afford to have children, and that their jobs and incomes are too insecure to allow them to plan their futures confidently. Yet also once again, birth rates have been sub-replacement for decades in many western countries. In the European Union in 2004 the highest birth

rates (per 1000 inhabitants) were in Ireland (15.2), France (12.7), then Denmark, Luxembourg and the UK (12.0 each). The lowest rates were in Germany (8.6), Latvia (8.8) and Lithuania (8.0). Overall, in the EU's new (in 2004) member states, in 2004 birth rates were below the continent's average, but still within rather than beneath the range in the older member countries (Eurostat News Release, 2006). Although marriage and fertility rates in the former German Democratic Republic fell around the time of Germany's reunification, they remained higher than in West Germany (Silbereisen *et al.*, 1996). Low birth rates is why the populations are ageing to such an extent throughout the western world (people living longer is also responsible). Europe faces decades in which the numbers retiring from employment will exceed new entrants to the workforces. Declining numbers in the economically active age group will need to support rising numbers of elderly citizens. The more prosperous EU countries regard immigration as a possible solution to their demographic problem, but this exacerbates the ageing 'burden' in the people-exporting countries, which include much of Eastern Europe.

Young people in Eastern Europe debate among themselves why they are marrying later and delaying fertility. In 2002 a discussion group of university graduates in Moscow finally agreed that, *'We're getting the same as Europe. It's due to western examples. We're much more aware than the older generation.'* In the same year, another discussion group of university graduates, this one in Dneipropetrovsk (Ukraine) concluded that, *'It's different than in the west. There people are delaying parenthood while they develop their careers. Here it's the low level of living. People will not take the risk, and for economic reasons they will not have more than one child.'*

Some countries in the west, and in the former communist bloc (the traditionally Muslim Central Asian states plus Azerbaijan), have maintained fertility at or above population replacement level. Other nations ask how Ireland, for example, manages to achieve this. What is the secret? Could it be transplanted? Governments wonder how to encourage their womenfolk to have more children, and in doing so these governments are not usually overlooking or overriding the women's own wishes. In the low fertility countries women's achieved fertility typically falls short of the levels that they say they desire (Fahey and Speder, 2004; Smallwood and Jeffries, 2003). In Brno (Czech Republic) and Yerevan (Armenia), Agadjanian (2002) found that the 16–17 year olds who were surveyed typically wanted to have two children, but explained that this would be expensive (maybe too expensive?). Governments wonder whether they should provide cash benefits, baby bonds, to reward mothers. Should they try to make it easier for women to combine employment and motherhood? Or should they offer more support to full-time mothers? Some East European governments (in Russia for example) have exhorted young women to have more children, but exhortation alone is unlikely to work even though women may agree that their countries need higher birth rates. This is another example of how individuals' and countries' interests have been decoupled. Individualised young women take decisions purely on the basis of what they regard as best for them as individuals and couples.

The crucial fact of this matter is that nowadays, all over the world, women can control their own fertility: sex has been decoupled from conception, and conception need not lead to a live birth. Many women will not have any children (or another child) unless they have a job and career position which they are confident that they can maintain, unless they have suitable housing for rearing children, unless they feel confident about maintaining a standard of living with which all family members will be comfortable, and, of course, unless they are in the right relationship. Ule and Kuhar (2003) have identified a new orientation to family formation and fertility among young people in Slovenia. The young people place a very high value on family life but insist that they are going to act responsibly, that having children will be a personal decision, and will not be until the time is right for them. Sometimes it evidently takes a long time before all the conditions are right at the same time. In some cases this never happens.

(iii) Single parents. Divorce and separation rates have risen throughout Eastern Europe and an outcome is more unpartnered parents. In Eastern Europe these parents (almost always mothers) are unlikely to be looking after themselves and their children unaided. Most return to live with their own parents, if they have left previously (Roberts *et al.*, 2003). Once again, economic conditions in the countries are usually blamed (by people within the countries) for relationship breakdowns. It is argued that relationships are placed under intolerable strain by inadequate and unreliable incomes, barriers to young couples obtaining their own dwellings and to the additional living costs if and when they manage to do so. The rising costs of formal childcare and reduced access to maternity leave (in practice if not in law) are said to amplify young couples' difficulties. Yet single parenthood has become more common than in the past in the relatively affluent west. In 2004 the highest proportions of all births that were outside marriage in the EU were in Estonia (58%), Sweden (55%), and Denmark, France and Latvia (45% each). The highest proportions of households with children where just one parent was present were in the UK (24%), Belgium

(18%), Estonia (17%), and Denmark and Germany (16% each) (Eurostat News Release, 2006). It is difficult to identify plausible explanations that fit all countries except that, for whatever reasons, unpartnered parenthood has lost its former stigma. This is another global trend. Within little more than a generation in South Korea, traditional extended families have been replaced by nuclear households, which have then become less stable (more divorces and separations, and more single parents). This is despite young people behaving 'responsibly' (as they describe it) – delaying marriage and fertility until the time and conditions are right (Bae, 2006).

Individualisation lurks in the background. This should not be equated with selfishness. There is no implication that young mothers who leave their partners, or the partner who leaves home, are not putting their children first. It is more a matter of people being unwilling to accept that whatever might be generally true applies in their particular cases. Young people seem as keen as ever to establish intimate relationships. They arguably have greater need than ever given the weakening of extended families and other 'communities'. Yet the very individualisation that magnifies partners' need for each other is likely to drive them apart if and when they perceive staying together as contrary to their own personal interests (Beck and Beck-Gernsheim, 1995). They are no longer content to 'make do' and 'get on with it' even if that is what other couples are doing, and even if they believe that this is usually the best course.

There is a worldwide debate about what might be done. It appears that the conventional intact family is usually still the best of all possible arrangements for both the adults and children, and it must be a universal aspiration at the time when couples marry. Among other things, conventional intact families are the most likely to be able to support their children effectively when the latter are making their own life stage transitions through higher education and out of the parental home (Goldscheider and Goldscheider, 1999). Do families need more support, or more inducements, to stay together? Or should we offer more support to unpartnered parents and try to lessen any problems for these parents and their children? Does the role (rights and responsibilities) of the non-resident parent need clearer legal and social definition?

(iv) Youth homelessness. This problem arises in very similar ways in east and west Europe. It occurs when young people who are unable to house themselves are also unable or unwilling to live with their families of origin. In Britain homelessness is often just one symptom of an inter-related set of problems: others may involve alcohol, drugs, trouble with the police and courts, and unemployment. Homelessness

is usually a temporary condition. It often follows spells of 'dossing' in the homes of friends (until their tolerance is exhausted). Before too long, the young homeless are normally assisted into regular housing, or into hostels, prison or hospital and then, if they are lucky, on to more stable accommodation (see Hutson and Liddiard, 1994).

All the above problems are products of youth life stage transitions becoming more prolonged and complicated, strewn with more pitfalls, and in many cases nowadays there are no happy endings.

Gender

Gender divisions do not appear only when young people embark on their family and housing transitions, or any of their other youth life stage transitions, but during these transitions the divisions deepen and are consolidated, irrevocably in most cases. Whatever the role of genetics might be, boy and girl infants are treated rather differently in most families, and then in elementary schools, though at this stage they usually study the same subjects and can play physical games (sports) as vigorously as each other. This changes during puberty and in secondary education. Males become physically stronger. Boys and girls opt for different subjects, then different kinds of employment. In peer relationships they learn to treat people differently, very differently, depending on gender. Learning and playing adult gender roles is thoroughly embedded in all the stages and processes of family and housing transitions. When couples marry and become parents, and when they become householders, decisions must be made, openly or tacitly, about who will earn the money, who will look after children, and who will do the various household chores. In principle, all kinds of tasks could be divided equally between the genders, but this is rarely what happens in practice, and once a division of labour is in place there is rarely any going back.

Western youth (males and females) are aware that second wave feminism has made a difference to all these processes. Today's young women feel that they can make choices that were denied to their mothers and grandmothers. Irrespective of whether they regard themselves as feminists, they acknowledge and invariably welcome the movement's achievements. Young males are also aware that the world has changed for them. They no longer expect to be sole 'breadwinners', and they are playing larger roles as fathers – being present at the birth of their children, taking paternity leave, etc.

Hence the surprise (for westerners) when the Iron Curtain came down and they found that young men and women in Eastern Europe were completely unimpressed by and indifferent to the mindset of western feminism. Rather than using their new freedom to unite in global women's movements, some young women in Eastern Europe were celebrating their new freedom to 'live normally' as full-time housewives, to flaunt their sexuality and even to earn their livings as sex workers (see Bridger *et al.*, 1996; Roberts and Jung, 1995). These responses to the end of communism become comprehensible when set in their own historical context. There was no second wave feminism in Eastern Europe (though people knew about it). Under communism women had formal, legal equality. They were told that they were already equal and that the demands of western feminism had no relevance in their own countries, and most women in Eastern Europe appear to have believed this. Under communism women had access to all programmes in education, all political positions, and all kinds of employment. There were women bricklayers and lorry drivers, and during the Second World War the German forces found themselves fighting against soldiers in skirts. Women under communism experienced all these equalities. Western feminism appeared to be offering no more than they already possessed. Equally to the point, by the 1990s many young women in Eastern Europe were feeling unimpressed by what communism's equalities had meant for women in practice.

The communist authorities had acknowledged that there were 'natural differences' between men and women. The authorities had revised their thinking following experience in Russia in the 1920s when the bourgeois family was regarded as an enemy of socialism, sex laws were abolished, divorce and abortion were made available on demand, weddings became bureaucratically functional (perfunctory), and when the birth rate plunged and many children were left destitute and uncared for. Subsequently weddings were made into attractive celebrations and motherhood was lauded. Women were expected to have unbroken full-time employment careers (they amounted to 50% of the workforces under communism) and this was made possible by the state recognising that women had other responsibilities. Communism provided maternity leave and childcare in nurseries and kindergartens. Moreover, mothers were treated indulgently at work. Managers understood when women needed to be absent due to children's illnesses, and when they needed to arrive late or leave early so that they could queue for household provisions. Women were expected to take on childcare and housework. The heroines of communism 'did it all' and smiled. There were no popular arts or commercial advertising that promoted women as sex objects. Although women had formal access to all programmes in education and all occupations, in practice most girls prepared themselves to work in shops, in light manufacturing, in office jobs, and in public service professions such as education and health care. Men occupied nearly all the power positions – as plant directors and in the communist party. Women were told that this was equality, and no organised opposition to this view was possible. In the 1990s women did not want to relinquish any of the rights that communism had conferred. At the same time, they were not impressed by the lives that these rights had delivered. They were aware of what they had been denied – the opportunity to be simply housewives, and to develop and use their sexuality to full advantage.

Under post-communism much has continued as before. Housework and childcare are still women's work. Girls take courses in education that prepare them for women's jobs. In some ways women in Eastern Europe have been net losers during the reforms. Their jobs (as under communism) are generally lower paid than men's. Even when women are doing similar work to men they are now paid significantly less (see Arabsheibani and Mussurov, 2003; Predborska, 2005). Young single women on average earn around 70% of their male counterparts' salaries (see Trapido, 2007). This is despite the fact that, as is now the case throughout most of the modern world, young women in Eastern Europe are out-performing males in education. Private sector employers try to avoid having to grant paid maternity leave. Nurseries have become more expensive. There are fewer women holding elected positions in political assemblies than was the case under communism. Women have been more vulnerable to unemployment than men (see Pollert, 2003; Watson, 1993). There are more young full-time housewives in Eastern Europe, not from choice, but usually because they are unemployed (and likely to remain so while their children are young) (see Jung, 1997). The role of the full-time housewife is far from that envisaged in the early 1990s – as in a well-off American household with multiple cars and other mod cons. Most young full-time housewives in Eastern Europe struggle against poverty, typically in 3-generation households, often in dwellings where water and electricity supplies are unreliable. Young women now have the right to express their sexuality (flaunt it if they wish): there are attractive omni-present role models in popular culture and advertising. However, the enthusiasm of the early 1990s has faded.

Young women today are not celebrating what post-communism has delivered. Nor are they all responding in the same way. The most common response is to study girls' subjects in education, enter a woman's job, marry and have children (maybe later than formerly), to continue in employment earning less than the husband (but not necessarily working fewer hours), and to cope with most of the housework. We shall see in Chapter 7 that there are class differences in how all this works out. Another response is to delay, delay and delay, and in the long run become a 'career woman' still working in a woman's job but with the commitment in hours and effort needed to get on. Single parenthood is another response (or outcome). The common element is that whatever their own responses, young women almost always insist that these are their own choices: that they do not have to marry, to become mothers, to do all the housework, but have chosen to do so. They do not feel that they need more choices, so what could feminism have to offer? They blame their problems on the economic conditions, often on their governments as well, but not on men or the rules of gender.

Male masculinity appears unscathed by the reforms in Eastern Europe except that so many of the old masculine jobs in heavy industries have disappeared, and unemployment and under-employment prevent young men from becoming effective breadwinners. This, of course, applies equally in the west where, as in Eastern Europe, it has not (yet) led to a wholesale revision of young men's ideas about what it means to be a man (see McDowell, 2003). In education males continue to predominate on technical courses, including computing. In Eastern Europe they have taken (and masculinised) some new occupations – business, private sector management, and finance (the new power positions). They are also the majority among young political activists. However, young women have been as likely to migrate, to work abroad, and to send remittances home or to return with savings (see Chapter 2). Young males are responsible for the greater part of the higher crime rates. When unemployed they hang about on the streets or in cafés (not necessarily buying anything) while their sisters help their mothers with household chores and look after any young children. There is no talk in Eastern Europe about 'new men' or 'new lads'. Heterosexuality is still hegemonic. Metrosexuality is unknown. Eastern Europe lags behind the west in these respects. Catch-up is obstructed by low incomes (less scope to make consumer choices) and also by the fact that young people of both sexes are most likely to stay at home until after they marry and become parents. Young men do not learn to be self-sufficient. Young women are socialised at home into long-standing female roles. Tomanovic and Ignjatovic (2006) have shown that in Serbia gender roles are more traditional when young adults live in extended families rather than as couples only or as couples with their own children.

We need to bear in the mind that the western 'genderquake' appears to be subsiding without having wrought a total transformation. Girls now outperform boys in education but the sexes are still tending to opt for traditional male and female subjects. Young men and women still tend to enter masculine and feminine occupations. Young single women may earn as much as young single men, but this changes following parenthood when men tend to increase their hours of work and earnings while women reduce theirs and interrupt their careers for various lengths of time with major consequences for their lifetime careers and earnings. Western men are doing more housework than in the past but women still do far more (see Roberts, 2006b). As in Eastern Europe, western women make varied choices (see Hakim, 1996). Some pursue hardly (if at all) interrupted labour market careers. Some opt for years as full-time housewives and mothers. Others decide to work part-time. These choices are class-related (as in Eastern Europe). These class differences are discussed in Chapter 7 where we shall also see that those concerned are rarely conscious of the role of class in their lives. Everywhere young men and women are most likely to explain how they live in terms of choice. Second wave feminism in the west, and communism plus the post-1989 reforms in Eastern Europe, are seen as having opened options that were formerly closed to women. Today's young women (and young men) feel no need to unite with others of their sex to fight a gender war: they take advantage of their options, and they make decisions and fight for gender equity (if they fight for it anywhere) within couples and households. Once again, individualisation and the reflexive self rule!

Summary and conclusions, and the contemporary relevance of the transition paradigm

We have seen that, in so far as they are able to do so, young people in Eastern Europe have been following (catching up) with western trends in new household and family formation, and appear to have leaped directly into a post-feminist era. The trends discussed in this chapter are among the reasons why some youth researchers have queried whether the transition paradigm is still appropriate for analysing young people's lives (see, for example, Cohen and Ainley, 2000; Wyn and Woodward, 2006). This paradigm (which is adopted throughout this book) assumes or implies that on either side there are relatively stable childhood origins and adult destinations, and that youth is a relatively unstable transitional life stage. 'Relatively' needs to be stressed, but often today, even relatively, this seems to be far from the case. A child today may experience one or more episodes of family reconstitution. Education is always a progressive experience, and is punctuated by hurdles at which a child may stumble. Parents' working lives may require or permit several changes of housing. Living standards may rise or fall depending, once again, on the adult family members' labour market careers (and family careers also). In some instances today adulthood is never achieved if long-term employment that will support an adult lifestyle, independent (of parents) housing, and a stable child-bearing and child-rearing relationship are key indicators. Youthful behaviour – serial partnerships and under-employment, and living with one's parents – may persist into later life. This happens to some people. At what point do these cease to be deviant exceptions and become a new norm? It is possible that recent cohorts of young people with their serial partnerships and under-employment who allegedly feel comfortable in flexible, insecure times (see Chapter 4) have been pioneering new adult ways of life, in which case sociologists of youth have been wrong about the life stage being prolonged. Rather, it can be argued, we should be presenting our evidence as indicating emergent adult norms.

These possibilities indicate why education-to-work, and family and housing transitions, are of fundamental importance. There has never been a guarantee that these transitions will be completed to the satisfaction of all parties, and there are so many different kinds of adult employment, and family and housing conditions, that can be the outcomes. These transitions are different in kind to becoming eligible to vote, subject to adult justice, and entitled to adult welfare benefits on reaching a given age. Moreover, experiences during education-to-work and family/housing transitions have implications, profound implications, for other transitions: whether one's relationship to state welfare is understood and learnt mainly as a tax-payer/funder or dependent; whether your experience is that the police and courts pursue you or protect you; how much you can spend and what you can consume.

The case for holding onto the transition paradigm is that in all modern societies, in Eastern Europe and the west, most young adults still achieve and settle in careers or jobs that will support an adult lifestyle, the majority still form new nuclear family households, and most marriages are still terminated only by the death of one of the partners. The paradigm is not outdated. Arguably, it needs to be retained if only to identify cases where, and diagnose the reasons why, transitions sometimes break down, and nowadays do so more frequently than in the past, and why youth transitions sometimes never reach a satisfactory conclusion.

Further reading

Bridger, S., Kay, R. and Pinnick, K. (1996), *No More Heroines? Russia, Women and the Market*, Routledge, London.

Heath, S. and Kenyon, L. (2001), 'Single young professionals and shared household living', *Journal of Youth Studies*, 4, 83–100.

Holdsworth, C. (2004), 'Family support during the transition out of the parental home in Britain, Spain and Norway', *Sociology*, 38, 909–26.

Predborska, I. (2005), 'The social position of young women in present-day Ukraine', *Journal of Youth Studies*, 8, 349–65.

Tomanovic, S. and Ignjatovic, S. (2006), 'The transition of young people in a transition society: the case of Serbia', *Journal of Youth Studies*, 9, 269–85.

6

Leisure

Introduction

International comparisons of young people's leisure are always complicated, much more so than comparisons of education systems, levels of pay, rates of unemployment, marriage and fertility – everything covered in previous chapters. On the one hand, nowadays there are massive global similarities in how young people spend their leisure time and money – clothing fashions, films watched, musical tastes and much more. Simultaneously, there are always country specifics and contrasts between groups of countries – Africa, Latin America, and for present purposes Eastern Europe and the west. Nilan and Feixa (2006) argue, correctly, that, 'Youth cultures are always emphatically local, despite globally derived details, since youth are embedded in immediate and embodied economic and political relations' (p. 8). The key features of the contexts of East European youth's leisure that are responsible for east-west differences are:

- Labour market conditions – not just the prevalence of youth under-employment (which is a global phenomenon) but that this occurs in countries where real earnings and living standards fell sharply when market reforms began and remain much lower than in the west. Alongside the decline in personal incomes, there were cutbacks in all public services, including leisure services. The countries that broke with communism had to set about creating capitalism before there were any capitalists in the countries. They also experienced the spread of (western) consumer cultures before most people had sufficient spending power to become active consumers. Low spending power has limited the ability of capitalist enterprises and consumer cultures to take charge of young people's leisure in Eastern Europe.

- Most young people remain living with their parents until some time after they themselves marry and become parents, and these life events are now typically occurring at older ages than was the case before the 1990s (see Chapter 5). This means that throughout youth and young adulthood individuals remain under parental surveillance if not control, and tend to be socialised into traditional gender roles. We should therefore expect (and we shall see that we do in fact find) pronounced traditional gender differences in East European young people's uses of leisure.

This chapter proceeds with some observations about the conditions experienced by children in Eastern Europe in the 1990s from which there is a 21st century legacy. We then examine how young people in Eastern Europe are spending their (often plentiful) leisure time and (usually very limited) money, and what has been stripped out of their leisure as a result of 'the reforms' that were accomplished in the early 1990s. The chapter then looks at the character of youth cultures in Eastern Europe, and the key differences and similarities *vis-à-vis* western youth cultures. The chapter concludes by identifying the rather different main class divisions among young people at leisure in Eastern Europe and the west. First, however, we note a major convergence, currently under way at a rapid pace, between young people's uses of leisure time in East and West Europe.

Online youth

Yahoo! launched in 1994 and that was the start. By the end of the 20th century virtually every business in the west, virtually every club, and virtually every school had its own website. By the end of the century households were going online. Early in the new millennium country after country passed the 50% threshold of online households. There was, and there is still a digital divide, but in the world's richer countries the proportions of the populations on the wrong side have diminished rapidly and continue to diminish. Take-up of the internet has spread at a similar pace to radio between the world wars and television after 1945.

At the end of the 20th century there was another digital divide – between the rich west and most of the rest of the world, but this gap is now closing. Internet use is now near universal among children and young people in the west. Access is currently spreading rapidly throughout Eastern Europe. During the first years of the new millennium internet cafés or clubs opened in all towns and cities. They were immediately filled by young people throughout the day and often throughout the night as well (when use is cheapest). They use the internet for the same purposes as western youth. There are some inter-country differences, but these differences are narrow (see Box 6.1). Some time during the next decade internet take-up by East Europe's households will take off and the internet cafés will be put to other uses. Online youth can join global communities, but we should bear in mind that the internet is not all in English. There are thousands of sites in all major languages and most of the world does not speak English. English language dominance in cyberspace is likely to be temporary.

Everywhere today there is the same moral panic about children and young people becoming online hermits and, in any case, accessing 'inappropriate' material. An examination of YouTube in 2008 found 117 'happy slappy' and 312 street fight videos that had been posted during the previous week. Children and young people (just like adults) receive unrequested 'inappropriate' messages via email and pop-ups. There are campaigns to raise parental awareness, to prompt parents to do more regulating, to prompt site owners to do more regu-lating, and to prompt governments to make all this happen. It is a replay of earlier moral panics sparked by horror comics, then televi-sion, and later on by video nasties. Children and young people at that time, the adults of today, survived the risks. In recent times the chil-dren and young people of Eastern Europe have experienced far more serious threats.

Box 6.1
Norton Online Living Report – Survey, 2008

An internet survey of a total of 4,687 adults and 2,717 8–17 year olds in the USA, UK, Australia, Germany, France, Brazil and China.

The 8–17 year olds who were internet users were:

- Spending 20–30 hours per month online, that is, around an hour a day on average.
- 20%–40% had created their own blogs.
- 30%–50% used social networking sites.
- 30%–40% had made friends online.
- Nearly all used the internet as a source of entertainment, mainly for playing games and downloading music.

The legacy of the 1990s

Since the mid-1990s most of East Europe's economies have been recovering. The benefits have been distributed unevenly, but even if everyone had benefited and if the losses of the 1990s had been wiped out completely (which is not the case), today's young people would still be victims of the earlier conditions. The children of the 1990s are the young people and young adults of today, and the 1990s was not a good decade for East Europe's children. For example, in Russia the number of children declined (due to the fall in the birth rate), but among those who were born, compared with children in previous decades:

- More became homeless.
- More became involved in crime.
- More were classified at school as having low mental ability.
- More were affected by chronic illnesses: 60% of school-children were diagnosed as suffering from a chronic condition.
- During the same period all forms of social protection became weaker, including assistance for disabled and other children with special needs (Petrov and Kantemirova,2004; Ponina,2004).

Moscow in the 1990s was one of the East European cities which acquired rising numbers of street children. Stephenson (2001) interviewed 123 of these children in Moscow who were all aged between 7 and 17. They had begun living on the streets to escape from unsatisfactory family lives, or following their parents becoming homeless, or simply to escape from poverty. In Moscow they were doing casual work on markets, street trading, a great deal of petty thieving, and forming themselves into support groups (some would say criminal gangs). Even if conditions were completely different today, the young adults who were reared in this way would still be a legacy from the 1990s, and their sub-cultures could be self-perpetuating. In any case, it is not possible to provide assurances that news stories that shocked the west in the 1990s have all become things of the past. In 2006 international NGOs applauded the announcement by the Kyrgyzstan government that funding was to be provided to revive the country's mental health services, but were appalled that the plan was to re-open large asylum-type institutions (Eurasianet, 2006). In the 1990s the tele-viewing western public was shocked by scenes from orphanages in Romania. These conditions arise partly because the countries have never known any other way, partly because high quality western-style community care is expensive, and in any case vulnerable children often reach the institutions because their families and 'communities' are unable to afford or otherwise cope with them.

One sequel to the vulnerable childhoods of the 1990s coupled with the difficult labour market conditions (which have endured for most young people) has been criminal teenage gangs, sometimes armed with weapons that have remained in circulation since the Soviet army broke up in 1991. Omel'chenko (1996) studied one such gang in Ul'ianovsk (Russia) whose principal activity was extorting money and goods from other young people. Salagaev and Shashkin (2000, 2003), based on fieldwork in Kazan (also Russia), have described how membership of a fighting gang has become an attractive career option, the 'young bandit' having been glamourised by the Russian media. Russian youth gangs have developed links with adult criminal organisations (sometimes described as mafia). Some have also become linked to political movements – nationalist movements. In the 6 months up to June 2006 in Russia there were 18 murders and over 100 recorded injuries as a result of hate crimes against non-Russians

Table 6.1   *Percentages who felt unsafe in different places and at different times*

	City centre daytime	Where live daytime	City centre night time	Where live night time
1988–90				
Liverpool	7	5	53	21
1997				
Donetsk	31	37	50	54
Lviv	10	13	50	44
Tbilisi	5	3	15	6
Armenia	1	1	12	10
1999				
Moscow	23	22	29	47
Vladikavkaz	33	37	41	43
Dneipropetrovsk	20	26	41	34
2002				
Yerevan born	2	3	15	6
Yerevan refugees	16	16	27	28
Vanadzor	1	1	4	4
Tbilisi born	8	7	15	15
Tbilisi refugees	10	10	23	22
Telavi	2	2	3	2
Makeeva	14	14	41	38
Khmelnitsky	17	6	47	31
Lviv	19	6	44	25

Source: see text.

(sometimes, however, Caucasian citizens of the Russian Federation). It may not be justification but it is part of the background that Russians have been victims of terrorist incidents in Moscow, Beslan (North Ossetia) and elsewhere allegedly committed by Chechens (from the North Caucasus) (see Avanisian *et al.*, 2006). The security situations have become poor throughout Eastern Europe. In Poland in 1987 three-quarters of the public described their country as a safe place to live: in 1997 three-quarters described it as unsafe (Oljasz, 1998).

In surveys among young people in different ex-communist countries (and in one western country – Britain) a standard question has been asked: 'Do you feel unsafe in the district where you live/in the city centre, during daytime/at night-time?' (see Table 6.1). One of the highest scores for feeling unsafe (53%) was recorded in Liverpool (UK) (in the city centre at night-time). In Eastern Europe feelings of vulnerability may have been exaggerated by the extent and speed of change following the security that prevailed during the communist era. However, some East European cities have recorded high scores for feeling unsafe not only in city centres at night-time, but also in the districts where young people live during daytimes (Donetsk in Ukraine, and Vladikavkaz in North Ossetia, neighbour to Chechnia, and scene of the Beslan school tragedy in 2004).

Young people's leisure in post-communist Eastern Europe

It is not only safety concerns that have been keeping East Europeans at home in their free time. Low income is the main reason. Out-of-home leisure became more expensive in the 1990s. Subsidies for state provisions for sport and culture were withdrawn or reduced (Council of Europe, 1996; Jung, 1994). Facilities closed, became run-down, or (if they could) raised admission prices thus becoming places for the new rich (or at least the better-off). State producers and distributors of culture (theatre, opera and ballet companies, and orchestras and film-makers) experienced seriously shrinking budgets. They could no longer offer employment (or pay, at any rate) to the graduates who were still emerging from their linked schools and higher education institutes. Before long classically-trained musicians and dancers were busking on the streets and working in strip joints. The old youth organisations disappeared. Their palaces (youth centres) closed unless taken over by local authorities (which was exceptional – see below). There are no successor bodies offering subsidised organised holidays, work brigades and fraternal visits to other (ex) socialist countries. Of course, there are new shops selling designer wear and other international brands, lots more bars and restaurants, and a few private sports clubs offering fitness training and sometimes tennis and indoor sports. However, access to this new leisure has depended on ability to pay. Admissions to theatres and cinemas (where western releases quickly replaced communist fare) are more expensive – too expensive for most people to go as frequently as formerly. Where and when state spending on culture was revived in or after the mid-1990s, as in Poland and Hungary, it was scaled down in comparison with communist times and concentrated on leading centres ('few but roses' – the long standing priority of UK Arts Councils) (see Jung and Moleda-Zdziech, 1998).

However, throughout Eastern Europe people had television which also changed – less serious talk and more cartoons, game shows, soap operas and old films. The audiences loved it. Hence the so-called 'mediatization' of leisure in Eastern Europe (Jung, 1996). By the mid-1990s people were going less frequently to the cinema, opera, museums, concerts and shows, and were reading fewer newspapers and magazines. They were spending much more time watching television and videos (see Jung, 1990, 1994, 1996). Research in small towns in lower Silesia (Poland) found that young people had more free time than other age groups but were constrained (just like other age groups) by lack of money. Women's leisure was particularly constrained. After they became mothers their own leisure became more or less synonymous with servicing their children's. Often the only thing that they did for their own enjoyment was watch television (Ferenz, 1998; Wozniakowa, 1998). A study in middle class districts in St Petersburg (Russia) in the early 1990s found that most households had been impoverished. They were among Russia's 'new poor' though some still had *dachas* and cars that they had acquired in communist times (Poretzkina and Jyrkinen-Pakkasvirta, 1995). Time budget research in western Siberia recorded a decline in free time between the 1970s and the 1990s. Most people had lost their jobs but were doing more work in total in their households and on private plots. Leisure, as in all the other places that have been investigated, was TV-dominated (Artemova, 1998; Gvozdeva, 1994, 1999).

Following a survey of the health of the populations in former Soviet countries, Pamela Abbott (2004) has summed up conditions after the turn of the millennium as follows. *'The security of the lives of the majority of the population has been shattered ... With an increase in crime, a rise in unemployment, a dramatic decline in living standards and a sharp reduction in public spending on education, health and housing, together with a dramatic increase in inequalities, creating an "hour glass society" ... The*

majority of our respondents were poor, with only a small proportion report-
ing the situation of their household as good: the proportion doing so varied
between just over two percent in Georgia to around a fifth in Kyrgyzstan'
(Abbott, 2004).

Young people's rates of participation in out-of-home recreation have
been low – consistently so. Table 6.2 lists the 'at least once a week' rates
for samples of 20-somethings in a variety of locations from 1997
onwards (when economic recovery was supposed to be under way in
most places). The rates vary from place to place but within low ranges
except in the cases of drinking alcohol (5% to 62%), playing sport (13%
to 44%), and going to pubs or cafés (1% to 36%). The percentages
watching live sport weekly ranged from 0% to 5%, and for going to the
cinema from 0% to 6%. The proportions who belonged to a recreation
(any type) club ranged from 0% to 18% (Table 6.3). The zeros are
mostly due to the absence (due to closures) of the relevant facilities in
the places in question.

Table 6.2 *Leisure activities: percentages who took part at least once a week*

	Play sport	Watch sport (Not on TV)	Cinema	Pubs, cafés etc.	Alcohol	Smoking	Church
1997							
Donetsk	27	3	1	14	16	34	7
Lviv	44	3	5	22	17	36	9
Tbilisi	22	5	6	18	25	50	9
Armenia	27	1	5	32	18	29	13
1999							
Moscow	34	2	5	13	22	41	2
Vladikavkaz	28	4	2	10	6	28	3
Dneipropetrovsk	25	3	4	11	21	40	5
2002*							
Yerevan born	17	3	3	36	31	44	9
Yerevan refugees	20	2	1	8	14	31	11
Vanadzor	17	0	0	13	15	44	1
Tbilisi born	8	3	3	12	20	57	8
Tbilisi refugees	15	3	0	9	20	44	10
Telavi	16	5	2	5	25	36	10
Makeeva	29	3	0	21	51	50	3
Khmelnitsky	13	0	1	12	37	34	9
Lviv	25	2	0	1	62	39	51

* 'Weak' alcohol (not spirits)

Source: see text.

Table 6.3 *Membership of voluntary leisure associations (in percentages)*

	Recreation club
1997	
Donetsk	5
Lviv	18
Tbilisi	11
Armenia	6
1999	
Moscow	4
Vladikavkaz	6
Dneipropetrovsk	5
2002	
Yerevan born	2
Yerevan refugees	5
Vanadzor	0
Tbilisi born	3
Tbilisi refugees	7
Telavi	5
Makeeva	4
Khmelnitsky	1
Lviv	3

Source: see text.

Puuronen and his colleagues (2000) conducted a comparative study of the lives (including the uses of leisure) of samples totalling 1731 young people in Petrozavodsk and Joenssu, both cities in Karelia, a region that straddles the Russia-Finland border. The Russian young people were spending more time at home, reading books, watching videos and listening to tapes. The Finns had higher participation rates in going to bars and cafes, taking holidays abroad, exercising, going to church, taking drugs and drinking alcohol.

Other researchers who have examined the leisure of young people in Eastern Europe have been pre-occupied with their uses of alcohol and drugs. An implication in the studies has been that levels of use have risen alarmingly. In fact all the studies show that the levels in Eastern Europe have been low compared with those recorded in western studies. Frantisek (1998) surveyed 1,253 secondary school students (typically aged 15–18) in Prague and Ceske Budejovic (Czech Republic). In this study a quarter of the sample smoked tobacco, and a quarter had experience of drugs but less than 10% were current users (cannabis was by far the most popular drug, as in all the other studies).

Goranskaya and colleagues (2000) found that 52.5% of 11th graders (typically aged 18) in Petrozavodsk (Russia) had been offered drugs. Pilkington (2004b) found that among samples totalling 2,814 14–19 year olds in Komi, Samara and Krasnador (all Russia), 21% had used drugs (a third by age 18/19), and 43% said that drugs were used by people in their immediate friendship groups. Pejic (2004) found that in Serbia only 11% of a sample of young people had used marijuana at least once, and only 16% consumed alcohol weekly or more often. Even the highest figures in these studies fall well short of levels recorded in the west, in Parker *et al.*'s (2002) north-west England project, for example (see Table 6.4). In this research, 76% had used drugs, and over 90% had been offered drugs and had at least one close friend who was using drugs.

Young people in Eastern Europe drink alcohol far less frequently, and when they drink they tend to drink far less heavily, than their counterparts in Western Europe. A survey of 2,000 15–16 year olds in Denmark identified three drinking styles – mainstream, experienced, and cautious. Mainstream and experienced drinking tended to earn status among peers. It was cautious drinkers who were at risk of social isolation and condemnation. Experienced drinking (which in this study meant starting young and drinking a lot) was not a sign of social disadvantage (Jarvinen and Grundelach, 2007). In Eastern Europe young (and older) adults may drink fulsomely at weddings and other celebrations, but 'binge drinking' is not the normal and regular (weekly or more frequently) leisure activity that it is among youth in many western countries. Alcohol consumption in Eastern Europe may have risen since the end of communism, but not, as yet, to anything like the levels achieved by western youth.

Another striking feature (to western eyes) of the leisure of young people in Eastern Europe is the starkness of traditional gender differences. Table 6.5 is from samples totalling 1,800 25–29 year olds in selected areas in Ukraine, Georgia and Armenia in 2002. The respondents in Table 6.5 are divided by gender and by education (according

Table 6.4 *Drug use, 1991–1999, 14–22 year olds, north west England*

	Ever	*Last year*	*Last month*
Offers	93%	-	-
At least one close friend	94%	-	-
Used	76%	52%	31%

Source: Parker *et al.* (2002).

Table 6.5 *Uses of leisure by education and gender: 25–29 year olds, Ukraine, Georgia and Armenia, 2002*

Percentages taking part at least once a month	Males, higher ed.	Males, no higher ed.	Females, higher ed.	Females no higher ed.
Playing sport	46	32	20	19
Watching sport	14	10	3	2
Pubs, cafes, etc.	54	50	33	27
Drinking weak alcohol	79	70	41	43
Drinking strong alcohol	56	47	18	21
Smoking	67	75	19	17
Disco/nightclub	17	12	10	7
Pop/rock concerts	4	1	6	1
Cinema	10	3	11	3
Classical concert, etc.	2	0	5	2
Theatre	8	1	11	4
Museums, galleries	3	1	6	1
Church	22	20	35	28
N=	443	434	482	439

Source: see text.

to whether or not they had received higher education). It can be seen that higher education was boosting participation in certain uses of leisure, specifically consumption of traditional high/classical culture. This was not an income effect: we shall see below that high earnings were boosting rather different uses of leisure. However, irrespective of educational level, males were the more involved in sport (watching and playing), smoking, drinking alcohol, and going to bars, cafes, discos and night clubs. The females' leisure was more oriented towards cultural consumption (classical and popular) plus church-going.

The studies in Eastern Europe that have focused upon drinking alcohol and using drugs by young people have all found higher rates among males than among females. In Pilkington's (2004b) study in three cities in Russia, 27% of the males and 14% of the females had used drugs. In Frantisek's (1998) research in the Czech Republic, 6.5% of the males and 3.6% of the females were using marijuana or hashish regularly, and a third of the males against a quarter of the females were drinking alcohol regularly. Omel'chenko (1996), in her case study of a criminal teenage gang in Ul'ianovsk (Russia), found that the role of female gang members was basically to service the males. This reminds one of studies of working class youth cultures in Britain in the 1960s and 70s when young women were glimpsed mainly as sisters or

Table 6.6   *Glasgow 15 year olds in 1987 and 1999*

	Males %	Females %
Currently smoke		
1987	14	16
1999	22	29
Current monthly (or more frequent) drinking		
1987	22	15
1999	61	66
Ever used drugs		
1987	11	6
1999	42	39

Source: Sweeting and West (2003).

girl friends of the principal male actors, when young men drove the motor cycles and scooters while young women rode on the pillions (Hall and Jefferson, 1976; Willis, 1978). There is no evidence from Eastern Europe resembling the findings from the West of Scotland study (see Table 6.6) which show that during the 1990s teenage girls caught up with or overtook boys in rates of smoking, drug and alcohol use, or the evidence from the mid-1990s of British teenage girls equalling boys' use of indoor sports facilities (Department for Education, 1995).

The reforms: the leisure debits

Older generations in Eastern Europe usually express some nostalgia for the past. Most refer to the security that they experienced under communism, and also the communality. Even those who expect the long-term benefits from the reforms to exceed the costs often regret that virtually everything created by communism has been jettisoned. They are particularly likely to feel this way when they compare their own youth with the lives of post-communist cohorts of young people. Under communism there were no commercial leisure provisions or any genuinely free voluntary leisure organisations. All organised leisure was under the auspices of the state and communist party.

Options were limited, but the menu on offer was quite attractive: sports, the arts (producing and consuming), travel, and work brigades. Zsuzsanna Clark, who grew up in Hungary before migrating to and settling in Britain in the 1990s, expresses it this way: *'communist Hungary, far from being hell on earth, was in fact rather a good place to live ... What I remember most was the overriding sense of community and solidarity, a spirit I find totally lacking in my adopted Britain and indeed whenever I go back to Hungary today. With minimal differences in income and material goods, people really were judged on what they were like as individuals and not on what they owned. Western liberals may sneer at movements such as the Young Pioneers, which sought to involve young people in a wide range of community activities, but they reflected an ambition to build a cohesive society – in contrast to the "atomisation" of the most advanced societies today ... Theatres, opera houses and concert halls were all heavily subsidised, bringing the price down to a level everyone could afford. The government opened up "cultural houses" in every town and village so that provincial based working class people, like my parents, could have easy access to the arts. Book publishing was similarly supported, so that prices remained low and book shops proliferated ... Now, after 13 years of "regime change", much of this cultural heritage has been destroyed. Museums, theatres and galleries have had to sink or swim in the new economic "realism". As ticket subsidies have been withdrawn, once again it is only the rich (and German tourists) who can afford to go to the opera. Hundreds of smaller art cinemas have been forced to close while the big Hollywood multiplexes move in ... Today Hungarians have the theoretical right to travel to the west whenever they like, yet the fall in real wages has been so dramatic that few of them can afford to go even to Lake Balaton'* (Clark, 2002, p. 18).

The communist authorities aimed to create cultural democracies. In the 1920s the Russian Bolsheviks debated whether there could be any place in communist societies for 'bourgeois' arts and sports. The decision (which was held onto until the end of communism) was that they would do sports and the arts better than the capitalist countries (beat them at their own games). The aim was always mass participation alongside the development of excellence (see Riordan, 1980, 1982). Equality of participation among socio-demographic groups was never achieved. For example, the intelligentsia strata were always the main consumers of high culture (see below). However, the aim was to make sports and the arts classless, and to develop a socialist way of life that would be superior to anything on offer in the west. It was possible in Eastern Europe to watch good quality opera and ballet for less than a US dollar. The view of the communist authorities was that popular western cultures were stupefying the masses (Hidy, 1982; Vitanyi, 1981). Under communism children did not grow up amid the sounds of western popular music. The music played on radio, in concerts and other public places was folk (traditional in the country or region) or classical. An outcome was generations of adults (still living today) among whom classical music is more popular than what the west regards as popular music (Roberts *et al.*, 2001).

In some (but only a few) parts of Eastern Europe, substantial chunks of the old leisure provisions for children and young people survived into the 21st century. Chances of surviving were well above average in Eastern Ukraine. Dneipropetrovsk, one industrial city in the region, was the home city of Leonid Kuchma, the country's president until 2004 (when his preferred successor was defeated in the 'orange revolution'). Kuchma's presidency was seen as having brought certain advantages to his home city. A new Pioneers Palace had been opened in 1990, and since 1991 this facility had been kept open by the city council (see Box 6.2)

Dneipropetrovsk was also the home of the Ice Palace which had been constructed in 1983–4 (see Box 6.3).

In Dneipropetrovsk the old Komsomol Palace (which had been built in the 18th century as a real palace) had been taken over by Dneipropetrovsk State University and was being run as its own Student Palace of Culture. This was not like a western students' union. A university-appointed director managed the facility in Dneipropetrovsk. The palace was well-equipped with modern sound equipment in

---

Box 6.2
Dneipropetrovsk Children's Palace

In 2002 the Children's Palace in Dneipropetrovsk was still operating more or less as when it had been planned as a communist facility. It contained an assembly hall, a theatre with seating for 500, a dance hall and 20 study rooms. The centre was open from 3.00pm until 9.00pm and sometimes 10.00pm each school day, and throughout the days at weekends and during school holidays. In 2002 it was being attended by 3,200 children and young people (age range 6–20). There were groups working on painting, arts and crafts, music, ecology, foreign languages and computing, and the centre produced a newspaper which was written and edited by the children. The older members acted as leaders, as had been the practice in Komsomol times. The centre employed 60 teachers. As well as its own programmes it coordinated the work of 8 district children's centres, some school-based facilities, and work with children at 29 sport facilities in the city. One change since 1991 was that originally everything was free whereas charges had been introduced for English language teaching, computing and dance classes. Another change was that the teachers' salaries had declined in real value.

Box 6.3

Dneipropetrovsk Ice Palace

In 2002 the Dneipropetrovsk Ice Palace was still functioning in much the same way as under the former communist system. As well as an ice rink it had a multi-purpose sports hall with seating for 5,000, a swimming pool and a 30 year old football stadium. The entire complex was attached to, and funded by, a Dneipropetrovsk enterprise that manufactured satellites, rockets and other items of aerospace technology. The Ice Palace employed 250 staff including 50 teachers/trainers. All the facilities were available for public use when not otherwise committed, but the facility had been designed and run as an elite training centre, and it was continuing to operate as an elite facility in 2002.

---

the music theatre, etc., and incredibly tidy. There was no bar. Approximately 20 student groups in painting, music and drama were using the facility.

The state of the sports centre at the Dneipropetrovsk Technological University in 2002 was probably more typical of the country (and Eastern Europe) as a whole. This sports centre had been built in 1986 with three large sports halls and a small swimming pool, which was dry and empty when visited in 2002. The entire facility had become run-down. The main work of the 25 teachers/trainers was organising the physical education classes for the university's students – all were required to take 4 hours of PE per week during term times. Children's sessions, which had been an important part of the programme in the past (sifting for child talent), had been scrapped.

To account for so much of the old system surviving the reforms in Eastern Ukraine, it is necessary to bear in mind that in 1991 the population had voted for independence from the Soviet Union, not a change of economic system. Enterprises had been given the formal structure of private companies with share capital and boards of directors, but in Eastern Ukraine the main blocks of shares in most large companies remained in state (*oblast* – regional government) ownership. Further reform, if this would have meant the closure of coal mines, steel plants and other enterprises, and facilities such as the children's and ice palaces, would not have been popular.

This is usually the reason why parts of the communist leisure system are still operating in other places. Butovo, a satellite town of 72,000 situated 27 kilometres from Moscow centre, had retained much of its collectivist character in 2002. Residents' committees were still running the shops in Butovo and the 'profits' were being ploughed into community facilities (supplementing the budget provided by

Moscow City Council). The ground floors or basements of most apartment blocks were dedicated to kindergartens, nurseries, after school classes (in dancing, crafts, computing and languages), senior citizens' clubs, and sports such as martial arts, aerobics, weights, and sauna rooms. The activists who helped to run these facilities realised that they were out of step with the new economic and political realities in Russia. *'The mayor has tried to close us down. We are an organised power. We are dangerous for the existing government. But we are still fighting and there are people in politics* (communists) *who help us.'*

Modernised versions of the old children's leisure time organisations have been revived in some places where they disappeared along with the Pioneers. In the aftermath of the colour revolutions in Georgia in 2003 and Ukraine in 2004, the Kremlin in Russia decided to create its own youth brigades – *Nashi*, the *Young Guard*, and *Young Russia*. By 2007 these movements claimed a total of 120,000 members. These members were reported to be a mixture of the ideologically committed (to Putin's presidency), the ambitious (who would formerly have joined the Komsomol), and those looking for some 'action' – for example, against Estonians who in Tallinn in 2007 moved the World War II remains of Soviet soldiers (Hammerschlag, 2007). Following its 'rose revolution' in 2003, in 2005 Georgia's government created the *Young Patriots* (with orange items of clothing as its uniform), which instantly became a popular mass organisation, capable of drawing together thousands of children in summer camps and at rallies in Tbilisi. Parents throughout Eastern Europe can recollect their own childhood experiences in the Pioneers, and usually conclude that there were some good features of the old system. Communism cared for and invested heavily in its children. They were the future. Today some western countries, including the UK, are struggling to develop similarly comprehensive children's services. A fact of this matter is that it is difficult to run an equivalent to the Pioneers in a democratic market economy. Georgia's *Young Patriots* have a title that appeals to the majority of the population. There is probably no other title that would have an equivalent appeal in Georgia. However, not all children in Georgia are ethnically Georgian. Dneipropetrovsk's Children's Palace teaches Ukrainian arts and crafts, but the entire ethos is not nationalist: a large part of the city's population is ethnically Russian and Russian is the main local language. In a post-communist city where the funds have been available, it has been possible to retain this kind of facility, but it would be difficult to develop an equivalent in western countries where various voluntary youth movements (scouts, guides, sports clubs, church organisations) already occupy the socio-cultural space.

Youth cultures

Two things have been missing from the preceding discussion. First, informal leisure – time spent 'doing nothing', just relaxing, hanging about. Informal uses account for a great deal of leisure time in all countries and in all socio-demographic groups. 'Doing nothing in particular' can be solitary; it may mean idly surfing the web, watching TV or listening to music. Alternatively, 'doing nothing in particular' can be social – sometimes intensely social. Sometimes the things that we do are secondary – watching television, listening to music, visiting the cinema – these activities can be just means to an end, which may be socialising with a particular person or crowd. Exactly where and with whom any 'hanging around' is done may depend on family and educational background, but not the basic ability or desire to spend time in this way. Their lower incomes do not disadvantage Eastern European youth *vis-à-vis* their western counterparts in this respect.

The second so far missing dimension of leisure is the cultural. Many of the things that we do in our leisure time have meanings, sometimes shared with intimates, sometimes general public knowledge, and sometimes just private meanings. Leisure is a part of life in which people are able to play with meanings. It is not only young people who do this, but since their adult destinations remain uncertain and they occupy no fixed long-term positions in their societies, leisure meanings may well play a heightened role in their lives, enabling them to express and signal to others who they are or who they want to be. This is why the study of young people's leisure is often conceptualised as the study of youth cultures. Adopting a particular style, thereby being seen as a particular kind of person, may require purchasing the appropriate clothing, footwear and hairstyle. Styles can be, but are not necessarily expensive in terms of money. East European youth show that the money costs can be minimal. Economic status (level of income) can be irrelevant, and likewise family and housing situations. Also again, therefore, in playing with meanings, in becoming and expressing who they are via their appearances and tastes, young people in Eastern Europe are not disadvantaged in comparison with western youth.

Up until the 1990s Eastern Europe was not completely cut off from western popular cultures. This was despite the communist authorities' disapproval of 'decadent' western popular culture which, therefore, was not available through official channels – shops, state radio or television, or concerts. Yet somehow western popular culture always seeped in. How strenuously the authorities tried to stem the tide varied from time to time and country to country, but knowledge about western music and fashions always got through the blockades. In private, in their homes, young people could sometimes tune in to western sounds on the radio. Audio cassettes, jeans and other fashion items found underground routes into the countries. When listening to the Beatles or the Rolling Stones in private, young people could experience the thrill of doing something that was officially off-limits (but which was surely harmless). By making their tastes known at school, college and where they worked, and on the streets by virtue of their dress and coiffure, young people could express dissent and defiance. Such cultural warfare has an elevated significance in any society where explicit, organised political opposition is prohibited. This is just one example of how global cultural products are always liable to be given local meanings.

Until the 1980s all this was underground. Under communism young people attended concerts where approved arts were performed, and they went to theatres and cinemas which offered officially approved productions. Young people did this at least partly because there was little alternative except to just 'hang about'. They took part in the sports and holidays organised by their schools and the communist party youth organisations if only because, once again, there was no alternative except to stay at home and loiter in the streets and parks. Alcohol, when acquired, was usually bought from kiosks and consumed at home or (by young people) in quiet streets or parks. In schools and universities students never lost the art of entertaining each other at end of term and other celebrations (held with the authorities' permission and support) with song, music and dance. Recorded music never swept all this aside.

During the 1980s the dams broke. Gorbachev, the Soviet leader, declared a policy of *glasnost* (freedom of expression). Leaders of the communist party youth organisations were instructed to listen to young people and give them what they wanted. Western popular culture instantly became overground. The music was played in student palaces (centres). Suddenly Eastern Europe had mods, punks, rockabillies and motor bike crowds on the streets and in city centres (see Pilkington, 1994). Music and fashion became overground means of political expression. Young people were able to use western cultural products to express a desire for change and their own identification with the western way of life. However, other 'conservative' youth cultures appeared – ultra-patriotic, muscular political cultures which in Russia attracted some young veterans from the war in Afghanistan who wanted to rid their country of western influences (Riordan, 1988). That said, the pro-western cultures became overwhelmingly ascendant towards the end of the 1980s. From that point onwards, Eastern

Europe had its own artists performing and recording what had previously been western-type popular music. Western fashions became regular student attire during the 1980s. In a sense, this period was the high point of the old underground. By 1989 young people in Warsaw and Prague, then elsewhere, were partying in the streets, expressing their desire for a change of system, for the western way of life. The most spectacular (and internationally televised) 'party' was when Berliners clambered over the wall in November 1989. As explained in chapter 2, thereafter the systems changed rapidly. The economies became market economies. Multi-party democracy replaced rule by the communist parties. All barriers to the inflow of western goods and culture were removed. The culture flooded in via satellite and was available on street stalls, local radio and local television, and the cinemas started showing western releases. As this happened, the meaning of western culture changed. The associations with defiance and dissent disappeared. Commerce took over (Pilkington, 1996). The market was offering what the people manifestly demanded. This was the new normality, the new conformity.

It would be wrong to imagine that western-sourced consumer cultures swept in and took over completely in Eastern Europe when communism ended. At the same time that western products and brands were flooding into Eastern Europe in the early 1990s, local production of western-type cultural products (as opposed to the old officially approved culture) was expanding. Western-type popular music was by then being produced and marketed locally, and older forms of culture, specifically recorded music, remained available, indeed plentiful. The cultural menu in every country, east and west, is always a mixture of the international and the local. East European countries have not proved exceptions to the worldwide 'rule' that the most popular TV programmes, musical compositions and performers, and sports teams and stars, are local. Nowadays young people throughout Eastern Europe can watch international top sport on TV, but their strongest support is nearly always for local teams and individual competitors. The pop stars about whom they are most enthusiastic are usually those who perform and record in their own countries, and in the national language. Following only or mainly western-sourced sounds is still taken to indicate enthusiasm for the western way of life to which there is now probably more opposition everywhere in Eastern Europe than was the case in 1989. In countries that have been absorbed into the EU, some adults and young people are now resisting Europeanisation. For example, in Poland a prevalent view is that western Europe is morally degenerate – too tolerant of abortion and 'deviant' sexualities. In all the new independent states of the ex-USSR, opinion is now divided over the senses, if any, in which the countries should become part of the west. There are invariably local cultures which claim superiority – more 'soul', as they say in Russia (Pilkington *et al.*, 2002). Eastern Europe's young people have learnt to distinguish between western standards of living (which they want) and western ways of being which are often regarded as deficient, less authentic than their own national cultures. That said, western styles, skinhead for example, might be adopted to express defiance towards any powerful groups – local or international.

It should now be apparent that the leisure of young people in Eastern Europe has never been as grim as their low (by western standards) participation rates in formal leisure activities may suggest. Living standards in Eastern Europe have never been as low as USA $ equivalents for salaries imply. When salaries are low, so are local costs of production and prices (of locally produced goods and services). Food, clothing, beer, wine – anything produced locally – has been available from markets, in shops and on street stalls or pavements at a fraction of western prices. Dollar equivalent sums reflect the international demand for the respective currencies, not what the currencies will buy when used in the countries where they are normally tendered. It is rather different with international goods – energy, cars, and electrical goods sourced in the Far East, for example. Here the prices are similar in $ in all parts of the world where they are bought and sold except that, in poor countries, sellers may need to depress their prices as far as possible in order to generate any effective demand.

The gap between spending power in East Europe and the west is also fudged by extensive pirating. DVDs now become available throughout Eastern Europe ahead of blockbusters being released on western cinema screens. Recorded music and computer software are pirated. Access to satellite TV is gained unofficially (in various ways). Designer label footwear and fashion clothing are rarely genuine. In the long run the official producers are likely to benefit. Pirating develops markets (demand) for products which, in the interim, local populations are unable to afford. The outcome of all this is that young people in present-day Eastern Europe are able to watch the same films and international top sport, listen to the same music, wear what appears to be the same clothing, and look much the same as their western counterparts, but at a fraction of the cost. Maybe they have fewer DVDs and CDs in their collections, and smaller wardrobes of clothing for sport, work and going out, but a conclusion to draw is that there is considerable flab in western consumption that could be cut away leaving the essentials intact.

Another mitigation for their relatively low incomes is that in Eastern Europe young people have still not lost the art of passing time without spending money. Cashless going out has become rare in the west. In Eastern Europe young people still hang about with each other outside their homes without purchasing any drinks or confectionery. They still know how to do holidays on the cheap – staying with relatives or in a family *dacha* in the countryside, or travelling to lake or mountain areas in their own countries with tents and enough food to last a week. No doubt commercial consumer cultures will eventually erode the art of enjoying cashless leisure. It has already become less attractive than under communism when this art was necessary in all strata. Nowadays it co-exists with higher profile, high spending lifestyles which young people, with rose tinted gazes, associate with becoming more like if not actually part of the west.

There is much about the leisure of young people in Eastern Europe that appears much the same as in the west, yet there are subtle and simultaneously basic differences. Young people in east and west Europe wear similar fashions, have similar hairstyles, have some common musical tastes, follow some of the same sports, teams and stars, and watch some of the same films and follow the lives of the same international celebrities. But all this is not really an instance of homogenous global youth. In Eastern Europe all of the above is usually done at a much lower cost, and the tastes, sounds and styles usually have specific local meanings. Even so, the main groups of youth sub-cultures in Eastern Europe bear canny resemblances to those noted in the west (see Box 6.4).

Despite the similarities noted in Box 6.4, the different contexts of youth in Eastern Europe and the west – the different histories of their countries, the countries' current positions in the world order, their 21st century politics and the present-day economic conditions – are bound to make at least as much difference to the 'meanings' as to young people's participation rates in different types of leisure activity.

The stratification of youth lifestyles

It is not unemployment *per se* that sets excluded youth apart in contemporary western societies. Unemployment is too common a transition experience during under-employed youth labour market careers to set apart those who are affected. The socially excluded are from neighbourhoods with unusually high rates of adult unemployment and poverty, and (in some countries) single parent families. They attend schools where overall attainment levels are well below average,

---

Box 6.4
Youth cultures in Eastern Europe and the west

Hilary Pilkington (2004a) conducted in-depth interviews, complemented by observations, with 134 young people in Moscow, Samara and Ul'ianovsk (all in Russia). Her evidence consists primarily of discourses – what the young people said rather than what they were actually doing – but as argued above, the cultural is an important dimension in all leisure, certainly young people's. Pilkington identified:

First, young people who described themselves as 'progressive'. They were westward looking and had definite musical tastes. These young people can be likened to the 'spectacular' youth noted by western youth researchers (the young people who identify with specific youth subcultures – skinheads or Goths, for example) except that in western contexts 'spectacular' young people are not necessarily (maybe not usually) enthusiastic about the western way of life.

Pilkington then distinguished Russian youth who described themselves as just 'normal', 'ordinary', or words to this effect. These are the kinds of labels that western youth are most likely to use when asked to describe themselves (see Brown, 1987; Jenkins, 1983). Whether in the west or in Eastern Europe, these 'mainstream' young people have no strong attachments to any particular sounds or fashions. In Russia when they went out they did not head for leisure places associated with any particular subcultures but spent a lot of time hanging about in the streets where they lived and around the schools that they attended.

Third, Pilkington distinguished 'oppositional' youth cultures, the subcultures of the 'antis' who acted in ways regarded by others as loutish, formed gangs and engaged in criminal activities. These young people were generally 'against' the ways in which their country was changing. In the west the corresponding groups would be called 'excluded youth' but in Russia, and elsewhere in Eastern Europe, the 'anti' young people are not necessarily from particularly disadvantaged backgrounds, and in the west the subcultures of excluded youth are not linked either organisationally or culturally to any political movements.

---

and where early leaving (at or before the first legal opportunity) is common. The young people in question may be from ethnic minority or national majority groups. They may live in depressed districts in generally prosperous cities, or in generally depressed de-industrialised towns. Irrespective of this, their neighbourhoods are no-go areas for children and young people from 'respectable' households, and likewise the schools are avoided by ambitious parents. Excluded youth are likely to experience trouble with the police and courts (which then exacerbates their labour market difficulties). The girls often become teenage mothers, and the boys become absent fathers or improbable 'breadwinners'. Other young people avoid these members of their age group. Door staff keep them out of mainstream pubs and clubs. They are 'flawed consumers' – not enough money to spend and liable to cause trouble (see Bauman, 1998). They hang about on the streets in their neighbourhoods beyond the age at which mainstream youth have moved on to other kinds of leisure. Recreational drug use is now mainstream, but not the glue sniffing or the dealing in heroin and crack cocaine that is part of life in some excluded neighbourhoods (see MacDonald and Shildrick, 2007; Shildrick and MacDonald, 2006).

The research in Box 6.5 shows that Toronto high school students could be divided into seven clusters according to their musical preferences, with many types of music occurring in several of the clusters. Note, however, that it is the *club kids* and the *black stylists* (names given to the groups by the researchers) who had the most distinctive musical tastes. Some of their favourite kinds of music – hip-hop, rap and reggae – do not feature in any of the other clusters. The *hard rock* group also had some distinctive preferences – punk and grunge. Now note that it is these very same musical taste groups whose musical preferences were part of broader patterns of leisure time use, uses which generally attract adult disapproval – hanging about with friends, hedonistic leisure (smoking, drinking and unsafe sex), drug use, and trouble with the police and courts. The *black stylists* and *club kids* were also distinctive in their educational records – plenty of school suspensions, low grades and modest ambitions. Similar youth sub-cultural groups have been identified in Britain. The young people generate worth and status among peers through their investments in styles which reinforce their disadvantaged positions in education and eventually in the labour market (see Archer *et al.*, 2007). In the present-day west, the young people whose musical tastes and other uses of leisure most clearly set them apart from the rest of their age group are 'at the bottom'.

In the relatively prosperous west the most easily recognised hierarchical schism in youth's consumption patterns is between the mainstream majority and excluded minorities. Eastern Europe is different in this respect. There are no underclasses (yet) in Eastern Europe (see Domanski, 2002). Unemployment is a risk for young people from all kinds of family and educational backgrounds. Young people without official jobs, even the long-term unemployed, are not always poorer than their employed peers. The former may be earning money in the second economy, or receiving spending money from their families, which allows them to participate in the same activities, with the same frequency, as other young people. As explained above, young people

---

Box 6.5
The musical tastes of young people in Toronto, Canada

A questionnaire study of 3,393 13–18 year old students from 30 Toronto high schools identified the following clusters of musical tastes:

(i)   *Club kids*, who enjoyed techno, dance, mainstream pop, hip-hop and rap.
(ii)   *Black stylists*, who enjoyed soul, rhythm and blues, hip-hop, reggae, and dance hall.
(iii) *New traditionalists*, who enjoyed classical music, jazz, opera, soul, rhythm and blues, country, and mainstream pop.
(iv)   *Hard rockers*, who enjoyed heavy metal, hard rock, alternative, punk, and grunge.
(v)   *Ethnic culturalists*, who enjoyed ethnic genres, soul, rhythm and blues, jazz, classical music, opera, country, techno, dance, and mainstream pop.
(vi)   *Musical omnivores*, who had above average appreciation of all kinds of music.
(vii) *Musical abstainers*, who had little interest in any kind of music.

Musical tastes were related to age, gender and ethnicity.

(i)   *Club kids* tended to be young, and mainly white.
(ii)   *Black stylists* were largely though not exclusively black.
(iii) *New traditionalists* tended to be older, female and Asian.
(iv)   *Hard rockers* tended to be young, male and white.
(v)   *Ethnic culturalists* were generally older and Asian.
(vi)   *Omnivores* tended to be older and Asian.
(vii) *Abstainers* tended to be male and white.

Certain musical tastes were clearly related to educational achievements and ambitions.

(i)   *Black stylists* and *club kids* had far more than average school suspensions, low grades, and modest educational goals.
(ii)   *New traditionalists* were high performing students who never missed classes.

Certain musical tastes were related to broader clusters of leisure activities.

(i)   *Club kids* and *black stylists* were into peer leisure and hedonistic leisure.
(ii)   *Hard rockers* and *black stylists* were into drug use.
(iii) *Black stylists* were the most delinquent taste group.

Source: Tanner *et al.* (2008).

---

in Eastern Europe have not yet lost the art of passing time without spending money, and they have been enterprising in keeping abreast of fashions and gaining access to the latest films and sounds on a low cost basis.

In Eastern Europe it is the high spending minority who are different and who therefore stand apart. They may live in the city centres or elsewhere, but they spend much of their spare time in big city centres. They may be from well-off families, or have high earnings from their own businesses or (more likely) from high salary jobs. They are different from the intelligentsia strata, a high status group under communism that had a distinctive and high profile lifestyle. The intelligentsia were highly educated, they were the principal consumers of official culture (art galleries, theatres, etc.), and they were also united by their interest in public affairs. The former intelligentsia have disintegrated and the strata are not being reproduced (see Roberts *et al.*, 2005). Some members of the old intelligentsia have been impoverished. Many of the young adults who would formerly have joined the intelligentsia have opted to exploit their marketable skills and knowledge. Highly educated young people in Eastern Europe are still the main consumers of high culture, but the same individuals, and especially those with high incomes, are also the big spenders in the new commercial facilities, and they go to bars and restaurants, etc. more frequently than they go to classical concerts.

There is nothing exceptional in the lifestyles of East Europe's better-off young people if set in a western context. They have modern cars, wear smart clothes, go to cafes and bars regularly, and nightclubs if they wish, and to the theatre and cinema, and take holidays at Mediterranean resorts. In Eastern Europe this makes them stick out. Their consumption is conspicuous, but not necessarily deliberately so. They are the group apart, high status role models for other young people, and they are likely to remain exceptional and to stick out until East Europe's economies and salary levels catch up with those in the west.

Endnote

This chapter, taken together with previous chapters, has most likely created the impression that life is better for young people in the west. If so, we need to pause. In 2007 a UNICEF report compared the well-being of children and young people in 19 European countries plus Canada and the USA. Six types of well-being were measured:

- Family and peer relationships (family structure, family relationships, peer relationships).
- Behaviour and risks (diet, smoking, drinking, sex, fighting, bullying).

- Subjective well-being (ratings of health, school life, and life satisfaction).
- Material well-being (income, unemployment, resources).
- Educational well-being (school achievement, staying on at school after age 15/16, transitions to other than non-skilled employment).
- Health and safety (health, preventative services, accidents and injuries).

When scores on the six types of well-being were aggregated for each of the 21 countries, the UK came right at the bottom of the well-being league table. The country that came next to bottom was the USA. According to the UNICEF measurements, children in Poland and the Czech Republic were faring much better.

Summary and conclusions

This chapter has shown that there have been both gains and losses for young people at leisure in Eastern Europe as a result of the post-communist changes in their countries. One difference between the losses and the gains is that most of the gains – locally available commercial leisure – have been rationed by ability to pay. We have also seen that there are many similarities between youth at leisure in Eastern Europe and the west. The former are less deprived than their low incomes suggest. Differences among young people according to their kinds of youth cultures, and how closely they identify with any, prove remarkably similar on both sides of the former Iron Curtain. Yet there are differences, inevitably so, given the labour market conditions faced by young people in Eastern Europe, the relative poverty of their families, and perhaps most of all as a result of the housing circumstances of Eastern Europe's youth. In Eastern Europe young people's participation rates in virtually all forms of leisure that cost money are much lower than in the west, gender divisions are wider, and unlike in the west where the major class division among youth at leisure is between the excluded and the rest, in Eastern Europe it is beneath the high spending minorities.

Further reading

Pilkington, H. (1994), *Russia's Youth and its Culture*, Routledge, London.
Pilkington, H. (1996), 'Farewell to the Tuscova: masculinities and femininities on the Moscow youth scene', in H. Pilkington, ed.,

Gender, Generation and Identity in Contemporary Russia, Routledge, London.

Pilkington, H., Omel'chenko, E., Flynn, M., Bliudina, U. and Starkova, E. (2002), *Looking West: Cultural Globalization and Russian Youth Cultures*, Pennsylvania State University Press, Pennsylvania.

Puuronen, V., Sinisalo, P., Miljukova, I. and Shvets, L. (2000), *Youth in a Changing Karelia*, Ashgate, Aldershot.

Riordan, J. (1988), 'Problems of leisure and glasnost', *Leisure Studies*, 7, 173–85.

Roberts, K., Povall, S. and Tholen, J. (2005), 'Farewell to the intelligentsia: political transformation and changing forms of leisure consumption in the former communist countries of Eastern Europe', *Leisure Studies*, 24, 115–35.

Class divisions

7

Introduction

This chapter opens by asking, 'What is class?' Class is a keyword that requires initial discussion rather than just a quick definition. We then visit the class structures that existed under communism, followed by some views from Eastern Europe on the subsequent changes. The chapter then discusses how class structures in the west changed during the twentieth century. We see that there have been broadly similar trends in post-communist Eastern Europe, but here the changes have been more rapid, and from and to more extreme start and end points. We see how Eastern Europe's working classes have become ideologically invisible and unrepresented in politics. This sets the context for discussing the positions of young people in Eastern Europe's transformed class structures where it appears that the only attractive future for today's youth is a middle class future.

What is class?

Every sociology student knows that there are different definitions of class, each embedded in a particular theory about how classes are formed and the expected consequences of class divisions for individuals and for their entire societies. Fortunately, all the main concepts of class – functionalist, Marxist and Weberian – share a great deal in common, and it is only these commonalities that we need to engage with here. All sociologists, irrespective of their theoretical persuasions, agree that classes have an economic foundation, and that the best indicator of a person's class position – not necessarily the only indicator, just the best – is how he or she earns a living, in which kind of job or occupation. Note that here we are talking about indicators, not how class is experienced or how it is lived. There is more to class than a way of making a living (see below), though our livelihoods are extremely important to all of us! There are hundreds of different occupations in any modern economy, and there are thousands, sometimes millions, of different jobs. How are these assigned to a more limited number of classes? This is usually on the basis of a combination of an occupation's typical market and work situations.

(i) Market situation. The strength of an occupation's market situation can be assessed by the rewards that workers receive – the pay, of course, then pensions, company cars, health insurance and any other fringe benefits – in other words, the total compensation package. Past rewards and prospective rewards can be just as important as those earned currently, and need to be taken into account. Earning a given sum per month or year has a different significance when it is the peak that is available in an occupation than when it is the bottom rung on an ascending career ladder.

(ii) Work situation. As regards class position, the crucial features are not the technical features of a job but the social relationships in which people are involved at work – how much job autonomy they possess, how closely they are monitored and managed, and whether they are responsible for and have authority over other workers.

Some class schemes use prestige/status/social standing to allocate occupations to positions in the class hierarchy, but these features of jobs are better regarded as products of, or just one set of elements associated with, an occupation's work and market situations than as the basic cause or generator of class divisions. Status rankings situate occupations along a continuous scale with no breaks, whereas the use of market and work situations (although more complicated) groups occupations into discrete classes, mainly on the basis of their work situations – whether people are owners or employees and, if the latter, whether they are primarily managers or managed, for example. These 'relational' class schemes are generally regarded as more authentic (closer to what the class structure is really like) than 'gradational' status hierarchies.

Box 7.1 presents the class scheme developed by John Goldthorpe, the UK sociologist, originally for use in his own large-scale survey of social mobility in Britain in 1972. With minor amendments, in 1998 the scheme was adopted by the UK government as Britain's official class scheme (for classifying the UK population), and in 2007 another slightly amended version was adopted by the European Union for collecting harmonised data from all member countries. Since the 1970s

---

Box 7.1

The Goldthorpe class scheme

1.1 Employers (large organisations) and senior managers	
1.2 Higher professionals	SERVICE CLASS
	MIDDLE CLASS
2 Lower managerial and professional	
3 Intermediate (e.g. clerks, secretaries, computer operators)	
	INTERMEDIATE CLASSES
4 Small employers and own account workers	
5 Supervisors, craft and related	
6 Semi-routine (e.g. cooks, bus drivers, shop assistants, hairdressers)	
	WORKING CLASS
7 Routine (e.g. waiters, cleaners, couriers)	
8 Never worked, long-term unemployed	

---

the Goldthorpe class scheme has been used by sociologists in most parts of the world, and in several cross-national research projects into class structures and mobility. There are other class schemes in use in present-day western sociology, but the Goldthorpe scheme is probably the favourite. The scheme groups people into eight classes according to occupations' typical market and work situations. The eight classes can then be collapsed into three groups. A service class or middle class is defined by its occupations' advantaged work and market situations. The working class is defined by its opposite characteristics – disadvantaged work and market situations. This leaves two intermediate classes – the self-employed and proprietors of small businesses, and an assortment of lower-level office, laboratory and sales occupations that are neither clearly middle class nor working class. This scheme purports to identify the main class divisions in western (and maybe other) societies. We shall return to the details later.

Sociologists will all agree that to justify labelling any occupational aggregate as a class its members need to share more in common than just work and market situations, and prestige. It is expected that social, cultural and political dimensions of class will arise from the economic foundations. As a result of working in the same or similar occupations, earning similar wages or salaries, and therefore being able to afford similar kinds of housing and other forms of consumption, it is expected that members of a class will have more frequent and stronger relationships with one another than with members of other classes. It is also expected that similar experiences in the labour market and at work, and in the rest of life, will lead to the development of distinctive class cultures – beliefs and feelings about the prevailing social conditions, the kind of society in which they live, their interests, and who is on their side and who is against them. Thereafter classes may become political actors, supporters of movements and organisations such as trade unions, professional associations and political parties that seek to defend a class's interests or to change a society in the interests of a particular class.

A fully formed class – maximally cohesive socially and culturally, and politically mobilised – is best regarded as an ideal type to which particular classes in particular societies at specific historical moments will approximate to varying degrees. Related to this, all classes are best regarded not as static entities but always in the process of formation or de-formation, and full class formation is more likely to take generations than just years or even decades. Britain, the world's first industrial nation, had an industrial working class as an occupational aggregate by the mid-19th century but it was only in the following decades that effective trade unions were formed, which founded the Labour Party in 1900, and the first majority Labour government was voted into office only in 1945. Class explanations work best when tackling major medium and long-term historical developments like the social and political implications of the original emergence of capitalism in the west, its replacement by communism in some countries, then communism's replacement by late 20th century global market capitalism.

It is difficult to maintain any discussion of class without introducing terms such as middle class and working class, and sociologists are agreed that these are two of the main classes that have been formed in the western world since the countries industrialised. These are the main groups of classes that are identified in the Goldthorpe class scheme (Box 7.1). The core members of the present-day middle class are people in management and professional occupations, who, as explained above, have advantaged work and market situations. They enjoy relatively high earnings and fringe benefits, employment security and career prospects. They also have autonomy at work, are subject to light supervision, and they typically command subordinates. All this is 'relative' to the working class whose occupations have all the opposite characteristics – lower pay, poorer fringe benefits, greater risks of unemployment, closer supervision, and rarely in charge of anyone else. Some occupations (and therefore people) do not fit clearly into either of these main classes: capitalists whose life chances depend much more on how they deploy their wealth than how they sell their labour power; lower ranked office, laboratory and other technical staff; factory chargehands; the self-employed; and the chronically sick and others who depend indefinitely on charity or state benefits. Whether to simplify things by squeezing all other groups into either the middle class or the working class, or whether to keep these main classes as 'pure' as possible, is an operational matter that all sociologists have to address when they engage in class research and analysis. Whatever course is taken, it is unrealistic and unhelpful to think in terms of classes being separated by fences or moats. There is far too much social mobility to justify such imagery, and too many borderline occupations. It is more helpful to think in terms of clumps or clusters of occupations with each clump possessing a core and a periphery.

Finally, before proceeding, the test of whether classes exist is not whether people believe in them or place themselves 'correctly' or 'incorrectly'. In ideal typical perfectly formed classes, members will identify with one another, and with their entire classes, but in imperfect real life situations there will always be some disjuncture between the objective and subjective aspects of class. It would be naïve in any modern society to expect children and young people to have clear and firm class identities. Nowadays most children and young people from all social class backgrounds and irrespective of their likely class destinations mix with one another in the same schools and colleges, they spend much of their spare time in the same places, wear the same fashions and listen to the same music. Yet despite this, and although they are unlikely to realise it, we shall see that most young people are securely locked into quite narrowly bounded class trajectories. These trajectories are created by push and pull forces. The initial push comes from families which have definite class positions depending on the parents' occupations. Middle class children tend to do much better at school than working class children (see Chapter 3). The reasons for this are hotly debated and need not concern us here. The crucial fact is that, for whatever reasons, middle class parentage is an advantage in education, and also afterwards because, again whatever the reasons, young people from middle class homes tend to get better jobs than young people from working class backgrounds who have identical qualifications. The pull forces are generated in the labour market. Young people are pulled towards some, and deflected away from other types of employment, by virtue of the qualifications that they can offer, and by other things as well, some stemming directly from their family backgrounds (ambitions and 'connections', for example). As we saw in Chapter 4, once in a given type of employment, young people tend to become locked in. They find it much easier to move (if they change jobs) into a similar kind of work than to a completely different level in the occupational structure. There are horizontal (middle class origins to middle class destinations and working class origins to working class destinations) and sloping (upwards or downwards) class trajectories. Over time, in all modern societies, there have been more upward than downward movements because the proportions of middle class jobs have been increasing and the proportions of jobs that are working class have been declining. This means that, over time, the chances of upward mobility for working class children have been improving, and the risks of descent for middle class children have been declining. These trends may appear incompatible, but they have been made compatible by the changing shape of modern class structures.

The trajectories into which they become locked show that, independently of whether they realise this, class exerts a powerful influence over young people's lives. The kinds of jobs that they are able to obtain influence the kinds of houses and flats that they are able to rent or buy, the districts where they can afford to live, and how much they can consume. Class is a powerful sociological concept because it summarises a lifetime of experience. The significance and explanatory power of class are not rooted entirely in the particular jobs that people occupy, or their lack of any employment, or any other aspects of their circumstances, at just one particular point in time. Class experience, like class formation, has a powerful life-long longitudinal dimension.

Classes under communism

Marxists have always argued that a person's class is determined by his or her relationship to the means of production, and that in capitalist societies there have been, and there still are, just two basic classes, owners and workers, or bourgeoisie and proletariat, and that other strata are either class factions or somehow derived from this basic class schism. If correct, once ownership of the means of production is collectivised, there should be no classes; communist societies would be classless by definition. The actual party line in the communist countries was that the societies were currently in a socialist stage of development, heading towards communism, a future golden age when the forces of production would be developed to a point where everyone's needs could be met, all grounds for conflict would have gone, and people would live together in harmony. This golden age would never have arrived, and this was recognised by virtually everyone in the communist countries long before the system collapsed. 'Dissidents' within the countries who risked imprisonment (and many writers outside the countries) argued that communism had produced a 'new class' of party leaders who controlled the means of production and appropriated surplus value (the value produced by workers that was not returned to them in wages, salaries and other benefits) (Djilas, 1957). One variant of this view was that socialist intellectuals (the intelligentsia) had become communism's ruling class (Konrad and Szelenyi, 1979). Needless to say, the communist authorities saw things differently. They classified people according to their occupations while preferring 'non-antagonistic strata' or some other alternative label to class (see Lane, 1982; Wesolowski, 1969). The strata whose existence was acknowledged officially and in everyday conversations at all social levels are listed in Box 7.2.

Box 7.2
Communist social strata

(i) *Nomenklatura*: key positions in all institutions (plant directors, heads of research institutes, senior posts in government departments etc) were reserved for named people who were all trusted and long-standing communist party members.

(ii) Intelligentsia and other specialist occupations which required advanced (higher) education and training, and correspondingly high levels of skill and knowledge.

The *nomenklatura*, intelligentsia and other specialists collectively can be said to have been the equivalents of the west's middle classes of professionally qualified staff and managers.

(iii) Other non-manual employees.

(iv) Workers (in manufacturing and extractive industries).

(v) Agricultural workers who were employed in manual occupations by state and collective farms (and who would also work on their own private plots).

The latter two groups, the 'workers' pure and simple, aggregated together, amounted to the majority of the populations in all the communist countries. Their interests were said to be prioritised, represented and acted upon by the communist parties, and therefore the countries were said to be run in the interests of their working classes.

There is general agreement throughout Eastern Europe that since the end of communism three things have happened to the old class structure as outlined above.

(i) Former strata have disintegrated. The *nomenklatura* no longer exist. An intelligentsia is no longer recognisable. The jobs and lives of farmers into whose ownership or control agricultural land has been divided in most of the countries are entirely different from under the old system. Likewise for workers whose establishments were once their collectives, the foundations of their entire ways of life.

(ii) Inequalities have become chaotic and delegitimised. Normal relationships between occupations and earnings were disrupted during the initial post-communist changes. For example, hotel employees were able to earn much more than medical doctors. Even today there is no official or any other justification for the new inequalities. A few people have become fabulously wealthy through 'honest robbery' privatisations. Business people appear to break the law with impunity. State officials and even the police are known to take bribes (when they can). University staff (some of them) expect or will accept gifts (bribes) to award admission to prestige universities and departments, and to make sure that students pass exams.

(iii) Inequalities have widened dramatically. The communist countries were the world's most equal societies (Yanowitch, 1977). Plant directors were paid more than ordinary workers, but not as much more as in the west. Even the *nomenklatura* lived quite modestly. They were allocated city centre flats, the use of *dachas* and state cars, and access to scarce (imported) goods, but a middle-ranking executive in a western corporation would have been insulted to be offered so modest a compensation package.

There is agreement on the above, then a wide variety of views on the details of the changes that have followed the collapse of communism (see Box 7.3).

It says much about the strength of basic class processes that three relationships, all longstanding in Eastern Europe and the west, and all centred around young people, have endured throughout all the flux and all the above pontifications.

- Parental class has continued to predict success in education. Children of highly educated professionals and managers have continued to be by far the most likely to enter higher education (see Chapter 3).

Box 7.3
How East Europeans interpret class changes in Eastern Europe

In Eastern Europe numerous views circulate in homes, on street corners, and in academic journals about the new inequalities. These views include:

- There are no classes as hitherto understood, just individuals and households with different amounts of money. Researchers based in ex-communist countries have rarely attempted to allocate people to classes in the conventional (western) sociological way. They are more likely to have grouped populations into income bands (see Bogomolova, 1998), or have asked people to rank themselves on (usually 5-point) scales according to their households' economic conditions, or to rate their social levels. When these methods have been used, most respondents have placed themselves in the middle, or just underneath the middle of the groups offered (for example, see Caucasus Research Resource Centre, 2005). When trends over time in subjective deprivation have been monitored, the results indicate a rise during the 1990s and a subsequent decline. For example, in Ukraine in 1994, 29% of the population said that they did not have enough money to buy food. By 1998 the proportion claiming such deprivation had risen to 51%. It then fell back to 22% in 2002 (Oksamytna and Khmelko, 2004).
- The societies have polarised into wealthy elites and impoverished masses (Tilkidjiev, 1996).
- New ruling classes, managerial elites, have been created during the reforms (Eyal *et al.*, 1998).
- The major new class division is between those who still depend on the old order (those in public sector jobs, and those relying on pensions or other state benefits, and other state services), and those who now operate in the private sectors to earn their livings and to consume (Piirainen, 1998).
- New middle classes are being formed. One new middle class group is said to consist of the owners of private businesses (*de novo* or privatised) and the salaried or fee-earning mangers and professionals who perform services for the owners, and in return receive a share of the profits in their pay (Kutsenko, 2002; Khmelko, 2002).
- Another new middle class group is said to be composed of the occupants of public offices which they are able to use for private benefit by taking bribes or sub-contracting profitable tasks to private firms which are owned by themselves or relatives (Khmelko, 2002).
- A further new middle class is said to be composed of 'experts' with highly marketable skills and knowledge (Kutsenko, 2002).
- The new middle class is said to be a mirage: the jobs do not offer salaries that will support a middle class lifestyle (Ilyin, 1998).

- Levels of educational attainment have remained strongly linked to the types of occupations that young people enter: those with higher education are the most likely to enter professional, management and other non-manual positions, while other young people enter other jobs (see Chapter 4).
- Once in the labour market, young workers have tended to stick within the segments that they initially entered (see Chapter 4).

In so far as the ex-communist countries have all become capitalist, market economies, one might expect their class structures to be converging with those in the west, possibly towards the classes identified in the Goldthorpe class scheme (see Box 7.1). The populations of East European countries can easily be placed in the Goldthorpe classes (simply from information about their occupations), and different occupations do in fact tend to possess the same characteristic work and market situations that are found in the west (see Evans and Mills, 1999). However, a problem with all class schemes is that they suggest static structures, and in themselves they say nothing about the social and cultural dimensions of class which are bound to differ according to political and economic conditions, and the recent histories and the historically rooted cultures of particular societies.

Class structure and social change in the west

If, as argued above, class formation can take generations, and if class positions – the economic foundations, then the social, cultural and political dimensions – are about lifetimes of experience rather than just current circumstances, it is clearly impossible for classes in present-day Eastern Europe to be basically the same as in the west. All countries in today's Eastern Europe and the west may be market economies, but they became market economies in different ways and at different times. No-one in the west has the same kind of lifetime experience as people who lived through the collapse of communism or who have been born in the aftermath.

All the countries in what we call the west became industrial societies during the 19th century or the first half of the 20th century. They have all, always, been basically capitalist market economies. Industrialisation in the west created new working classes, which became the majority of the populations, and a common theme in the 20th century histories of western countries was the rise of their working classes as social, cultural and political entities – how workers formed trade unions, which helped to create working class political parties, which then mobilised the working class and made this class and its representatives into figures who commanded respect, and thus the west's working classes became powerful political forces (see Roberts, 2001c). The exceptional country (a very important exception) was the USA where, compared with western Europe, the proportion of the workforce in trade unions remained rather low, and neither of the main political parties – Republicans and Democrats – could be described at any point as basically a working class party (see Lipset and Marks, 2000). Where the working class became an influential political force (as happened throughout western Europe) it sought and achieved, with inter-country variations in detail, three kinds of change.

- First, if not already enfranchised, the working class demanded votes – democracy.
- Second, when they achieved power trade unions and working class political parties demanded the regulation of market economies. Sometimes this meant nationalising major industries. Sometimes it meant agreeing wages, salaries and other conditions of work with trade unions. Sometimes it meant requiring the owners of businesses to accept trade unions and governments as partners in macro- and sometimes in micro-economic planning.
- Third, working class political parties demanded that the provision of some goods and services – always education and health care, and sometimes transport, culture, sport and housing – be wholly or partly withdrawn from the market so that access and enjoyment could become rights of citizenship. Working class political parties also demanded that governments should guarantee the welfare of all citizens via some combination of full employment policies, minimum wage regulations, unemployment and sickness benefits, child benefits and pensions, etc.

The above were all achievements of working class power. Where the working class was not mobilised industrially or politically (as in the USA) the consequences just did not happen.

During the 20th century one can say either that the west's middle classes were re-formed or that new middle classes were created. Many new salaried middle class jobs were created and before the mid-century the people in these new salaried jobs (sometimes called the salariat or the service class) far outnumbered the older middle class of business people and self-employed professionals. They key point here is that the social, cultural and political development of the west's middle classes in the early and mid-20th century was in the context of, and at least partly in response to, the rise of working class power. The

20th century middle classes were always a very mixed occupational aggregate – owners of substantial capital, owners of small businesses and self-employed professionals (the core members of the old middle class), plus salaried managers and professionals, and any other grades of workers – chargehands, foremen, laboratory workers, office staff and technicians – who did not feel part of the working class and who felt threatened rather than represented by working class power. The middle classes were united by little more than a common concern to defend their privileges against the threat from beneath, which meant supporting a political party of the right that was against nationalisation and other forms of state intervention, and high taxes to pay for state welfare, that were favoured by the left.

In the second half of the 20th century the earlier historical trend was reversed and the west's working classes became weaker (see Roberts, 2001c). As indicated above, the working classes have declined numerically. This is partly due to the transfer of production jobs to lower cost countries, and partly to new technologies and more efficient working practices which usually lead to employment reductions. New working class jobs have been created but these tend to be in service sectors rather than 'traditional' (as they have become known) manufacturing and extractive industries. The new jobs are generally less skilled and lower paid than the working class jobs that have been disappearing. The new service sector jobs also tend to be in smaller establishments (such as shops and restaurants) where it has been and still is more difficult for trade unions to recruit and represent members than in the industries from which working class jobs have been lost. Overall, working class employment has declined in quantity and in quality, and the jobs and workers are now less likely to have trade union protection. In many countries trade union membership has fallen as employment has declined in the industries and occupations that were unionised most densely. However, in some countries this source of decline has been offset by the spread of trade union membership among non-manual employees, but the effect of this has been to change the character of the trade union movements. The change has meant that trade unions collectively can no longer be regarded as representing the working class. Working class political parties have faced a similar choice of somehow widening their appeal beyond their traditional working class supporters or becoming permanent opposition parties. In most western countries the old parties of the left have repositioned themselves and have become centre or even centre-right parties (like New Labour in Britain).

As their working classes have declined, western countries have become middle class societies in several senses.

- First, the working classes are no longer the majority, the mass of the people.
- Second, the middle classes are always better organised and represented. All serious political parties compete for middle class votes. The middle classes supply most of the activists, elected representatives and national leaders even in what were once working class political parties. The middle classes are the main joiners and are the most likely to hold office in virtually all kinds of voluntary associations – charitable, cultural and sporting (Li *et al.*, 2003).
- Third, the middle classes are now the main consumers of nearly all types of goods and services. All businesses want their money. The working class market is no longer the mass market. Mass consumer culture today is the culture of the middle classes. Now the working class at leisure just does less and buys less rather than different things which are valued within the class's own culture (see Roberts, 2006b).
- Fourth, the working classes are no longer respected as 'the salt of the earth', a source of virtues admired by all – industriousness, loyalty, and the ability to smile and cope through adversity. Rather, the present-day working classes are denigrated. It is said (by politicians and the media) that the working class lacks parenting skills, that their children under-achieve at school, and behave badly at school and on the streets, and that the adults lack the skills and knowledge that are relevant in today's economies and are liable to be seduced by a 'dependency culture' – expecting and content that the state should provide for them (see Skeggs, 2004).
- Fifth, more young people are from middle class homes: the kind of homes where the parents want, and the children expect to achieve in education and thereby qualify for middle class careers.

Meanwhile, positional competition within the middle classes has intensified. One example is the competition to get children into the best schools and universities. In Spain a rise in the divorce rate early in 2007 was attributed to parents seeking the extra points awarded to single parent families so as to secure places in (what were believed to be) good secondary schools. Some judges had found parents seeking reconciliations as soon as school applications were completed (Keeley, 2008). Another example of positional competition is different professions comparing their salaries and social standing. The gap between the middle and the top of western countries' wealth and income ladders has widened, thus increasing the rewards for success and the penalties and frustrations of those who, despite their achievements in education and their ambitions, are left in the middle. Meanwhile, the threat of working class power has evaporated and can no longer be relied on to unite the middle classes socially, culturally or politically.

Class in Eastern Europe after communism

Eastern Europe is an extreme case and is currently prototypical as regards recent changes in the class structure and the implications for young people's life chances. The changes have been in exactly the same directions as in the west – from working class to middle class societies in economic, cultural and political terms – but in Eastern Europe the changes have been more rapid, and both the points of departure and destination have been more extreme.

Communist societies claimed to be workers' states. Whether or not they really were run by the workers, or in the workers' interests, is beside the current point. The regimes legitimised themselves by claiming to be guardians of working class interests. The ways in which communism changed all the countries were supposed to be of particular benefit to workers. The workers were the heroes, portrayed in posters on streets and factory walls with spanners and pickaxes, celebrated for breaking production records. However cynical actual workers may have been, their jobs, their contributions to their societies, were portrayed in glowing terms. They were the producers whose glorious efforts were building communism. Workers whose endeavours were especially heroic – coal miners for example – were among the highest paid employees. They earned far more than schoolteachers and medical doctors. Being a worker, and for a young person becoming a worker, were sources of pride.

With the end of communism the Marxist worldview that celebrated the working class was discredited. Suddenly the workers' state was a thing of the past. Many jobs in mining and manufacturing disappeared. The employees learnt suddenly that their technologies and working practices were out-of-date historical relics. When the jobs survived the reforms, conditions of employment were usually degraded. Fringe benefits – holidays at centres run by the industries and trade unions, and workplace-based health care – were usually jettisoned along with other 'frills'. The heroes of the transition were businessmen and bankers. Trade unions (which had been an integral part of the old system) became functionless. Managements no longer needed trade unions to help in exhorting workforces to meet production targets. Factory bosses had new incentives. Failure to meet the market's requirements meant the sack or even the closure of a plant. Under communism the trade unions did not have a genuine bargaining role, and the new owners of businesses have not wanted to be tied down by having to negotiate and respect agreements. Trade unions in Eastern Europe have lost members and have sometimes ceased to exist, or they continue to exist as hollow shells. The communist parties have been able to survive only by changing their names and often completely overhauling their policies. The working classes in the new Eastern Europe have no representatives. They have no theory, no ideology that celebrates their role and gives them a future (see Stenning, 2005b). Simonchuk (2004) argues that although the working class still amounts to around a half of the population in Ukraine, and although nearly a half of the people describe themselves as belonging to the working class, this class's voice has been silenced and the class has become ideologically invisible. The working class is the past. Few young people today aspire to become workers.

In Eastern Europe the middle class is the new promised land (see Kivinen, 1998). It has been said again and again inside the countries and internationally that consolidating and securing the reforms depends on creating middle classes with stakes in the new societies. Communism's unproductive workers (bureaucrats) and criminals (spivs and profiteers) are now celebrated. Riding with the tide of post-communist history means somehow jumping aboard the new middle classes. There have been different ways of accomplishing this. One has been to start a new business and develop it into a profitable enterprise. Another has been to take over a state establishment that has become available for privatisation. Business people who accumulated substantial capital in the early 1990s were able to acquire oil and gas resources in some countries, plus TV stations and telephone companies, and thereby become multi-billionaires (in USA $). Young and older people who had accumulated more modest sums could bid for a meat processing plant or some other small but potentially profitable enterprise. Another route into the new middle class has been as a professional or management functionary, performing services for the new class of owners as an accountant, lawyer or as a general 'fixer'. Some officials in some state departments have been able to generate earnings that will support a middle class lifestyle by performing services for international companies and NGOs, local private businesses and ordinary citizens – resolving tax and customs problems, or obtaining health and safety certificates, or planning permission for a new building, for example. Is this corruption? One view has been that state officials are paid by the state to work for the state: if they assist anyone else, the beneficiary should reward them appropriately. As the post-communist governments have become more successful in taxing earnings and profits, it has been possible to raise the salaries of public sector employees thus lessening their need, though not necessarily diminishing their motivation, to use their positions for private gain. Another route into the new middle classes has been in a job with an international organisation, or through a key position in a local firm or government department that performs services for international bodies.

Young people in the new class systems

In some Eastern European countries only tiny minorities of young people make it into the middle class proper. In other countries where the economies have recovered and developed more strongly, the proportions are larger, but they are always minorities. There are always a lot more 'wannabes'. Many young people find that, when approached, the middle class really is a mirage; their nominally middle class jobs will not supply the incomes to support a middle class lifestyle. Even so, young people clamber towards this new heavenly state. They crowd onto academic courses in upper secondary education, then progress through higher education. They improve their foreign language and ICT skills by paying for private coaching or courses at the private colleges that have opened in all Eastern European cities. It is an extreme version of the situations that already exist, or which are emergent, in western countries. In the USA, always the western country with the weakest working class, college is the only attractive route forward that high schools can dangle before their pupils (see Rosenbaum, 2001). Europe's vocational tracks through upper secondary education are weakening, becoming less attractive, and parents and young people are becoming more ambitious as the populations become more middle class (see Chapter 3). Graduates from higher education discover that their qualifications do not guarantee middle class jobs – merely admission to the pools that are allowed to compete for these jobs. Once in their first jobs they are likely to discover that even then they are not on career ladders leading into the middle class proper, but have simply joined smaller pools within which they must compete strenuously for career preferment (Brown and Hesketh, 2004).

Who 'makes it' in Eastern Europe? The same kind of young people who 'make it' in the west. As explained in Chapter 2, they are usually higher education graduates who can offer something in addition – foreign languages, familiarity with information technology, and evidence of an aptitude to work in commercial environments. Connections can be useful. So is living in the right place, and being a man. Graduates in Eastern Europe and the west tend to marry one another (Blossfeld and Timm, 2003), and a middle class lifestyle usually depends on a household being able to combine more than one income. The typical middle class partnership in Eastern Europe is between a graduate wife in a modestly paid but secure short-hours public service profession (such as teaching) and a graduate husband with lighter domestic responsibilities who is able to work longer hours, maybe travel abroad, and earn a much higher salary, or a set of incomes, in business or in public or private sector line management, or a combination of these. The young people who succeed know that they owe a great deal to the families who supported them through their own education, who paid for private coaching when necessary, and maybe used influence to get them into a particular university or job. The young adult members of Eastern Europe's new middle classes are determined to do the same for their own children by paying for private education when this seems advisable whether at nursery, kindergarten, or the secondary stage. Eastern Europe's new super-rich may well decide to have their children educated partly in a western country. Thus, as is the worldwide norm, Eastern Europe's new middle classes will tend to reproduce themselves, passing on advantages from generation to generation (see Roberts *et al.*, 2002).

A group of Moscow university graduates who took part in a discussion group in 2002 were broadly agreed on how they would educate (or try to educate) their own children. None had children yet, but all expected and intended to become parents eventually. They were determined that their children should learn foreign languages either at school or at home or in some other way. *'IT skills are nothing special nowadays. It's foreign languages that make a difference.'* All expected to use the private sector at some stage. Some envisaged sending their children abroad for part of their higher education. Most wanted to avoid state kindergartens: *'Classes are very large...They spread diseases. They don't give enough education.'*

Other young people in Eastern Europe can only hope and dream that one day, when their countries' transitions are completed, their own turns will come. Some are trapped in rural villages, trying to plan routes out. Marriage and parenthood usually slam the door: the young people know that they have no way of obtaining equivalent housing and family support in child-rearing if they move. Other young people are working in coal mines, steel plants and other industrial establishments. Some are well paid, but even they are likely to worry that their industries and jobs have no future. Many who work for foreign companies (in oil and gas exploration and extraction, for example) find that the top jobs are held by foreigners. Attempts to build businesses often never get beyond survival self-employment. Beginning workers take temporary jobs in bars and shops. They hope that time will improve their prospects, but as the years go by, and the longer their countries remain allegedly in transition, the less likely this becomes.

Note that nothing above implies that the young people are even mildly class conscious. They rarely speak and it is unlikely that they think about themselves in class terms. Young people are always unlikely to be sure of their own class positions given that, for so many, their futures are difficult to predict. This remains the case even when young people agree that they live in class societies. Young people are most likely to be sure of their own class locations when children from different class backgrounds attend entirely different elementary and secondary schools, then progress immediately into different kinds of employment. This applied in many countries in the past. Does it apply anywhere today? Young people with different class origins and destinations rub shoulders in the same schools, have similar leisure preferences and activities, and face similar problems in finding jobs. They may be aware of problems and opportunities shared by all young people, possibly by all members of their societies, but thereafter they are most likely to be aware of their own individuality, the specificities of their own biographies, their own past achievements (recorded on their CVs), and their current and longer-term prospects.

Even so, if we step back, as sociological observers, we can see clearly how young people's lives and biographies are shaped by class structures and processes. We can see the implications for young people of historical trends – the shrinkage, de-formation and disempowerment of the working classes, and the growth and formation of new middle classes, currently composed of people with diverse social origins, doing many different kinds of jobs, with mixtures of what were once described as highbrow and lowbrow tastes which they are able to indulge, albeit to varying extents, because although advantaged *vis-à-vis* the working classes, there are huge inequalities and rivalries within the present day middle classes in Eastern Europe and the west.

Class and political representation

There is no East European country whose party politics can be described as firmly class-based. Even when different parties' policies can be situated on a left–right axis, the support that they attract is likely to have as much to do with what their leaders were doing before 1989 (their roles under the old system), and the leaders' stances on whether national traditions and independence are at risk through too much or too little integration into the west. However, there are class-related differences in voters' views, which are much as one would predict from class differences in opinions and political partisanship in western Europe (Gijsberts and Nieuwbeerta, 2000). Young people's attitudes on political issues are class-related, though not necessarily the parties or politicians they would vote for.

Tables 7.1, 7.2 and 7.3 are from the surveys of a total of 1800 25–29 year olds that were conducted in Ukraine, Georgia and Armenia in 2002. The samples are sub-divided, first, according to whether or not they had been through higher education, then according to whether their personal reported monthly incomes were over or less than $50. The young adults who were the most likely entrants to Eastern Europe's new middle classes had received higher education and had decently paid jobs at the time of the survey ($50 a month was decent pay in 2002 in the places where the research was conducted). It can be seen in Table 7.1 that the potentially middle class groups were the less likely to believe that life had become more difficult since the reforms, the more likely to support the USA-led military action in Afghanistan, and were the most supportive of their countries joining NATO. The issue in Table 7.1 that most clearly separates the classes is their feelings about the disintegration of the USSR. The middle class groups tended

Table 7.1 *Attitudes on social and political issues (in percentages)*

Percentages who agreed or agreed strongly	HEd	No HEd	Monthly income $50	Monthly income less than $50
The USA was right to bomb Afghanistan	37	26	39	27
This country should be in NATO	51	41	50	41
Life is more difficult since the reforms	77	82	68	84
Views on disintegration of USSR:				
Positive	36	15	34	14
Negative	21	39	29	37
N=	927	873	491	766

Source: see text.

to regard the end of the USSR as a positive development, whereas the working class groups tended to feel negatively about the loss of the Soviet Union.

Young people in Eastern Europe have been the most pro-reform age group (for example, see Machacek, 1994, 1996). Ex-communists would not have regained power anywhere had the vote been restricted to the under-30s. It is mainly older people who are nostalgic and sensitive to what has been lost during the reforms. The overwhelming majority of young people in all East European countries are against any turning back or slowing down. They want their countries to press ahead and become successful market economies and western-type democracies. However, different classes of young people differ in how overwhelmingly, and how enthusiastically, they endorse the reforms. Those who are securing middle class positions for themselves are by far the most enthusiastic. They are the least likely to believe that the reforms were a mistake, the most likely to argue that markets are preferable to the old system, and to favour western-type democratic politics. They are more likely than other young people to feel that the new wider inequalities are justified. They certainly feel that their own rewards are no more than fair returns for their own efforts and talents. While they are likely to want the state to look after the weakest members of their societies, they themselves do not want to depend on state welfare but are determined, if they can, to make their own provisions for health care and pensions. The evidence from the 2002 surveys in Ukraine, Georgia and Armenia (see Table 7.2) shows that the young adults who were on middle class trajectories were far more likely than their working class counterparts to intend to mobilise private resources for their own children's education.

The political agendas of the young potentially middle class adults in this research were geared to making their countries more hospitable for people such as themselves. Young people who were clearly on working class life trajectories (whether they realised this or not) were less enthusiastic about the reforms. They were less likely to feel that rewards in their reformed countries are being distributed according to merit. While they might have preferred to be self-sufficient, they were not confident that they would be able to pay for their own health care and save for their retirement. They were also less enthusiastic about the west. Some were uncertain about western-type democracy. Some felt that what their countries really needed was strong leaders (see Chapter 8).

However, in present-day Eastern Europe there are very few working class young people who are politically active. The middle class activists are a small minority from their own class, but they comprise

Table 7.2 *Educational ambitions for own children (in percentages)*

	HEd	No HEd	Monthly income $50 and over	Monthly income less than $50
Wants private education for own children	30	17	36	18
Expects to pay for coaching for own children	85	69	79	72
Very keen for children go to university, even if has to pay	47	24	41	27
Very keen for children to attend a university in the west, even if has to pay	33	14	24	14
N=	927	873	491	766

Source: see text.

most of the young activists in political parties and in other civil society organisations as well (see Table 7.3). It is their voices that are heard in politics. They also have a vision of what their countries should become which, in a phrase, is more like western countries – successful democracies and successful in global markets. Young people with reservations do not have an alternative inspirational vision of where their countries might head.

Table 7.3 *Political activity (in percentages)*

	HEd	No HEd	Monthly income $50 and over	Monthly income less than $50
Political party member	5	3	7	3
Been to at least one political meeting in last 12 months	11	5	10	6
Very/quite interested in politics	28	19	32	19
N=	927	873	491	766

Source: see text.

The west is following Eastern Europe in all the above respects but is travelling more slowly because western political parties carry 'baggage' and 'traditional support' that were built-up in the era of working class power, and in the west the break with the past has been less thorough than in Eastern Europe. Young people in the west who become long-term political activists, then have careers as professional politicians and become leaders of their parties, are nearly all products of higher education nowadays, and any work experience that they obtain outside politics is usually in middle class occupations. Former socialist parties have shifted onto the centre ground. They no longer seek to eliminate or even gradually reduce the roles of the market and private capital. However, these parties still carry at least remnants of working class culture. The old visions – regulating markets and strengthening welfare states – are not dead even if they can no longer mobilise sufficient support to win an election. In Eastern Europe young people on all class trajectories tend to regard such ideas as backward looking.

Maybe during the 21st century an attractive alternative to the global capitalist market economy will be envisioned, inspire young people, then be created. At present the most likely creators appear to be the governing elites in Russia, China and the Central Asian republics. They may draw closer together as an economic and security zone of state regulated markets and managed democracies, but if so this will not be in response to bottom-up demands, certainly not from their young people. The alternative will be developed top-down, with support among those below mobilised by those above.

Summary and conclusions

Class is a powerful sociological concept because it can reveal otherwise hidden links between economic life, social life and politics. Without introducing class into an analysis it becomes difficult to understand how changes in a country's economy and politics can have vastly different implications for different sections of the population, or the sources of social movements that press for and sometimes achieve political and economic changes. Young people are affected by class because their social class origins have much to do with their levels of attainment in education and the kinds of employment that they are able to enter, but this does not exhaust the implications of class for a country's youth. The class locations into which they become locked, initially by labour market processes, soon after commencing their working lives make a difference to whether young people feel able to benefit from how their countries are changing, whether they feel part of their countries' likely futures, whether the media and political leaders are offering visions of a future that they personally wish to enter, and whether their countries' elites are sensitive and responsive to the young people's own concerns and interests. The broad directions of change in the shape of class structures, and in the balance of class forces, have been basically the same in Eastern Europe and the west, but currently the outcomes are somewhat different. In western countries working class youth face new risks of social exclusion. In Eastern Europe minorities of young people, the most likely winners from the post-communist transformations in their countries, are exceptional in their enthusiasm for the future possibilities that have opened up for themselves and their countries.

Further reading

Kivinen, M. (ed.) (1998), *The Kalamari Union: Middle Class in East and West*, Ashgate, Aldershot.
Stenning, A. (2005), 'Where is the post-socialist working class? Working class lives in the spaces of (post)-socialism', *Sociology*, 39, 983–99.

Politics

'The 20th century was undoubtedly the century of youth. It was in this century that it first became established as a social group rather than an age group. Young people have become the prime agents of innovation and progress in a majority of areas of life. Youth movements of the 20th century undeniably played a part in the ideology of progress – evident in the firm connection between social and critical awareness on the one hand, and the utopian social projects produced by these movements on the other…. at the beginning of the new millennium it seems that the prominent role of young people that characterised the whole of the previous century is coming to an end' (Ule, 2005, p 9). *'The value system of individualisation carries within it the seed of a new ethic that rests on "obligations towards oneself"'* (*ibid*, p. 17). These observations are based largely on Ule's research among young people in Slovenia, but she could be writing about young people anywhere in present-day Europe.

Introduction

Any discussion of youth and politics, like youth and anything else, needs to be guided by clear questions. Failure to ask such questions results in discussion being swamped by the sheer volume of data on young people's attitudes to political parties, events and policies, and examples of young people's involvement in political action. This is especially so when 'political' is defined broadly to encompass any action that is intended to influence politicians or, irrespective of the intentions, that does influence or elicit a response from politicians, plus, possibly, all acts of 'citizenship' – holding office or just participating in any voluntary association, assisting in fund-raising, or even informally doing good deeds. There is a lot of information that could be presented with the whole of Eastern Europe and the west to draw from.

170

The main questions that need to be addressed to the data derive from the character of youth as a transitional life stage.

- Are the outlooks, the mindsets, of upcoming cohorts of voters, activists and leaders changing the character of politics in the relevant countries?
- How do young people in a given country or a group of countries at a particular time (the present time, for our purpose) differ from young people in other times and places?
- Which young people are being recruited into political careers? Are they representative of the entire cohorts?

This chapter opens with an account of young people's forms and levels of political engagement under communism, then discusses the 'class of '89' – young people who were in life stage transition when communism ended and their successors. We see that these young people are extreme examples of contemporary global youth. They are distinguished by historically low levels of political engagement combined with high levels of cynicism towards politics and politicians' motives. The chapter then introduces the concept of political generations and proceeds to argue that although the generational divide is clearest in Eastern Europe, in most parts of the world in the late 20th century new political generations were formed that are distinguished from their predecessors by their detachment from public affairs. This is despite the anger felt by many young people in Eastern Europe, in the west, and in other parts of the world, about the state of their countries and how their countries are being led. The chapter then explains why politically significant expressions of this anger tend to be spasmodic rather than sustained: the most plausible main explanation is the absence of alternative inspirational future visions to multi-party democracy and the global market economy.

Young people and politics under communism

Under communism young people were highly aware, interested and participant in politics – more so than has been the case in any other modern societies (see Bronfenbrenner, 1971; Grant, 1968; Lane, 1976; Matthews, 1972). They were politically aware if only because Marxism was a compulsory subject at all levels in education – from elementary school to university. Young people knew (even if they did not agree with) the theory that was used to legitimise the regimes in their countries. They also knew the names of leading political figures. They knew all about communism's triumphs, especially its victory over fascism in the Great Patriotic War.

All children became members of the Octobrists (up to age 9) and the Pioneers (9–16 year olds). These movements were in many ways akin to the Boy Scouts/Girl Guides except that membership was universal and there was no competition from other voluntary associations or commerce. There were uniforms. The activities were basically recreational in after-school and holiday clubs, but everything was surrounded by and sometimes pervaded with a political message (as can happen to the entire curriculum in faith schools). The leaders of these movements were Communist Party cadres (paid functionaries). When they outgrew the Pioneers, between a third and a half of all young people (including most of those who entered higher education) joined the Komsomol (for 16–28 year olds). This was a serious political organisation. The Komsomol was the normal first step towards full party membership (between 10% and 20% of adults became full party members – the exact proportions varied by regions, countries and time). Party membership was an honour that needed to be earned. Entry was selective rather than open door. The Komsomol organised sports, cultural activities and holidays for the entire age group, but members were also required to participate in political discussions and propaganda activities. Young people who joined the Komsomol were not necessarily committed in an ideological sense, as most have stressed (since 1989). They could join simply because this was expected of them or for career reasons. Komsomol membership could make it easier to enter a prestige university. Students could earn higher grants through Komsomol activity. Membership opened the possibility of a career as a party functionary – the ladder to the most powerful positions that existed in communist countries. Party membership was an asset in any other career – a requirement if one was to reach the *nomenklatura*. All this required at least an indication of political commitment, and all Komsomol members attended events addressed by political leaders (local and sometimes national), and were involved in propaganda activities and discussions about public affairs.

Communism did not require or expect citizens (or party members) to learn political dogma by rote and to accept the party line without questioning. There were debates, and party members (including Komsomol members) did not have to pretend that they agreed with every decision that the party took. The requirement was simply that they abided by decisions that were taken following democratic (on communism's definition) procedures. Personal dissent was not unlawful. The prohibition was on organised opposition.

This system of political socialisation produced some (it is impossible to say exactly how many) true believers who were genuinely committed and who believed that they were engaged in building better societies and better lives for all their countries' people. The system involved more young people (and more adults) in politics than any western democracy has ever achieved. In 1989 there was an expectation in Eastern Europe that following the overthrow of communism young people would become even more interested and active in politics. After all, they were to have a choice of parties and would be able to play parts in determining the future directions of their countries. At that time East Europeans knew far more about western democracy in theory than how it worked in practice.

1989 and what happened afterwards

In 1989 students all over East-Central Europe were on the streets demonstrating for change. They won, and they were surprised by the speed and finality of their victory. Communism was history in their countries by the end of the year. The futures that the old system had laid out for young people disappeared. They felt liberated. There would be new and better opportunities. People could think whatever they wished and say whatever they thought. There was another new option, not to care, but in 1989 most young people did care and their preferred leaders were in power by the end of the year. The countries celebrated, and young people were at the centre of the partying in Warsaw, Prague then in November on the Berlin Wall.

What happened next? The 'classes of 1989' returned to their homes, schools, colleges and jobs, and got on with the business of daily life. This turned out to mean coping with rampant inflation and a sharp drop in the real value of most households' incomes, akin to the impact of a major war. In the Balkans and Caucasus young people were fighting in real wars. Daily life was a struggle, and amid these changes nearly all young people quit politics. This was unexpected. It was believed that the new freedoms of expression and association would unleash sustained civic activity among enthusiastic young people. It was believed that with a choice of parties young people would become more involved, more interested, more committed citizens than under communism. In the event exactly the reverse happened. Interest in politics and party membership among young people fell to extremely low levels – lower than in the west where young people's political apathy concerns politicians in most countries, and is well beneath the levels under communism. Table 8.1 lists the proportions in successive surveys in Eastern Europe who said that they were 'interested' or 'very interested' in politics. As benchmarks, the list is headed by answers to the same question by samples of young people in Britain and Germany. The levels of expressed interest in Eastern Europe are generally well beneath the western range. There are variations by place within Eastern Europe: the highest scores in Eastern Europe in Table 8.1 are from the west of Ukraine (Lviv in 1997, and Lviv and Khmelnitskiy in 2002, where support, sometimes enthusiastic support, was overwhelmingly for nationalist parties which triumphed in the 'orange revolution' in 2004).

Table 8.1 *Percentages who were very interested or quite interested in politics*

1988–90	
Liverpool	53
Swindon	38
Bremen	75
Paderborn	67
1993	
Gdansk	18
Katowice	10
Suwalki	12
1997	
Donetsk	38
Lviv	46
Tbilisi	18
Armenia	14
1999	
Moscow	20
Vladikavkaz	30
Dneipropetrovsk	20
2002	
Yerevan born	17
Yerevan refugees	15
Vanadzor	15
Tbilisi born	19
Tbilisi refugees	18
Telavi	33
Makeeva	22
Khmelnitsky	37
Lviv	45

Source: see text.

Despite young people's leading role in innovation and progress throughout the 20th century noted by Ule (see above), it has been normal in all modern societies for young people to be less interested in politics, and less likely to be politically active, including less likely to vote, than the adult populations. Nowadays researchers in western countries note how much lower levels of youth political activity have become compared with the 1960s. In the 1980s Breakwell (1985) noted that although many young people in Britain still held radical views, they had become quiet (inactive) rebels. Since then young people in Britain have become even 'quieter'. Between 1994 and 1999 the proportion of 12–19 year olds who 'felt close to' or hoped that a partic-ular party would win an election declined from 68% to 39% (Park *et al.*, 2005). In Canada Adsett and McKellar (2002) have documented the recent decline in voting by younger cohorts. In France in the late 1970s 25% of 30–34 year olds said that they frequently engaged in political discussions with friends: the proportion had fallen to 12% by the late 1990s. In 1982 in France the average age of trade unionists and politi-cians holding elected positions was 45; in 2000 it was 59. At France's *Assemblée Nationale* in 1981 38.1% of the deputies were aged under 45 but only 15.1% in the new *assemblée* that was elected in 2002 (Charvel, 2006). There have been comparable trends throughout the modern 'democratic' world. Thus it is helpful to recall that even in the 1960s and 70s researchers were noting, and deploring, young people's generally low levels of political knowledge, interest and participation (see Crick and Heater, 1977). The political activists who shut down campuses were minorities among the students of that era (see, for example, Blackstone *et al.*, 1970; Fendrich, 1973; Feuer, 1969; Kahn and Bowers, 1970).

There are several reasons for young people's tenuous relationship with politics. First, young people have less political knowledge – about the parties, their leaders and policies – than people who have been reading newspapers, voting in elections (or able to do so) for many years. Second, adults build up track records of voting in elec-tions and thereby acquire 'default options' – parties that they normally support and will vote for unless they have specific reasons for not doing so. Young people cannot possess default options unless these have been inherited from their families, local communities, religious or ethnic groups. Nowadays there are additional reasons. One is that, as stressed in previous chapters, today's young people's adult desti-nations are usually unknown (to themselves and to others) at the time in their lives when they are first becoming fully politically aware (see below), so it is difficult for them to identify with any particular inter-est groups and parties with corresponding policies. Another reason is that young people are remaining in education for longer and are sheltered from the full impact of experience in the labour market and employment which in the past acted as powerful milieux of teenage political socialisation.

The proportions of young people in Eastern Europe who have joined political parties are miniscule. Very few belonged to trade unions in any of the places listed in Table 8.2 except in Ukraine (once again the exceptional country). Up to the time of the relevant surveys, trade unions had fared better during the reforms in Ukraine than in any of the other listed countries, and the Ukraine regions also had the highest proportions who had joined political parties. Despite this, even in Ukraine few young people had been involved in any political activity in the year preceding the interviews, and in some places high proportions (up to 70%) said that they had decided definitely not to vote in the next elections (see Table 8.3).

There are easily identified reasons (now) why everyone should really have expected political interest and activity among youth in Eastern Europe to subside to lower than normal levels after 1989. It is always easy to be wise with hindsight! First, all the countries' political parties (except the communists or ex-communists) have been new and

Table 8.2 *Memberships (in percentages)*

	Trade union	Political party
1997		
Donetsk	57	1
Lviv	48	7
Tbilisi	4	2
Armenia	4	3
1999		
Moscow	13	2
Vladikavkaz	17	5
Dneipropetrovsk	37	3
2002		
Yerevan born	5	1
Yerevan refugees	7	1
Vanadzor	7	2
Tbilisi born	4	6
Tbilisi refugees	4	3
Telavi	2	4
Makeeva	44	10
Khmelnitsky	15	3
Lviv	27	6

Source: see text.

Table 8.3 *Political participation (in percentages): next election*

	Intend to vote for named party	Will vote, but not sure who for	Will not vote	Attended at least one political meeting during last year
1997				
Donetsk	12	47	41	8
Lviv	9	51	40	24
Tbilisi	12	57	31	7
Armenia	11	32	57	17
1999				
Moscow	23	55	22	11
Vladikavkaz	29	41	30	12
Dneipropetrovsk	16	61	23	8
2002				
Yerevan born	13	32	55	7
Yerevan refugees	13	17	70	5
Vanadzor	18	49	33	0
Tbilisi born	22	35	44	10
Tbilisi refugees	27	28	45	17
Telavi	32	33	35	11
Makeeva	29	30	42	4
Khmelnitsky	35	19	46	9
Lviv	52	27	21	14

Source: see text.

often unstable in terms of both leaders and policies. Hardly any of the new parties have sunk deep and broad grassroots composed of stable memberships and supporters. The main exceptions are, first, the (ex) communists who attract little support among young people anywhere (see below), and second, in some countries, the new 'parties of power' (usually formed through amalgamations of smaller parties that join together basically so that these coalitions will hold office without serious challenge). Where these parties exist they are the real successors to the old communist parties. Examples are *United Russia* (which was formed to support President Putin) and the *Party of the Regions* in Eastern Ukraine. Kazakhstan and Uzbekistan have similar parties, and in Georgia the coalition that gained power following the 2003 'rose revolution' has been developing into a party of power. Individuals entering public sector employment or who simply believe that political connections will work to their advantage are likely to join such parties where they exist (as noted above, people joined the communists for the same reasons when the communists were the party of power). These parties of power should not be dismissed instantly as undemocratic let alone anti-democratic. In the relevant countries and regions the parties probably enjoy overwhelming support. They guarantee political stability, which many members of the public value. Also, it can be argued that any country can benefit from a prolonged period of stable government while developing a successful market economy. This happened, for different reasons and in rather different ways, in Sweden, Singapore and Japan.

A second reason for most young people's non-involvement in politics is that throughout Eastern Europe people of all ages have typically been disappointed by the performances of their post-communist governments. Expectations in 1989 turned out to be unrealistic. The new governments have possessed far less power than their citizens expected. Often they have appeared (and have been) subservient to the World Bank, the International Monetary Fund and the European Union. Related to this, voters have been disappointed by their govern-

Table 8.4 *Percentages who agreed or agreed strongly that politicians are more interested in themselves than the good of the country*

1993	
Poland	78
1997	
Donetsk	79
Lviv	76
Tbilisi	83
Armenia	80
1999	
Moscow	64
Vladikavkaz	52
Dneipropetrovsk	54
2002	
Yerevan born	94
Yerevan refugees	83
Vanadzor	88
Tbilisi born	92
Tbilisi refugees	92
Telavi	92
Makeeva	83
Khmelnitsky	89
Lviv	59

Source: see text.

ments' apparent inability to alleviate poverty, reduce unemployment, and maintain social protection. Young (and older) voters have often decided that none of their countries' politicians or parties deserve their support. There was widespread cynicism – massive levels – towards politicians in all the places where young people were investigated which are listed in Table 8.4.

The East European countries are extreme cases. Kutsenko (2004) notes that by the beginning of the new millennium most Ukrainians had decided that their country was not truly democratic. What about western countries? In 2006 a survey in all the EU27 countries found that 62% 'tended not to trust' their national governments, and 72% 'tended not to trust' political parties (European Commission, 2007). This research found that trust varied by countries. In Poland 81% trusted neither their city/village council, the national parliament, the government or political parties. Somewhat fewer in the UK, but still a majority, 63%, trusted none of these bodies. The figure was only 19% in Denmark, Europe's most trusting country according to these measurements.

Political generations in Eastern Europe and the west

There are particular reasons why young people in present-day Eastern Europe should be less engaged politically than their contemporary western counterparts even though the latter's involvement in politics falls well short of the levels of their predecessors in the 1960s and 70s. As noted above, even at that time investigators were seeking explanations of young people's lack of interest in politics, but by present-day standards young people of that era were highly political. This is so whatever measurements are used – voting, membership of political parties, or participation in political events. Middle class western youth cultures in the 1960s were entwined with protests against the threat of nuclear war, for civil rights in the USA, against American military engagement in Vietnam, and for all the liberations to do with sexuality, gender and drugs. There has been nothing similar since then. In 1974 the war in Vietnam ended and so did all the protests. Researchers in the 1990s and subsequently have sometimes tried to show that young people are still political by broadening the definition to include active support for any causes (the environment, animal rights, etc.) and any forms of active citizenship (voluntary work in local communities for example) (see Smith *et al.*, 2005; Weller, 2006), but however far the concept of politics is stretched it proves impossible to conceal the truth – today's young people may be interested and knowledge-able (possibly more knowledgeable than in the past) but they rarely try to intervene in and influence public affairs. In recent years in Britain it is industrial action by academic staff, not student action, that has disrupted the universities. The political protesters who have been sent to prison in Britain have been pensioners, not young people. The over-40s have been more likely than younger people to engage in political consumption by supporting buycotts and boycotts (see Stolle and Micheletti, 2005). Other new political movements – the Greens and anti-EU nationalist parties such as the UK Independence Party – draw most of their active support from older cohorts (Gillham, 2008; Searle-Chatterjee, 1999). There has been no shortage of efforts by politicians and their nominees to turn young people into active citizens. The World Bank (2005) is encouraging countries to adopt national youth service programmes. In 2006 the European Commission announced a 885 million Euro programme of youth exchanges and other initiatives to encourage young people to participate in democratic life and voluntary service, with the aim of inspiring a sense of European citizenship and involving young people in constructing the future of Europe. Young people throughout Europe have remained stubbornly indifferent.

Clark, the recent migrant from Hungary to Britain whose reflections on life under communism were presented in Chapter 6, proceeds as follows: *'I have seen both communist and western news management and I know which is the most devious – and therefore the most effective . . . Put simply, the communist regimes educated their people to such an extent that they developed the critical faculty to challenge, and eventually overthrew the system. After three years of living in Britain, I see no danger of that happening here'* (Clark, 2002). One might add, and Clark would not dissent, that there seems equally little chance of present-day Hungarian youth challenging and overturning the system in which they live today.

We now know (it was not obvious at the time) that the student movements of the 1960s and 70s indicated that a new political generation was coming of age in the west. New political generations are formed during periods of major historical change. Youth is the life stage when individuals form opinions about the world in which they live which they are likely to retain throughout their lives. In later life we are most likely to recall events which occurred when we were first becoming socially and politically aware. This tends to be at 15-plus. When younger, children may 'know' about political events and people, but before age 15 they rarely have any grasp of ideologies and political party policies (Nossiter, 1969). It is during the years immediately following age 15, the late-teenage years and early 20s, that most people first become fully politically aware. These are critical years. Events such as the death of Kennedy (1963), and the impact of Prime Minister Margaret Thatcher (1979–1990) on life in Britain, are most likely to be recalled in some detail afterwards, and to have made a lasting impression (thereafter you always knew whose side you were on) if these were among the first political events in which you felt involved (see Schuman and Corning, 2000). Afterwards we do less learning because we already know what needs to be defended and what needs to be changed in our countries.

During periods of major historical change, young age cohorts are exposed to different formative experiences than their predecessors. They are likely to feel that their own views are not only unrepresented, but maybe not even understood, by elders who occupy positions of power. Under these circumstances young people can be mobilised in new movements that express their own concerns and aspirations. Karl Mannheim (1952) coined the concept of 'political generation' in noting how young people whose transitions to adulthood coincided with the First World War and its aftermath were attracted to the communist and fascist movements of the 1920s and 30s. The so-called baby boomers, the products of the high birth rates that followed World War II, became a subsequent new political generation in western countries. Inglehart (1977, 1997) originally noted that these were the first cohorts to grow up under post-scarcity conditions. The concerns that they expressed as they grew towards adulthood during the 1960s were different than those of the cohorts who had been brought up during the 'hungry 30s' and when their countries were preparing for or threatened by conventional war (as it is now described). Since then, in the west, there have been no further new political generations which have expressed their arrivals in 20th century ways. Western economies have de-industrialised. Unemployment has once again become a serious and persistent problem in some countries. Despite these changes, since the 1960s no new cohorts of young people in the west have felt that their countries' politicians (often the same people who led student protests in the 1960s and 70s) are completely out-of-touch and simply do not reflect their own concerns and interests, and have therefore become the core activists in new political movements. AIDS and 9/11 could have led to the formation of new political generations but up to now, since the 1960s, there have been no events which have triggered exceptional and sustained political excitement and activity among young people in the west. However, we may be misled by expecting, in 21st century conditions, that further new political generations will express their arrival in the same ways as in the 20th century (see Edmonds and Turner, 2005).

In Eastern Europe the history of political generations has been rather different than in the west. New political generations came of age after communist regimes were installed throughout East-Central Europe following the Second World War. There were different generational factions, as there usually are – communists and fascists in the 1920s and 1930s, for example. Some members of the first generations that grew up under communism decided to live and work within the new system (enthusiastically in some cases). This was undoubtedly the majority response, though since 1989 many of those concerned appear to have re-invented their biographies. Other members of the post-1945 political generation in Eastern Europe became part of the resistance movements that were behind the riots in Poznan (Poland) in 1956, the confrontation with Soviet tanks in Budapest (Hungary) also in 1956, the Prague Spring (Czechoslovakia) in 1968, and who eventually created the *Solidarity* movement in Poland and *Civic Forum* in Czechoslovakia which challenged communism successfully in the 1980s. These were not youth movements though the young people of that era became involved, caught up in the events. The collapse of communism has led to the formation of another new political generation in Eastern Europe. This is 'the class of 1989' – those who were completing their education at the time when communism ended. They and those who have followed them age-wise have no personal experience of adult life, and no political consciousness, formed under the old system. These young people were not part of the change movements of the 1980s. They came afterwards, when change was actually taking place or had been accomplished. For students who were on the streets in 1989, and for cohorts who began their life stage transitions subsequently, a market economy and multi-party democracy are not breaks with former experience which they had to spend years, sometimes decades, fighting for; they have simply been parts of the adult world into which they have grown. This latest political generation is fundamentally different from previous 20th century political generations. It is distinguished by its detachment from public affairs. It is a political generation whose character has been shaped by end of/new millennium conditions. It is an extreme and, in this sense, a prototypical version of the relationship with politics that characterises present-day western youth.

The class of '89

The young people who took part in the events of 1989 and those who have followed them towards adulthood have a different mindset – a view of the world in which they live – which sets them apart from older cohorts in their own countries and (for the present) young people in the west. They may not be expressing their distinctiveness in 20th century ways – by joining parties and other movements, campaigning on the streets, etc. – but they are a new political generation.

(i) Pro-reform. Young people in Eastern Europe are overwhelmingly pro-reform. They are on the side of the market economy and multi-party democracy. They know that 'life has become more difficult since the reforms' (see Table 8.5). Despite this, the vast majority prefer a market economy to the old system (Table 8.6). For them, there can be no argument. They were not personally involved in the struggles that brought down communism. They never fought for the market or democracy. These have always been taken-for-granted features of the adult world into which they have grown. Their superiority to the planned economy and the one party state is taken as self-evident.

Table 8.5 *Socio-political attitudes: percentages who agreed or agreed strongly that life is more difficult since the reforms*

1993	
Poland	65
1997	
Donetsk	65
Lviv	67
Tbilisi	77
Armenia	68
1999	
Moscow	41
Vladikavkaz	45
Dneipropetrovsk	54
2002	
Yerevan born	78
Yerevan refugees	87
Vanadzor	92
Tbilisi born	93
Tbilisi refugees	86
Telavi	90
Makeeva	74
Khmelnitsky	80
Lviv	23

Table 8.6 *Market economy versus the old system (in percentages)*

	Prefer market economy	*Prefer old system*
1997		
Donetsk	74	26
Lviv	95	5
Tbilisi	93	7
Armenia	73	27
1999		
Moscow	95	5
Vladikavkaz	70	30
Dneipropetrovsk	74	26
2002		
Yerevan born	89	11
Yerevan refugees	72	28
Vanadzor	71	22
Tbilisi born	96	5
Tbilisi refugees	89	12
Telavi	89	12
Makeeva	68	28
Khmelnitsky	84	16
Lviv	87	7

Young people today have no personal experience of adult life under the old system but they have been told about it, and they are not nostalgic. They know that people were guaranteed jobs, health care, pensions, etc., and that life was more secure and in this sense more comfortable in the old days, but they prefer the new uncertainties and opportunities to the old guarantees. Ex-communists would not have been returned to power anywhere had the vote been restricted to the under-30s (see Williams *et al.*, 1997). The issue, for the younger generations in Eastern Europe, is not whether to be for or against reform but how to make the market and democracy work properly so that their own countries can become successful 21st century societies. Success, for most young people, means becoming more like the west and, in some senses, part of the west by bringing at least the material aspects of the western way of life into their countries. Most young people who live in adjacent states have travelled to western Europe. They have seen what it is like (including the 'warts') and overall they like what they have seen. After the events of 1989 young people throughout Eastern Europe exhibited what has been described as a spontaneous

Eurocentrism (Niznik and Skotnicka-Illasiewicz, 1992) which has not been extinguished. They have been the continent's most enthusiastic Europeans. The anti-globalisation movement strikes few chords in the mindset typical of East European youth. They want their countries to become integrated in the international economy and western political communities. They want inward investment. They want western corporations to educate their own countries' managers and they hope that western politicians will show their own countries' leaders how to do their jobs effectively.

(ii) Optimism. Eastern Europe's youth are optimistic. They believe that life will become better for people in general in their countries and for themselves in particular. They believe that their own lives will be an improvement on the lives that their parents have led. *'It's better for us than it was for our parents. Most young people feel that things are better at the moment. Our parents pity us but we're optimists. We hope that things will not get any worse. We hope, and we expect, that things will be better still for our own children'* (young female university graduate, Dneipropetrovsk, 2002). All generations in Eastern Europe believe that their countries are progressing. However, older generations often feel that it is their children or grandchildren rather than they themselves who will experience the full benefits of the changes. This sets Eastern Europe apart from the west where parents and young people tend to feel that the youth life stage was much easier and that the prospects ahead of young people were better in the past (see Halsey and Young, 1997). *'On average, less than one European in five believes that the life of those who are children today will be easier than the life of those from their own generation (17%) while around two-thirds of Europeans believe that life will be more difficult for the next generation'* (European Commission, 2006, p. 49). The new millennium west lacks a vision of a better future. Economic growth, once it has lifted people out of poverty, ceases to make them happier (Layard, 2005). Depression and other mental illnesses and crime rates have reached record levels in the west. Parents worry about whether their children will ever establish themselves in secure careers and experience happy marriages and family lives. Young people in Eastern Europe 'know' that life in the west is better, and they believe that the lives of people in their own countries will improve. They often point to how even the unemployed in the west have higher incomes than workers in their own countries. They are confident that their countries, and their own lives, will progress despite the difficulties that they typically encounter in making education-to-work and family/housing life stage transitions.

Their optimism is sustained by a belief that their countries are still in transition. It is arguable that the transitional stage ended some time in the 1990s by when privatisation had been more or less completed, basic market reforms had been introduced, and multi-party systems were operating, since when change has been incremental in most places, at a similar pace to change in western countries, but this is not the view of most young people in Eastern Europe. They believe that the historical transformation of their countries is still in process and that their own life stage difficulties will be resolvable once their countries' transitions are completed successfully. Young people who are experiencing difficulties in obtaining decent jobs and moving into independent housing also sustain their optimism by insisting that they themselves are still in life stage transition. They are assisted in this view by the manner in which communism consolidated an elongated concept of youth. The Komsomol (the main communist party youth organisation) enrolled 16–28 year olds. The East European concept does not truncate youth at age 18 or 21. They have no need for terms such as post-adolescence or emergent adulthood.

(iii) Anger. Despite the above, East Europe's post-1989 generation is composed of angry young men and women. They are angry that their countries have not made faster progress. They are angry about the difficulties that they themselves, their families and friends face in their daily lives. They are angry about the new inequalities in their countries and the majority do not believe that rewards are being distributed according to merit. They are angry about politicians whose lifestyles are clearly beyond what their official salaries will support. Hence the cynicism revealed in Table 8.4. Older generations compare the present with communism, and their evaluations of the present are sometimes boosted by the mere fact that it is not communism (see Rose, 1991). For young people this is insufficient. Communism is just history rather than a part of their personal experience. They compare the present in their countries not with 'what was' but with 'what could be'.

Towards whom is young people's anger directed? Mainly towards their countries' politicians – the entire 'political class' – though young people are unlikely to use this expression. Nevertheless, they regard politicians as a distinct class or career group who are more interested in personal betterment than improving life for ordinary people. They know that the small minority from their own age group who are politically active are more interested in building political careers for themselves than serving the people. Corruption is a major issue in all the East European countries. Any political campaigner who can present himself or herself as a clean outsider can rely on attracting support on this basis alone.

(iv) Private solutions. Despite their anger, few young people in Eastern Europe have been forming or joining political parties or any other organisations that promise to manage the transition successfully, eradicate corruption, and fulfil the upcoming generation's hopes. Rather, young people are investing their energies and hopes in engineering private solutions to their problems. Young people rarely trust any big institutions. They trust only their families and close friends. These are their main sources of assistance (see Ceplak, 2006). These are the supports in which they have confidence and which they believe will be sufficient. This is one of the senses in which young people in Eastern Europe have become the prototypical Europeans. *'One of the realities that the survey has revealed is the schism of opinion that European citizens exhibit between their own personal futures and the collective future . . . This social reality implies a sense of self-dependency – "the country may not be doing well, but I will take good care of myself"'* (European Commission, 2006, p. 67).

Market reforms in Eastern Europe have de-coupled individuals' prospects from the fortunes of their countries. As explained in Chapter 4, it was different under communism. Then, when the economies expanded and living standards rose (as happened in the 1970s) everyone experienced the benefits. When the economies stuttered (as in the 1980s) everyone felt the pain. Things are different in any market economy. Particular firms and particular individuals' careers can prosper even when a national economy is depressed. Conversely, weak firms and individuals can flounder even when an economy is booming. The less any economy is regulated by government and other collective organisations (employers' federations, trade unions and professional associations), and the smaller the scale of state services and welfare in any economy, then the looser the coupling between individuals' and countries' experiences. Most young people in Eastern Europe believe that over time their countries' economies will become stronger, but they have even greater confidence that they personally will fulfil their ambitions. Even though the majority were currently under-employed, most of the 25–29 year olds who were interviewed in 2002 in Ukraine, Georgia and Armenia thought that within five years they would be established in good jobs or successfully self-employed (Table 8.7). Young people in East and West Europe have high internal locus of control and efficacy scores (when measured on psychological scales), meaning that they feel that they themselves can influence the development of their own lives (see Puuronen *et al.*, 2000). Provided they have confidence in themselves and can rely on the support of families and friends, individuals can be optimistic about their own futures even when they have serious doubts about their countries' prospects.

Table 8.7   *Expectations in five years' time (in percentages)*

	Full-time job or self-employed	Unemployed	N =
Tbilisi born	95	2	177
Telavi	76	12	200
Tbilisi refugees	82	2	200
Yerevan born	77	9	185
Vanadzor	66	8	200
Yerevan refugees	78	11	190
Makeeva	87	2	300
Khmelnitsky	87	5	150
Lviv	79	2	150

This de-coupling is helping to de-politicise young people through-out the entire modern world. It is a consequence of the deregulation of economies and labour markets, the declining role of state welfare, and the accompanying individualisation (as noted by Ule, 2005; see above). In Eastern Europe the pace of change has been rapid. The economies have changed from being near totally regulated to extremely unregulated. State welfare has become pathetically weak. Cohorts who have become socially and politically aware since 1989 do not trust politicians to deliver anything. In this sense they are proto-typical and western youth are following. The latest new political generation in Eastern Europe is distinguished not by any particular kind of political activity but by its inactivity.

Disengaged and disaffected

Needless to say, young people in Eastern Europe are not all pro-reform and optimistic. As everywhere, opinions are spread around central tendencies, and the pro-reform optimists are rarely complacent and few have confidence in their countries' politicians. It is also relevant, highly relevant, that young people in Eastern Europe are no more likely than western youth to possess perfectly coherent views on the condition of their countries and what needs to be done. Social theorists are expected to be coherent. They are exposed to criticism if their state-ments are contradictory. Lay people are not subject to equivalent pres-sures. At different points in the same conversation young people will express views that appear, and really are, contradictory (see Muljukova, 2003). They will say that market systems are better than planned economies then argue that governments should somehow manage their countries' economies in the interests of all the people. Young (and older) people usually expect their governments to somehow guarantee the security of gas, electricity and water supplies. Governments are blamed when these supplies break down, which is still a frequent occurrence in many parts of Eastern Europe. These are the same people who argue confidently that in general markets do things better. Most young people believe that their governments should assist and protect weaker members of the populations such as the elderly and the chronically sick. These are the same young people who prefer to rely on themselves and their families for their own health care and security in later life. Young people who want their countries to become integrated in the global market economy and who want direct foreign investment in their industries will later on express disquiet about the sale of national assets to foreigners (especially energy resources and supply systems). In some ways and to some extent, most young people in Eastern Europe are nationalists who are worried that their own countries' independence, traditions and cultures are at risk whether from Russia, the EU, missionaries who represent foreign-based sects, or ethnic minorities within their own countries' borders. The same young people who claim to be ardent democrats will, moments later, argue that their countries really need strong leaders who will discipline self-interested party politicians and stamp out corruption. There was general agreement in a student discussion group at the Lviv Commerce Academy in 2002 when one participant argued that, *'Ukraine needs a strong leader for a few years at least – someone like Stalin or Peter the Great.'*

There are undercurrents of opinion within all age groups in Eastern Europe that are critical of the market economy and democracy. In 2002 86% of a representative sample in Georgia agreed that democracy was not effective and that the country needed a firm hand (Sumbadze and Trakhan-Mouravi, 2003). This is the same country that in 2003 staged the 'rose revolution' which swept Saakashvili to the presidency with over 90% of the vote on a pro-democracy ticket. Presidents who stifle opposition (including, according to his critics, Saakashvili) do not always thereby forfeit popularity. In Russia and the Central Asian states international observers report a decline in democracy, judicial and media independence, and in the autonomy of civil society organ-isations, during the early years of the 21st century (Goehring, 2006). There can be (though it is not always the case that there is) popular support for strong and decisive leaders. In many countries there is hostility towards foreigners. In 2003 less than 20% of Georgians thought that (foreign-based) sects should be allowed to perform religious services in the country (Sumbadze and Trakhan-Mouravi, 2003) and there were reports of a rise in the number of attacks on missionaries and members of such sects (Parsons, 2003). In 2006 a survey in Moscow found that a half of all Muscovites disliked people from the Caucasus (Avanisian *et al.*, 2006). In 2003 Sikevich (2003) found 71% of 18–25 year olds in St Petersburg expressing dislike towards non-Russian ethnic groups. According to Edelstein (2000), 30% of young East Germans are hostile to foreigners. All countries in East and West Europe have nationalist parties. In 2006 Russia had The Great Russian National Party, the Union of Slavs, the National Bolshevik Party, and the Movement Against Illegal Immigration. None of these parties have built mass memberships (yet) and up to now they have looked unlikely, even in a coalition, to win an election, but the views that they express strike chords in the minds of many (albeit still minorities among) young and older voters. In 2005 in Poland the Law and Justice Party was elected into office with a programme that included purging politics and public administration of former communist informers and corrupt politicians and officials while defending Polish traditions, culture and interests in international arena.

As indicated in the last chapter, dissent from the pro-market, pro-democracy, take-care-of-yourself, and optimistic norms is most common among young people on working class life trajectories, but a crucial point is that there are no effective leaders (though there are plenty of would-be leaders), no movements that are developing such dissent into alternative inspirational visions of the future. Neither the nationalists nor the advocates of strong leadership have visions of the future that inspire even substantial minorities of the young, though they may offer an outlet for their anger. Working class young people are no longer being recruited into politics via the Komsomol or trade unions, or inspired/provoked by sustained labour market and employment experience while they are still teenagers. This applies equally in Eastern Europe and the west. These routes into working class political careers have closed in the west due to fewer young people entering the labour market during the period in their lives when they are first becoming politically aware, and in some countries on account of the decline of the trade unions themselves. The young people who become political activists and who then embark on political careers are nearly all university-educated nowadays. This applies in both the west and Eastern Europe, and in the latter part of the world those concerned, the members of the age group who gain a public voice, are overwhelmingly pro-reform and supportive of the general direction of change in their countries since 1989. For these young people there really is 'only one show in town', one inspirational vision, which is a local version of the western way of life, which is to be delivered by making market reforms and multi-party democracy work effectively (as is believed to happen in Western Europe and North America). Young people in the west are less enthusiastic about their western way of life. They do not find it inspirational. However, they resemble their eastern counterparts in that they are not being presented with, or at least they are not learning about and being inspired by, any alternative vision of the future.

Youth in political action

Contemporary youth are not totally passive. From time to time some of them erupt in public demonstrations of discontent. Exactly how discontents are expressed, of course, varies according to time and place.

(i) The colour revolutions. Young people played a part in the revolution in Belgrade in 2000 (the fall of Milosevic), then the colour revolutions in Tbilisi, Georgia in 2003 (the rose revolution), Kiev, Ukraine in 2004 (the orange revolution), then Bishkek, Kyrgyzstan in 2005 (the tulip revolution) (see Collin, 2007). Except in Kyrgyzstan, organised movements of young people campaigned for change: *Otpor* (Resistance) in Belgrade), *Kmara* (Enough) in Tbilisi, and *Pora* (It's time) in Ukraine. These revolutions have proved that it is possible to mobilise the anger felt by young people towards politicians in Eastern Europe. In each of the colour revolutions protesters took to the streets enraged by the alleged falsification of election results (further evidence, if any was needed, of the corruption of politics). Actually it is difficult to eliminate vote rigging in countries where public officials who run elections believe that their jobs depend on the re-election of the incumbent, and that their career prospects depend on demonstrating impressive support in the cities, towns or districts for which they are responsible. However, all the revolutions were actually triggered by splits within the countries' political classes. The usurpers were current or former insiders. After the revolutions politics continued as before (the business of the political classes), and young people returned to their families, schools or jobs (as in 1989) and soon recovered their anger.

On the basis of qualitative studies of young people in western and ex-communist European countries, Spannring concludes: *'Political reasoning is characterised by doubt and scepticism. No political leader or*

organisation has the monopoly on truth, and ideologies have lost their credi-
bility. For this reason, young people find it difficult to remain loyal to any one
organisation or even to become "party soldiers", indoctrinated with the
organisation's ideology...It is closer to their approach to politics to take part
in demonstrations, petitions and short-term initiatives (Spannring, 2005, p
33). Eastern Europe's colour revolutions have been examples of this.

(ii) Anti-globalisation, anti-capitalism, anti-war. Meetings of the world's
financial leaders have become regular occasions for huge demonstrations protesting about the global capitalist economy. In some countries, particularly the USA and the UK, there were massive street
demonstrations against the 2003 invasion of Iraq by the USA-led coalition. Many young people were involved in all these events. They are
also active in the 'green' movements. However, all these movements
and events have been adult-led. The activists have included young
people, but the issues have not divided the generations so much as
split all age groups.

(iii) Youth issues. Young people are occasionally mobilised into political action on specifically youth issues such as the proposed changes in
the employment laws (to allow young people to be engaged on temporary contracts) in France in 2006. However, it is always difficult to
engage young people in sustained campaigns on specifically youth
issues. This is because youth is a life stage with a rapid population
turnover, and each cohort is normally divided in various ways – by
gender, race, social class origins, those who are in education, those
who are in jobs and the unemployed, and so on. In the UK young
people did not become mobilised in sufficient numbers, on a sustained
basis, to mount a serious challenge to the withdrawal of higher education student grants in the 1990s, or the introduction then the steep rise
in tuition fees to £3000 a year in 2006.

(iv) Urban riots. These have erupted in several countries at various
points in time over the last 30 years. In the UK there was one wave of
riots in 1981 and another (the so-called Milltown riots) in 2001–02.
Perhaps the best-publicised revolts occurred in France in 2005. High
youth unemployment has been a consistent part of the background to
these eruptions. Race has been a common (but not always present)
part of the cocktail. These riots may be treated (by the media and
politicians) as criminal rather than political, but they clearly have
political significance if only because they pitch young people in direct
confrontation with the authorities. However, the uprisings lack clear
political objectives. Usually the rioters can explain what they are

against – unemployment, ethnic discrimination, poor housing and community facilities in their areas, the police and their tactics – but what are they for? In any case, the disturbances are too irregular, and involve too few young people, to be equated with a generation in revolt.

(v) Youth cultures and politics. It can be claimed that all youth cultures have some political significance irrespective of whether the participants use this phrase (see Bennett, 2000; Bennett and Kahn-Harris, 2004). Some pop/rock performers intend to convey political messages. They are able to mobilise large numbers of young people in support of certain political causes – for example, anti-racism in Britain, and Live Aid internationally. However, one wonders whether these short-term spasmodic instances of youth mobilisation owe more to the politics or to the music.

Summary and conclusions: the historical inversion

We can now answer the questions posed at the beginning of this chapter. First, how many young people are developing the motivation and skills required to build political careers? Nowadays these skills may involve the use of the mobile phone and internet rather than leaflets and public oratory. How many young people develop firm attachments to any ideas or movements? The policies may be about new rather than old issues. The movements may be new, possibly the cyber-variety, rather than traditional political parties. If individuals do not develop these attachments and skills when they are young, it is unlikely that they ever will. Very few young people are developing such skills or attachments (to ideas or movements) and most of those who are doing so are from the best-educated of their generation who are heading towards middle class careers. Working class young people are no longer being socialised into working class politics through immersion in workplace cultures and trade unions from age 15/16. This alternative route into political careers has closed.

The next question to ask is whether the upcoming politicals have mindsets that set them apart from the established political classes. In Eastern Europe the answer is an unequivocal 'yes': the newcomers from the class of '89 are different in their pragmatism. In the west the answer is 'no': the newcomers are similar to the political incumbents in their pragmatism. In Eastern Europe and in the west the political classes of the future will have to appeal to new generations of voters who have no firm party attachments or ideological commitments. Mindsets in Eastern Europe and the west are most likely to converge. In Eastern Europe enthusiasm for the western way of life will probably subside into a bland acceptance that there is no better deal on offer. Optimism will subside into hope that conditions and opportunities will not deteriorate. Anger will be dowsed as expectations of politicians are lowered.

We await the formation of the next truly new politically active generations. It is impossible to forecast either exactly when this will happen or the character that future political generations will take. One requirement will be an alternative vision of the future. This could be supplied by the Greens. It could be supplied by nationalism. Majority youth across Europe could be mobilised against various 'outsiders' – immigrants or supra-national bodies such as the EU. The vision would be a future of genetic or cultural purity. Confrontation politics could appeal to ethnic minority young people, the second and third generations who are citizens of European and North American countries who believe that they should not need to ask for special treatment or even equal treatment but that they should be able to rely on equal opportunities in education and the labour market, and equal respect for their ethnic cultures, just like other citizens (see Hussain and Bagguley, 2005). Some minority groups are able to gain support (material and ideological) from overseas. Islamic minorities can feel that they are part of a global struggle, a clash of civilisations, which has been rumbling for over a thousand years. Marxist minorities in western countries used to derive similar encouragement from the certain 'knowledge' that global history was on their side. However, the other pre-condition for the formation of new political generations is major historical change that sets normally non-political citizens seeking new answers. The change (which will surely come at some point) could be welcome, like the new prosperity that spread throughout the west after 1945, or painful – global financial meltdown or ecological calamity. In the meantime we have entered an era of historical inversion.

Mitev (2004) has argued that in former communist countries, alongside the great historical transformation, there has been another historical upheaval. Throughout the 20th century young people were the idealists and older people were the realists. Today, he argues, those roles have been reversed: young people are the pragmatists, willing to operate in the world as they find it, while radicalism burns brighter among 'the greys'. The same reversal that Mitev notes in Eastern Europe has occurred in the west. The baby boomers who were involved in Paris 1968 and similar events of that era (some of them at any rate) have retained their radical ideals and their taste for political activity.

Longer life spans and low fertility rates are making the greys a weightier demographic force. Politicians want their votes. Businesses want their consumer spending. It is possible that Eastern Europe's movers and shakers of the 1980s – the activists in *Solidarity* and *Civic Forum*, and other members of the intelligentsia who took advantage of *glasnost*, the predecessors of the class of '89 – will be reborn as a radical postcommunist generation. They may well have retained their original ideals (many feel betrayed by what has followed communism in their countries), and they know how to form effective social movements. This is one possible scenario, but this generation will eventually die with no radical successor in sight at present.

Further reading

Edmunds, J. and Turner, B. S. (2005), 'Global generations: social change in the twentieth century', *British Journal of Sociology*, 56, 559–77.

Inglehart, R. (1997), *Modernization and Postmodernization: Cultural, Economic and Political Change in 43 Societies*, Princeton University Press, New Jersey.

Mannheim, K. (1952), 'The problem of generations' in *Essays on the Sociology of Knowledge*, Routledge, London.

Schuman, H. and Corning, A. G. (2000), 'Collective knowledge of public events: the Soviet era from the Great Purge to glasnost', *American Journal of Sociology*, 105, 913–56.

Conclusions: global youth in the 21st century

Introduction

This concluding chapter reviews some of the evidence presented earlier – about youth under-employment as a normal 21st century global phenomenon, the expansion of education (especially general, non-vocationally specific education), on family and housing transitions, deconstructed transitions, youth cultures, and young people and politics. Doing so underlines some of this book's core contentions: that despite young people's heightened self-awareness, structural determinants of their futures remain as powerful as ever; and that recent cohorts are not best viewed as scarred for life but simply as having rather different life stage experiences and facing different adulthoods than earlier cohorts. This chapter also highlights how, in major respects, the situations of young people and their responses in different parts of the world are converging, and argues that this convergence is not the outcome of imperialism by any 21st century super-power but the result of indigenous processes of modernisation that are currently in play all over the world, sometimes, as in Eastern Europe, only recently unleashed. One of the convergences is that 21st century global youth are far more likely to be pre-occupied with private goals and discovering private solutions to their problems than engaged in any form of political action. This concluding chapter also notes senses in which, despite East Europe's prototypicality in many respects, the USA is the country in which most characteristics of global 21st century youth are most evident and well-established.

There have always been some global similarities in youth's condition; those that necessarily arise from youth being a life stage – a universally recognised life stage – situated between childhood and adulthood. Some global similarities follow from this elementary feature of youth. However, when Margaret Mead (1935, 1971) studied the coming of age in Samoa her comparisons emphasised the contrasts with North American realities, and throughout the second half of the 20th century most comparative youth research emphasised contrasts – according to differences in countries' education systems, ways of absorbing young people into the workforces, according to young people's ability to consume products endowed with meanings developed by or for the age group, and the extent to which serial affairs and unmarried cohabitation were accepted behaviour during the life stage.

Youth (the life stage) is unlikely to become an identical experience throughout the world even in the most distant foreseeable future given the continuing differences in languages, religions and other cultural phenomena, levels of economic development, and so forth. Even so, this book's contention is that we are encountering greater similarities in the 21st century than were found earlier on. This book has suggested that in some respects youth in Eastern Europe have become world leaders – at the forefront of current global trends. Despite this, most (though, again, not all) of the emergent global similarities became common features of youth's condition in America prior to their internationalisation. America is arguably the most modern among modern societies, a status achieved by its willingness to jettison European traditions such as separate academic and vocational tracks through secondary education, and pioneering modern youth practices such as 'dating'. Thus America has a strong claim to the global leadership title.

One important implication of this, if correct, is that increasingly common features of global youth's condition should not be read as signs of crisis, the permanent scarring of young people, a breakdown in life stage transitions or the wider socio-economic-political order. America is one of the world's strongest countries, with one of the strongest economies, with a population that enjoys one of the world's highest standards of living. The new global similarities are signs of youth transitions throughout the world adjusting to global 21st century contexts.

Under-employment

A contention implicit in the order of topics in this book has been that education-to-employment, and family and housing transitions are pivotal youth life stage transitions in that young people's experiences during and progress through these transitions have implications for all other aspects of their lives. Thus the globalisation (shorthand here for global normalisation) of youth under-employment creates many further similarities in young people's experiences. As Chapter 2 explained, unemployment is now a worldwide youth problem. In 2002 the International Labour Office estimated that globally 88 million 16–25 year olds were unemployed, amounting to a half of all the unemployed persons in the world. Moreover, the quality of the jobs that are available for young people is deteriorating globally. Both problems (unemployment and poor quality jobs) are currently most severe in the less developed countries where 85% of the world's young people live.

From the 1940s to the 1970s most of Europe (communist and western) could offer enough jobs (sometimes far more than enough) to accommodate all school-leavers. In contrast, the USA had serious unemployment among high school drop-outs, and youth unemployment was a major problem in much of the under-developed world where young people were drifting from rural areas into towns and cities. However, it was then believed that growth and enlightened economic management would eventually lead to full employment everywhere. Today it looks as if the '30 glorious years' (following the Second World War) of full employment (where this was achieved) was an exceptional interlude. Ever since the 19th century, in capitalist market economies, it has been sufficiently common to be described as normal for school-leavers to face exceptional risks of unemployment and poor quality (part-time, temporary, low-paid, dead-end) jobs. There are some countries where present-day youth unemployment is still quite low (the UK and the Scandinavian countries in Europe, and in Germany youth unemployment remains low relative to the adult rate). Today, however, these countries are the exceptions. We saw in Chapter 2 that in Japan, one of the economic success stories from the 1950s to the 80s, demand for youth labour has declined, support from families and schools has become less effective, and many of the jobs that are still available for school-leavers are low-paid and temporary (Inui, 2003; Nagasawa, 2004). In Germany, once famous for its protective dual system, labour market openings for young people have narrowed, especially for young people who complete full-time education at age 18 or earlier, and training is increasingly regarded as a dead end (see Evans *et al.*, 2000; Kuda, 1998).

There is no generally agreed diagnosis or remedy for the current youth unemployment. Western political elites (and many academics) believe or say that current youth labour market problems have arisen due to a decline in demand for low-skilled labour and that the remedy lies in more youth education and training. Yet we saw in Chapter 3 that all over the world young people today are better educated than ever before, and there is still plenty of low-grade employment in all countries. Another fact of this matter is that economic growth can no longer be relied on to generate an equivalent increase in labour demand (Bowring, 1999; Forrester, 1999), and all over the world low-level jobs are less at risk of elimination than 'Brazilianisation' (see Beck, 2000). When young people take these jobs (as many do, every-where) this is invariably as temporary stop-gaps and because they are unable to obtain the kinds of employment that they are seeking and to which they feel entitled.

This book has argued that under-employment is a better term than unemployment for describing the typical condition of young people in today's labour markets. When the official youth unemployment rate is 20% (a typical rate for 16–25 year olds in present-day Europe) this does not mean that a fifth of school-leavers are becoming long-term unem-ployed while the rest experience continuous employment. It is closer to the reality to imagine all youth in the labour market being out of work for 20 percent of the time. This is one sense in which youth are under-employed: they are working less than continuously, often for less than full-time hours when they are in work, and for less than full adult salaries. A second sense in which young people are under-employed is that their typical jobs are well beneath the levels for which they are qualified. Even though 'investment in human capital' usually pays a satisfactory 'dividend', this often takes years, some-times decades, to arrive. This has been the case in the USA for many years, and likewise a period of so-called 'floundering' before young people find jobs in which they are able and willing to settle. In these respects, where America led, other countries now follow.

The expansion of education

Are there any countries today that cannot envisage at least 50% of their young people progressing into higher education? Schools, colleges and universities are now the most likely places to find 16–25 year olds. I realise that in some less developed countries significant proportions of children still fail to complete primary/elementary school, but even in these countries, in urban areas, higher education is becoming a normal aspiration.

Chapter 3 explained that there are several reasons for this expansion of education. One is a generation ratchet. Every generation of parents wants its children to do at least as well, and preferably even better, than they themselves performed in education. A second reason is that education is seen as the best route to a good life. Teachers and governments give this message their seals of approval. 'Investing in human capital' is supposed to lead to economic prosperity for a country and good jobs for the young people who invest. Bornschier *et al.*, (2005) claim that there is a double economic dividend. The first instalment is from more productive workers. The second is said to be via the legitimation of inequalities (everyone is seen to have stood a fair chance) and the enhanced social cohesion, which diminishes conflict and results in everyone pulling together. However, these authors explain that both dividends depend on the private sector creating sufficient jobs, and in many countries (not just in Eastern Europe) the private sectors are manifestly failing to deliver. They argue that absorbing additional graduates into bloated public sectors imposes a drain on wealth producing sectors, while disaffected, unemployed, highly educated young people may foment social and political unrest. This 'may' happen, but Chapter 8 explained that the overall condition of youth in the 21st century makes this less likely than was the case during the 20th century.

Do young people trust higher education to open the doors to the good life? Unemployment and under-employment have spread among the world's highly educated young adults. It seems more likely that young people feel that they need to accumulate as many, and as advanced, qualifications as possible in order simply to remain in the competition for good jobs and the associated lifestyles. Most will know from experience that the labour market opportunities for young people without higher education are extremely limited. They may be aware that there are plenty of temporary, part-time jobs (unacceptable as long-term career positions) through which they can part-finance their studies. A circular process appears to be operating all over the world. As general standards of attainment in education rise, it becomes easier for employers to recruit well-qualified young people, and so demand for the less-qualified drops, which adds to the incentives for young people to prolong their studies. This process has been noted and analysed in detail in, but is not confined to, Sweden and Germany (see Aberg, 2003; Solga, 2002).

The USA was the first modern society to develop a mass higher education system. By the end of the 1960s a half of young Americans were graduating high school and proceeding to college. Today around two-thirds take this step. The USA is no longer the world leader in the proportion of young people who go to college, but it led the way historically, and today other modernising countries are catching up in some cases or have caught up and overtaken America (South Korea, for example; see Bae, 2006).

Family relationships

Young people's situations *vis-à-vis* their family and housing life stage transitions also have profound implications for all other aspects of their lives, but unlike with education and labour markets, it is difficult to detect any signs of global convergence except that the nuclear family has become a normal residential unit, and marital partners are normally selected on the basis of mutual attraction in all parts of the modern world. The much-derided Talcott Parsons (1954) has proved correct in these respects. These features of modern family life require a redefinition and a loosening of parent-child relationships during a child's transition to adulthood. Peer relationships (friendships) strengthen during the youth life stage. This, of course, is among the basic pre-conditions for the development of consumption-based youth cultures.

All that said, there continue to be important inter-country differences in patterns of family life. Whether it is normal for young people to leave the parental home prior to marriage to live singly, in shared housing, sexually cohabiting or not, varies according to what is considered right and proper (between northern and southern Europe, for example) (see Holdsworth, 2004). Likewise, there are huge inter- and intra-country differences in how easily young people can obtain independent accommodation. Housing shortages under communism, which continue to the present in most parts of the relevant countries, usually prevent young singles, and often prevent couples (even young parents) moving into their own places (Roberts *et al.*, 2003). Western-style sex equality is not becoming fashionable worldwide. Its appeal diminishes whenever and wherever single person households, and even more so when couple-only households, are not economically viable. 'Late' parenthood (30s rather than 20s and teens) has become the norm in some, but not in all countries. In Europe, but not in the USA, birth rates have sunk well beneath population replacement levels.

Alongside these differences there are several new, to set alongside the enduringly modern, similarities:

- Young people's dependence on their parents is being prolonged as a result of the extension of education and young people's difficulties in establishing themselves in adult employment. Everywhere parents appear to want to support their children for as long as is necessary, moderated in some countries by also wanting to teach them independence and responsibility (see Holdsworth, 2004).

- Meanwhile, many families have become less able to offer the support that they feel their children need. A common reason is the fragility of present-day conjugal relationships. In Britain, at age 16, nearly 90% percent of children born in 1958 were still living with their two biological parents whereas for the cohort born in 1984–86 this proportion had fallen to 65% percent (Ivacovou, 2004). More teenagers than in the past are being cared for by single parents, and more are living in reconstituted families. In some parts of the world, mainly sub-Saharan Africa, AIDS is orphaning huge numbers of children while simultaneously threatening young adults' own health.
- While making their extended life stage transitions, and with many families unable to offer satisfactory support, young people face increased risks of poverty and homelessness.
- Parents want governments to do more, not instead of, but to complement families' efforts. In practice, however, the trend is towards governments offering less support – transferring the costs of education onto young people and their families, and guaranteeing only 'employability' rather than jobs for all.
- One former set of options (where it once existed) is being eliminated globally due to the inability of teenagers and young people in their early 20s and even mid-20s to afford their own family dwellings and to become child-rearers.

Again, in several ways America has been the prototypical country. College in the USA has never been free. Students have always relied at least partly on their families (when their families have been able to offer support). The USA is also one of the world's most unequal modern countries, and held this status throughout the 20th century. The financial support that poorer families have been able to offer to young people has usually been inadequate. The USA also led the world towards high divorce rates, single parent and reconstituted families which tend to be less able to support young people during extended life stage transitions than the conventional intact two-parent family.

De-constructed transitions

Collectively the above trends (in labour markets, education, and in family and housing practices in some places) have provoked the bout of conceptual innovation in youth sociology that was discussed in Chapter 4 – about transitions becoming extended, protracted, destandardised and non-linear, and about young people being thrust into a post-childhood limbo. Wallace and Kovacheva (1998) have argued that in Europe youth has been 'de-constructed'. James Cote (2000) talks of 'arrested adulthood' – a condition where individuals outgrow youth without becoming fully adult. Arnett discusses 'emergent adulthood', a life stage when individuals are no longer 'youth' yet not fully adult (see Arnett, 2005, 2006; see also Bynner, 2005). The prolonging, complication and individualisation of youth biographies (the three components of deconstruction) are another set of global trends, variously rooted in developments in education, labour markets, housing and family arrangements, that are creating a common, global 21st century youth condition.

The big controversy in youth sociology has been not about whether these trends have occurred, but about whether the 'de-constructing' has created new possibilities for reflexive young people to take charge of their own development and build choice biographies, as claimed, for example, by Dwyer and Wyn (2001) and Lagree (2002). Parents worry endlessly that their children will flounder amid the new uncertainties. They feel that the road to adulthood has become more dangerous than when they themselves were young (see Halsey and Young, 1997). However, it appears that most young people the world over have confidence in their own ability to cope (Dwyer and Wyn, 2001). On the other side of this debate stand sociologists who stress that the ability to choose a biography is distributed unequally, and that for most young people choices have to be made within externally (structurally) defined limits (Cote, 2002; Evans, 2002; Furlong and Cartmel, 1997; Roberts *et al.*, 1994).

One plain fact of this matter is that historically young people have not broken free from former structures. It is rather a case of the structures themselves having weakened. Dropping-out and breaking free were possible only when youth trajectories were more tightly and transparently structured (and also when it was usually quite easy to opt back in). Nowadays young people struggle to get in. Beneath all the deconstructing, it is surely evident that as young people progress through the life stage they become increasingly divided from one another – into those who do and those who do not enter higher education, and into those who get good jobs, the under-employed, and the seriously unemployed, for example. Moreoever, young people's destinations remained linked as firmly as ever to their social class family origins, and to the places where they are born and grow up. Class awareness among young people may be low (the reasons for this are not difficult to detect) but all over the world class inequalities in origins and destinations are growing wider than ever. As they progress through youth, gender divisions among young people also become increasingly clear as males and females enrol for different programmes in education, enter different kinds of employment, and take on different roles in their parents' homes or in the homes that they create with one another. All young people may be equally reflexive in taking all the relevant steps in their life courses, but they all act within structures that are not of their own making.

Youth cultures

There are always social class differences in young people's uses of leisure. These arise from different family origins that provide different kinds and levels of financial, social and cultural support; according to whether young people progress or do not progress through higher education; according to the kinds of employment (if any) that they obtain, how much they earn, and how much they are able to spend on their leisure. There are also gender differences, and the width of these differences in young people's leisure is related to the extent of gender differences in education, employment and domestic arrangements. These differences (not the details but the existence of differences with class and gender bases) are common throughout the world. There are many inter-country differences in young people's uses of leisure. Some arise from local cultural specificities, others from the economic and political contexts. That said, young people's leisure is where global convergence is most easily illustrated.

Any international traveller will surely see that contemporary youth cultures are incredibly mobile. This convergence is partly, but not mainly, due to the spread of youth travel. More young people are crossing national frontiers for education, work and leisure, but 'more' does not mean 'most'. The jet-setters are still a tiny minority of global youth. International travel remains an elite perk. It may become even more exclusive in the future as the costs of aircraft fuel and pollution rise. However, in the European Union it is increasingly common for university students to spend a semester or a year at an institution in a second member country. Those who benefit from this may develop a particular kind of European consciousness and identity which separates these cosmopolitans from other Europeans. However, cultural products flow globally irrespective of whether human beings travel. Music, fashions and sports teams, sports stars and sports events now play to global audiences. The internet is currently hosting thousands of cross-national virtual communities (see Mattar, 2003).

During the 20th century the globalisation of popular cultures helped to inspire a cultural imperialist, global Americanisation thesis.

Commentators noted that the mass media (the content at any rate) were largely American in origin, so the cultural colonisation of the rest of the world by the USA was said to be underway. It was true at that time that America was the leading source of globally marketed music, films and TV programmes. Now America has also given the world shopping malls and McDonald's. However, 21st century global culture is less America-centric. This is due to a mixture of reasons, some old, others new (see Hesmondhalgh, 2002). First, international cultural products have always been given localised meanings in particular local contexts, as illustrated by Bennett (2000) in the case of popular music. So in the 1970s listening to the Beatles, wearing Levi's and adopting a skinhead appearance did not have exactly the same meanings in London and Moscow. Country and regional cultural specificities are not being wiped out by the global. The global village of the 21st century contains a variety of fusions between the global and the local, mixtures of the internationally hyper-modern and the locally and traditionally rooted (see Luping Wu, 2002). Second, more and more countries have been developing their own cultural industries. New technology (ICT) has facilitated this: the costs of market entry have fallen. Everywhere today, the most popular musicians, TV programmes and sports stars tend to be locally based or sourced. Finally, the internet permits the creation of virtual, cross-national interacting communities that have no single centre. There is a digital divide, but this does not run between north and south, or between countries, so much as within all countries, and everywhere there are processes of diffusion from those who are switched on to the rest of the populations.

Cultural domination by America is not among the reasons why the future of global youth looks suspiciously American. There has always been considerable American exceptionalism, maybe most of all in the country's popular cultures. America's favourite sports (American football, baseball, basketball and ice hockey) have not become the global favourites. Young Americans who visit Europe recognise instantly that European youth scenes are different (see Thornton, 1995). In global terms, as regards youth cultural scenes, America is exceptional in many important (to young people) respects. In most parts of the USA alcohol cannot be served or sold legally to anyone under age 21. The modal young American lives in a smallish town or suburb, in a largish house (by international standards) in which teenagers are given or create their own space. Soon after the Second World War the automobile became central in American teenage life in a way that still does not apply anywhere else. Drive-in movies have not been a successful export. American 'straightedge' (Christian fundamentalist) youth cultures (no sex, alcohol, cigarettes or drugs) are not setting a global trend (see Wood, 2003).

However, there are senses in which present-day America does represent the future of global youth. This is because, as argued above, features which are now part of global youth's condition developed earlier in the USA. These features are the high rate of participation in college education, which passed 50% during the 1960s in the USA, high unemployment among the least educated school-leavers, high risks of under-employment for others, and high rates of separation and divorce coupled with wide economic inequalities which make the nuclear family an unreliable support system during youth transitions. In the 21st century these features of youth's condition are spreading globally, but not as American exports. They are spreading through indigenous processes generated by modernisation in every country that becomes part of the new millennium's global, capitalist market economy, and where the nuclear family is the normal child-rearing unit.

Youth and politics

The closing decades of the 20th century saw the formation of new political generations in Europe. The contrast with older generations is clearest in Eastern Europe where recent changes in the economic and political contexts have been most thorough, but in east and west Europe alike recent cohorts of young people have shared a common generation-defining political characteristic, which is disengagement. There are some very important exceptions (see below), but disengagement from politics is a widespread feature of global youth in the early 21st century. We saw in Chapter 8 that levels of expressed interest in politics and political activity among young people are currently at a low ebb. This is not to say that the young have no political opinions. Many are highly opinionated, including those who are most emphatic, positive, that they are 'not interested' in 'official' politics. This may be despite acknowledging that politics is important and despite being aware and indeed knowledgeable about their countries' politics and international affairs. Today's young people tend to mistrust politicians' motives and do not believe that any will offer solutions to their own age group's problems, or their countries' problems. In the former communist countries there has been a huge turnaround since the heady days of 1989–91. Post-communist youth have been concentrating on discovering personal solutions rather than seeking collective solutions to their difficulties (see Roberts *et al.*, 2000). Investigators often try to show that young people remain political by broadening the definition of politics to include any civic activity including volunteering and participation in new social movements (concerned with animal rights, ecology or whatever) (see Smith *et al.*, 2005), but even with the broadest possible definition it is impossible to conceal the truth. Commentators on post-Second World War western youth cultures were able to find political meanings in most of them. In 1985 Mike Brake argued that all youth cultures were 'an expression of the mini-politics of rebellion against obscure forces' (p 198). Bennett (2000) has argued that all the post-war music-based youth cultures carried political messages (with politics broadly defined). That was then! Some commentators recognise that things are rather different today, and claim that youth are now living in a post-subcultural era (Bennett and Kahn-Harris, 2004).

Experience during the early and mid-20th century encouraged sociologists to associate young people with radical politics. Following the First World War a new political generation came of age in Europe and produced supporters for the new political movements of that era — communist and fascist. In the post-Second World War decades young people in the west's 'post-scarcity societies' decided that their countries' leaders did not speak for them, and the young people campaigned on the streets for 'post-materialist' causes such as civil rights and women's rights, against war, and perhaps most of all for greater personal freedom (see Inglehart, 1977). Most young people in that era were not politically active, but there were senses in which those who were active spoke for their generation, and they produced many of the leaders who subsequently held and who currently hold high political office. In the colonised countries young people became active supporters, and actively involved in, the independence and democratisation movements that won their battles. Subsequently, former terrorist leaders (in the colonial powers' eyes) became prime ministers and presidents. The 'old guards' are still in power in some ex-colonies and throughout the west and Eastern Europe, and their issues still dominate electoral battles and parliamentary and press debates in some countries. In Eastern Europe, 'What were you doing in the 1980s?' remains a salient issue for older voters. In the west the core issues in official politics are still a mixture of issues that pre-date the post-1945 generation (economic security and growth), and issues that the baby boomers pushed onto political agendas (gender and race equality, peace, the environment).

Today, in the developed countries, it is not young people who are joining new political parties and movements that seek radical change. We saw in Chapter 8 that nowadays the over-30s are more likely than the under-30s to take part in boycotts and buycotts (for fair trade,

among other things) (see Stolle and Micheletti, 2005). Europe's nationalist parties (which oppose subordination to the European Union)
draw most of their support from older voters. This also applies to the
'Greens' (see Searle-Chatterjee, 1999). In Britain in 2005 the protesters
who went to prison were pensioners! The anti-capitalist, anti-globalisation and feminist movements are no longer young people's
crusades. All the causes listed above are supported mainly by older
political generations who feel not just disappointed but angry at how
recent history has frustrated their one-time hopes for the future.

There are exceptions, as with all generalisations. We also saw in
Chapter 8 that in Europe some groups of second-generation 'immigrant' minority youth have become openly critical of older moderate
spokespersons for the communities in question (see Hussain and
Bagguley, 2005). The upcoming generations are dissatisfied with
anything less than treatment as full and normal citizens, just like other
locally born groups. In some Islamic countries young people are
mobilised in movements demanding greater respect for their culture
both domestically and internationally. There are no equivalent youth-
inspiring movements in the west, or in the former communist countries, or in most of the less developed world. Rather than urging
political restraint on the impatient young, today's older generations
are typically perplexed at youth's political passivity.

How are we to explain this passivity? I believe, from the evidence in
earlier chapters of this book, that there are three contributing explanations:

- The individualisation of youth life courses which reduces the like-
  lihood of young people aligning themselves with any wider social
  categories and encourages a search for private solutions to problems.
- Delayed entry into adult occupations. Nowadays young people's
  occupational futures typically remain unknown until long after
  they have become socially and politically aware. They are no
  longer experiencing political socialisation in workplaces wherein
  they learn their places, their positions and their associated interests, within their countries' occupational and class structures.
- New political generations have been formed in all parts of the
  world – in post-colonial countries, in post-communist countries,
  and in the western countries which have undergone economic
  restructuring since the 1970s, in the sense that we now have
  cohorts of young people who have never experienced anything but
  post-colonial, post-communist or (in western countries) neo-
  liberal, post-industrial conditions. A common feature of all these

new conditions is the absence of powerful, juxtaposed ideologies. There appears to be no serious option to ignite young people's enthusiasm except making the present a little better.

In conclusion

Much youth sociology is written in a crisis mode. Researchers draw attention to high unemployment, glaring inequalities, and cynicism towards all politicians. The message, explicit or implicit, is that something needs to be done. This is despite the now abundant evidence that some favourite cures fail to work. Civic education is unable to countervail against broader depoliticising forces. More education and training simply produce better qualified and more highly skilled under-employed young workers. The USA is an important case because it demonstrates that nothing needs to be done. It is possible for the features of youth's condition that are currently being internationalised to persist for decade after decade during which the vast majority of young people continue to make satisfactory life stage transitions – satisfactory to their societies and to themselves, not necessarily in the sense that all or even most young people are able to realise all their hopes, but in so far as the economies continue to grow, families continue to reproduce the populations, and governments remain effective. High levels of non-participation in politics, indifference, ignorance, and cynicism towards politicians are all fully compatible with the long-term stability of democratic and non-democratic regimes. Young people's current condition, *vis-à-vis* politics, is not a problem that requires urgent attention and solution.

Life stage transitions are loose joints in all modern social systems which enable the macro-structures to cope with change. The youth life stage is one such loose joint; the transition from adulthood into later life is another. One way of coping with an ageing population is somehow to persuade older people to work a little longer. At other times, reduced labour demand can be addressed through earlier retirement. Alternatively, or in addition, it can be addressed by lengthening young people's life stage transitions. Housing shortages can be addressed by young people remaining longer in their parents' homes. If the transition to economic independence takes longer, then family formation and parenthood can also be delayed. Youth is the life stage when populations are most easily redistributed from contracting to expanding sites. The sites may be occupational strata, regions or entire countries. Once people are settled in adult roles, such transfers are usually more difficult, and more painful for those who are involved.

At present, all over the world, low level jobs are being subjected to what Ulrich Beck (2000) calls 'Brazilianisation'. This is the result of freer trade and fiercer competition between countries, and the deregulation of labour markets as part of the currently dominant neo-liberal economic agenda. National governments can try to resist Brazilianisation by regulating their labour markets and closing their borders, but the most likely end result in today's global conditions is economic stagnation or even decline. Jobs which offer neither the security nor the salary to support an adult lifestyle are usually filled by secondary earners – 'secondary' in variety of ways. Married women have often been one such group. The semi-retired are another. Young people who are living with their parents, and students who need to part-finance their studies, are another. An alternative is for the jobs to be filled by (legal or illegal) immigrants who may be primary earners for households in their countries of origin.

The expansion of education systems and the prolongation of schooling are responses to the push from increasingly ambitious parents and young people, the pull from the expansion of professional and management grade occupations, and the push from the limited opportunities available for younger school-leavers (amplified by the Brazilianisation of the relevant employment). As explained above, extended education no longer guarantees a good job but while they are students young people's hopes can survive. Ambitious young adults who are dissatisfied with their current jobs can be an asset, injecting drive and dynamism into an economy. In other words, young people's difficulties in realising their aims may be an advantage rather than a calamity for the surrounding socio-economic order.

In every known society there has been a powerful tendency for high status families to transmit their status down the generations. In all modern societies the rate of social fluidity (social mobility in excess of the volume enforced structurally by changes in the proportions of positions at different levels, and differential fertility) has been remarkably constant over time and between countries (Erikson and Goldthorpe, 1992). However, there have been differences, and changes over time, in the stages in the 'status attainment process' when life chance inequalities become apparent. Once upon a time access to any formal education was class-related. Then universal elementary education eliminated class inequalities at this level. Access to and achievements in secondary education then became class-related. Throughout the world, as completion of full secondary education becomes the norm for young people from all social strata, the reproduction of class inequalities is displaced into post-secondary, tertiary levels. Families in higher-level positions continue to advantage their children through the transmission of what Bourdieu terms economic, social and cultural capital (Bourdieu and Passeron, 1977). Some would add genetic capital to this list. The value (which is considerable) of a good family background is not incompatible with sufficient social mobility (much of it structurally enforced) to persuade populations that everyone has stood a fair chance, thus producing one of the dividends that Bornschier *et al.*, (2005) attribute to mass enrolments in tertiary education. Young people from modest backgrounds are able to rise with assistance from various combinations of scholarships, sacrifices by their families, and the individuals' own motivation and talent.

None of above suggests that today's young people live in the best of all conceivable conditions in which to be young; only that there are no structural imperatives which can be relied on, one way or another, to change the definitive features of global youth's condition in the 21st century, and that bringing about changes in these conditions will in fact be rather difficult. Today's youth in Eastern Europe and the west are not going to change the world, but the world will change radically at some point. We cannot say exactly when, or what the cause will be – ecological calamity and financial meltdown are both possible. Youth's condition will then change again, there will be youth and other problems that simply have to be addressed and solved, and young people may well be provoked into radical, epoch-shaking political action. This book's conclusion is 'not now' which is not the same as 'not ever'.

Bibliography

Abbott, P. (2004), 'Place, control and health in post-Soviet societies', paper presented at *International Institute of Sociology Congress*, Beijing.

Aberg, R. (2003), 'Unemployment persistency, over-education and the employment chances of the less educated', *European Sociological Review*, 19, 199–216.

Adamski, W., Zaborowski, W. and Pelczunska-Nalecz, K. (2001), 'The dynamics of structural conflict in the process of systemic change: Poland from 1980 to 2000', *Sisyphus*, 15, 147–62.

Adsett, M. and McKellar, C. (2002), 'An analysis of the crisis in the political participation of young Canadians: looking at period, cohort and life cycle interactions', paper presented at *International Sociological Association Congress*, Brisbane.

Agabrian, M. (2006), 'Relationships between school and family: the adolescents' perspective', *Forum: Qualitative Soziaforschung/Forum: Qualitative Social Research*, online journal, 8, 1, article 20. http://www.qualitative-research.net/fqs-texte/1-07/07-1-20. Accessed 22 January 2007.

Agadjanian, V. (2002), 'Adolescents' views on childbearing, contraception and abortion in two post-communist societies', *Journal of Youth Studies*, 5, 391–406.

Aksentyeva, E. and Gumenyuk, E. (2000), 'The state of youth reproductive health in Karelia', paper presented to conference on *Youth on the Threshold of the Third Millennium*, Petrozavodsk.

Aleshonok, S. (1998), 'Russian youth: searching for new channels of influence in society', paper presented at *International Sociological Association Congress*, Montreal.

Anderson, B., Ruhs, M., Rogaly, B. and Spencer, S. (2006), *Fair Enough? Central and East European Migrants in Low-Wage Employment in the UK*, Joseph Rowntree Trust, York.

Anderson, M., Bechhofer, F., Jamieson, L., McCrone, D., Li, Y. and Stewart, R. (2002), 'Confidence and uncertainty: ambitions and plans in a sample of young adults', *Sociological Research Online*, 6, 4.

Anderson, M., Bechhofer, F., McCrone, D., Jamieson, L., Li, Y. and Stewart, R. (2005), 'Timespans and plans among young adults', *Sociology*, 39, 139–55.

Andres, L., Anisef, P., Krahn, H., Looker, D. and Thiessen, V. (1999), 'The persistence of social structure: cohort, class and gender effects on the occupational aspirations and expectations of Canadian youth', *Journal of Youth Studies*, 2, 261–82.

Andres, L. and Grayson, J. P. (2003), 'Parents, educational attainment, jobs and satisfaction: what's the connection? A 10–year portrait of Canadian young women and men', *Journal of Youth Studies*, 6, 181–202.

Arabsheibani, G. R. and Mussurov, A. (2003), 'Education, earnings and discrimination in Kazakhstan', paper presented at World Bank Workshop on *Enhancing Poverty Monitoring in Azerbaijan, Kazakhstan and the Kyrgyz Republic*, Issyk-Kol.

Archer, L., Hollingworth, S. and Halsall, A. (2007), '"University's not for me – I'm a Nike person": urban working class young people's negotiations of "style", identity and educational engagement', *Sociology*, 41, 219–37.

Arnett, J. J. (2005), *Emerging Adulthood: The Winding Road from Late Teens Through the Twenties*, Oxford University Press, Oxford.

Arnett, J. J. (2006), 'Emerging adulthood in Europe: a response to Bynner', *Journal of Youth Studies*, 9, 111–23.

Artemova, O. (1998), 'Changes in the labour structure of the rural Siberian working population in the 1970s-1990s', paper presented at *International Sociological Association Congress*, Montreal.

Asmailzade, F. (2007), 'Study abroad becomes a new priority for Azerbaijani government', *Central Asia-Caucasus Analyst*, 9, 24, 3–4.

Atkinson, W. (2007), 'Beck, individualization and the death of class: a critique', *British Journal of Sociology*, 58, 349–66.

Avanisian, V., Ahmedbeili, S. and Bukia, S., 'Hard times for Caucasians in Moscow', *Caucasus News Update*, 23 June 2006.www.iwpr.net. Accessed 24 June 2006.

Bae, K. (2006), 'General features and conditions of Korean youth', paper presented at *World Congress of the International Sociological Association*, Durban.

Bagatelas, W. and Kubicova, J. (2004), 'Bulgarian emigration – a closer look', *South-East Europe Review*, 6, 4, 27–35.

Ball, S. J., Maguire, M. and Macrae, S. (2000), 'Space, work and the new urban economies', *Journal of Youth Studies*, 3, 279–300.

Bauman, Z. (1998), *Work, Consumerism and the New Poor*, Open University Press, Buckingham.

Beck, U. (1992), *Risk Society: Towards a New Modernity*, Sage, London.

Beck, U. (2000), *The Brave New World of Work*, Polity Press, Cambridge.

Beck, U. and Beck-Gernsheim, E. (1995), *The Normal Chaos of Love*, Polity Press, Cambridge.

Bennett, A. (2000), *Popular Music and Youth Culture*, Macmillan, Basingstoke.

Bennett, A. and Kahn-Harris, K. (2004), 'Introduction', in A. Bennett and K. Kahn-Harris (eds), *After Subculture: Critical Studies in Contemporary Youth Culture*, Palgrave, Basingstoke, 1–18.

Bernadi, F. (2003), 'Returns to educational performance at entry into the Italian labour market', *European Sociological Review*, 19, 25–40.

Bills, D. B. (2004), *The Sociology of Education and Work*, Blackwell, Oxford.

Blackstone, T., Gales, K., Hadley, R. and Lewis, W. (1970), *Students in Conflict: LSE in 1967*, Weidenfeld and Nicolson, London.

Blossfeld, H.-P. and Timm, A. (eds) (2003), *Who Marries Whom? Educational Systems as Marriage Markets in Modern Societies*, Kluwer, Dordrecht.

Bogomolova, T. (1998), 'Income mobility in Russia in the mid-1990s', paper presented at *International Sociological Association Congress*, Montreal.

Bornhorst, F. and Commander, S. (2006), 'Regional unemployment and its persistence in the transition countries', *Economics of Transition*, 14, 269–88.

Bornschier, V., Herkenrath, M. and Konig, C. (2005), 'The double dividend of expanding education for development', *International Sociology*, 20, 506–29.

Bourdieu, P. (1984), *Distinction: A Social Critique of the Judgement of Taste*, Routledge, London.

Bourdieu, P. and Passeron, J. D. (1977), *Reproduction in Education, Culture and Society*, Sage, London.

Bowring, F. (1999), 'Job scarcity: the perverted form of a potential blessing', *Sociology*, 33, 69–84.

Brake, M. (1985), *Comparative Youth Culture*, Routledge, London.

Breakwell, G. M. (1985), *The Quiet Rebel*, Century Press, London.

Bridger, S., Kay, R. and Pinnick, K. (1996), *No More Heroines? Russia, Women and the Market*, Routledge, London.

Bronfenbrenner, U. (1971), *Two Worlds of Childhood: USA and USSR*, Allen and Unwin, London.

Brown, P. (1987), *Schooling Ordinary Kids: Inequality, Unemployment and the New Vocationalism*, Tavistock, London.

Brown, P. and Hesketh, A. (2004), *The Mismanagement of Talent: Employability and Jobs in the Knowledge Economy*, Oxford University Press, Oxford.

Burkeman, O. (2002), 'More black inmates than students', *The Guardian*, 29 August.

Bynner, J. (2005), 'Rethinking the youth life phase: the case for emerging adulthood?', *Journal of Youth Studies*, 8, 367–84.

Bynner, J., Elias, P., McKnight, A., Pan, H. and Pierre, G. (2002), *Young People's Changing Routes to Independence*, Joseph Rowntree Foundation, York.

Caucasus Research Resource Centre (2005), *Data Initiative Survey 2005*, Baku/Tbilisi/Yerevan.

Ceplak, M. M. (2006), 'Values of young people in Slovenia: the search for personal security', *Young*, 14, 291–308.

Charvel, L. (2006), 'Social generations, life chances and welfare regime stability', in P. D. Culpepper, P. A. Hall and B. Palier (eds), *Changing France: The Politics that Markets Make*, Palgrave Macmillan, Basingstoke.

Chuprov, V. and Zubok, J. (1997), 'Social conflict in the sphere of education and youth', *Education in Russia, the Independent States and Eastern Europe*, 15, 47–58.

Clark, Z. (2002), 'Goulash and solidarity', *The Guardian*, 2 November, p. 18.

Clarke, S. (2000), 'The closure of the Russian labour market', *European Societies*, 2, 483–504.

Cohen, P. and Ainley, P. (2000), 'In the country of the blind? Youth studies and cultural studies in Britain', *Journal of Youth Studies*, 3, 79–95.

Collin, M. (2007), *The Time of the Rebels: Youth Resistance Movements and 21st Century Revolutions*, Serpent's Tail, London.

Conant, J. B. (1965), 'Social dynamite in our large cities: unemployed out-of-school youth', in A. Kerber and B. Bommarito (eds), *Schools and the Urban Crisis*, Holt, Rinehart and Winston, New York.

Corso, M. (2007), 'Georgia: NGOs promote family planning awareness', www.eurasianet.com. Posted 9 May 2007, accessed 14 May 2007.

Cote, J. (2000), *Arrested Adulthood: The Changing Nature of Maturity and Identity. What Does it Mean to Grow Up?*, New York University Press, New York.

Cote, J. E. (2002), 'The role of identity capital in the transition to adulthood: the individualisation thesis examined', *Journal of Youth Studies*, 5, 117–34.

Council of Europe (1996), *Cultural Policy in the Russian Federation*, Culture Committee, Strasbourg.

Crick, B. and Heater, D. (1977), *Essays on Political Education*, Falmer Press, Ringmer.

Dementieva, I. (1998), 'The family and professional orientations of teenagers in the changing Russian society', paper presented at *International Sociological Association Congress*, Montreal.

Department for Education (1995), *Young People's Participation in the Youth Service*, Statistical Bulletin 1/95, London.

Devadason, R. (2007), 'Constructing coherence? Young adults' pursuit of meaning through multiple transitions between work, education and unemployment', *Journal of Youth Studies*, 10, 203–21.

Dikici, H. (2003), 'Armenia after independence from the perspective of migration', *Review of Armenian Studies*, 1, 2, 88–98.

Dingsdale, A. (1986), 'Ideology and leisure under socialism: the geography of second homes in Hungary', *Leisure Studies*, 5, 35–55.

Djilas, M. (1957), *The New Class*, Thames and Hudson, London.

Domanski, H. (2000), *On the Verge of Convergence: Social Stratification in Eastern Europe*, Central European University Press, Budapest.

Domanski, H. (2001), 'The rise of the meritocracy in Poland', *Sisyphus*, 15, 115–46.

Domanski, H. (2002), 'Underclass and social stratification in post-communist societies', *Sisyphus*, 16, 109–21.

Domanski, H. (2005), 'Between state socialism and markets: effect of education on incomes in 27 countries', *European Societies*, 7, 197–218.

Dore, R. (1973), *British Factory – Japanese Factory*, Allen and Unwin, London.

Dore, R. (1976), *The Diploma Disease*, Allen and Unwin, London.

Dronkers, J. and Robert, P. (2004), 'Has educational sector any impact on school effectiveness in Hungary? A comparison of public and the newly established religious grammar schools', *European Societies*, 6, 205–36.

Du Bois-Reymond, M. (1998), '"I don't want to commit myself yet": young people's life concepts', *Journal of Youth Studies*, 1, 63–79.

Du Bois-Reymond, M., Plus, W., te Poel, Y. and Ravesloot, J. (2001), '"And then they decide what to do next . . ." Young people's educational and labour trajectories: a longitudinal study from the Netherlands', *Young*, 9, 2. www.allifi/nyri/young/2001-3/duBois.htm.

Dubsky, V. (1995), 'Czech youth and social change', in A. Cavalli and O. Galland, (eds), *Youth in Europe*, Frances Pinter, London, 115–26.

Duffy, C. (2005), 'Barter, veksels and "nei zyvie den gi": between normalization and new forms of exchange in contemporary Russian inter-company relations', paper presented at *37th World Congress of the International Institute of Sociology*, Stockholm.

Duncan, R. and Goddard, J. (2005 2nd edition), *Contemporary America*, Palgrave Macmillan, Basingstoke.

Dunstan, J. (1978), *Paths to Excellence and the Soviet School*, National Foundation for Educational Research, Windsor.

Durkheim, E. (1895, 1958), *The Rules of Sociological Method*, Free Press, Glencoe.

Dwyer, P. and Wyn, J. (1998), 'A new agenda: changing life patterns of the post-1970 generation', *International Bulletin of Youth Research*, 17, 27–34.

Dwyer, P. and Wyn, J. (2001), *Youth, Education and Risk: Facing the Future*, Routledge Falmer, London.

Edelstein, W. (2000), 'Pathologies of the politics of youth: violence, cynicism and educational remedies', paper presented at conference on *Adolescents into Citizens: Integrating Young People into Political Life*, Marbach Castle, Switzerland.

Edmunds, J. and Turner, B. S. (2005), 'Global generations: social change in the twentieth century', *British Journal of Sociology*, 56, 559–77.

Elder, G. H. (1974), *Children of the Great Depression*, University of Chicago Press, Chicago.

Elliott, A. and Lemert, C. (2006), *The New Individualism: The Emotional Costs of Globalization*, Routledge, London.

Erikson, R. and Goldthorpe, J. H. (1992), *The Constant Flux: A Study of Class Mobility in Industrial Societies*, Clarendon Press, Oxford.

Ermisch, J. and Francesconi, M. (1999), *Cohabitation in Great Britain: Not for Long but Here to Stay*, Working Paper, Institute for Social and Economic Research, University of Essex, Colchester.

Eurasianet (2006), 'NGOs call on Kyrgyz government to revise mental health care strategy', <eurasianet.org> Posted 22 August 2006, accessed 26 August 2006.

European Commission (2006), *Report on the Functioning of the Transitional Arrangements set out in the 2003 Accession Treaty (Period 1 May 2004 – 30 April 2006)*, Brussels.

European Commission (2007), *European Social Reality*, Special Eurobarometer, Directorate General Communication, Brussels.

European Commission, DG Education and Culture (2006), *Youth in Action 2007–2013*, Brussels, http://ec.europa.eu/youth/index_en.html. Accessed 23 January 2007.

European Group for Integrated Social Research (EGRIS) (2001), 'Misleading trajectories: transition dilemmas of young adults in Europe', *Journal of Youth Studies*, 4, 101–118.

Eurostat News Release (2006), *The Family in the EU25 Seen Through EU Figures*, Eurostat Press Office, Luxembourg, 15 May 2006.

Evans, G. and Mills, C. (1999), 'Are there classes in post-communist societies?', *Sociology*, 33, 23–46.

Evans, K. (2002), 'Taking control of their lives? Agency in young adults' transitions in England and the new Germany', *Journal of Youth Studies*, 5, 245–69.

Evans, K., Behrens, M. and Kaluza, J. (2000), *Learning and Work in the Risk Society: Lessons for the Labour Markets of Europe from Eastern Germany*, Macmillan, Basingstoke.

.s, K. and Heinz, W. R. (1994), *Becoming Adults in England and ermany*, Anglo-German Foundation, London.

.yal, G., Szelenyi, I. and Townsley, E. (1998), *Making Capitalism Without Capitalists: The New Ruling Elites in Eastern Europe*, Verso Books, New York.

Fahey, T. and Speder, Z. (2004), *Fertility and Family Issues in an Enlarged Europe*, Office for Official Publications of the European Communities, Luxembourg.

Fendrich, J. M. (1977), 'Keeping the faith or pursuing the good life', *American Sociological Review*, 42, 144–57.

Ferernz, K. (1998), 'Ways of women's behaviour during leisure as the example of copying the culture', in J. W. te Kloetze (ed.), *Family and Leisure in Poland and the Netherlands*, Garant, Leuven/Apeldoorn, 107–14.

Festinger, L. (1957), *A Theory of Cognitive Dissonance*, Row, Evanston.

Festinger, L., Riecken, H. W. and Schachter, S. (1956), *When Prophecy Fails*, University of Minnesota Press, Minneapolis.

Feuer, L. S. (1969), *The Conflict of Generations*, Heinemann, London.

Fierman, W. (n.d.), 'Inside Kazakhstan's education system: linguistic Kazakization and economic realities', www.indiana.edu/~isre/NEWSLETTER/Vol15no2/fierman.htm. Accessed 14 March 2006.

Forrester, V. (1999), *The Economic Horror*, Polity Press, Cambridge.

Fox, F. E. (2004), 'Missing the mark: nationalist politics and student apathy', *East European Politics and Societies*, 18, 363–93.

Frantisek, D. K. (1998), 'Modernisation and the lifestyles – lifestyle of Czech adolescents', paper presented at *International Sociological Association Congress*, Montreal.

Franzen. E. M. and Kassman, A. (2005), 'Longer-term labour-market consequences of economic inactivity during young adulthood: a Swedish national cohort study', *Journal of Youth Studies*, 8, 403–24.

Freeman, R. B. (1976), *The Over-Educated American*, Academic Press, New York.

Furedi, F. (2004), *Therapy Culture*, Routledge, London.

Furlong, A. and Cartmel, F. (2007), *Young People and Social Change*, Open University Press, Maidenhead.

Furlong, A., Cartmel, F., Biggart, A., Sweeting, H. and West, P. (2005), 'Complex transitions: linearity and labour market integration in the West of Scotland', in C. Pole, J. Pilcher and J. Williams (eds), *Young People in Transition: Becoming Citizens?*, Palgrave Macmillan, Basingstoke, 12–30.

Gangl, M. (2001), 'European patterns of labour market entry: a dichotomy of occupationalized and non-occupationalized systems', *European Societies*, 3, 471–94.

Gachechiladze, R. (1997), *Population Migration in Georgia and its Socio-Economic Consequences,* Caucasian Institute for Peace, Democracy and Development, Tbilisi.

Gerber, T. P. and Hout, M. (1995), 'Educational stratification in Russia during the Soviet period', *American Journal of Sociology,* 101, 611–60.

Gerber, T. P. and Hout, M. (1998), 'More shock than therapy: market transition, employment and income in Russia, 1991–1995', *American Journal of Sociology,* 104, 1–50.

Giddens, A. (1991), *Modernity and Self-Identity,* Polity Press, Cambridge.

Gijsberts, M. and Nieuwbeert, P. (2000), 'Class cleavages in party preferences in the new democracies of Eastern Europe: a comparison with Western democracies', *European Societies,* 2, 397–430.

Gillham, P. F. (2008), 'Participation in the environmental movement: analysis of the European Union, *International Sociology,* 23, 67–93.

Goehring, J. (ed.) (2006), *Nations in Transit 2006,* Freedom House, Washington DC.

Goldscheider, F. and Goldscheider, C. (1999), *The Changing Transition to Adulthood: Leaving and Returning Home,* Sage, London.

Goldthorpe, J. H., Lockwood, D., Bechhofer, F. and Platt, J. (1969), *The Affluent Worker in the Class Structure,* Cambridge University Press, London.

Goodwin, J. and O'Connor, H. (2005), 'Exploring complex transitions: looking back at the "golden age" of from school to work', *Sociology,* 39, 201–20.

Goranskaya, S., Vinogradova, I. and Ivanova, L. (2000), 'Prevalence of drug taking among the young people who study in Petrozavodsk', paper presented at conference on *Youth on the Threshold of the New Millennium,* Petrozavodsk.

Grant, N. (1968), *Soviet Education,* Penguin, Harmondsworth.

Gros, D. (1997), 'A comparative study of the causes of output decline in transition economies', *ACE Quarterly,* 9, Autumn, 15–16.

Grunert, H. and Lutz, B. (1996), 'A double process of destablisation in post-socialist societies: the case of Germany', paper presented at *Workshop of the European Science Foundation Scientific Network on Transitions in Youth,* La Ciotat.

Gvozdeva, G. (1994), 'Changes in free time utilization by rural residents in West Siberia under the ongoing economic reform', paper presented at *International Sociological Association Congress,* Bielefeld.

Gvozdeva, G. (1999), 'Time balance changes and women's use of their right to rest', *Society and Leisure,* 22, 127–44.

Hakim, C. (1996), *Key Issues in Women's Work,* Athlone Press, London.

Hall, S. and Jefferson, T. (eds) (1976), *Resistance Through Rituals,* Hutchinson, London.

Halsey, A. H. and Young, M. (1997), 'The family and social justice', in A. H. Halsey, H. Lauder, P. Brown and A. S. Wells (eds), *Education, Culture, Economy, Society*, Oxford University Press, Oxford.

Hamilton, S. F. (1987), 'Apprenticeship as a transition to adulthood in West Germany', *American Journal of Education*, 95, 314–45.

Hammerschlag, M. (2007), 'Putin's children', *International Herald Tribune*,   http://www.iht.com/articles/2007/07/05/opinion/edhammer.php?page=1. Posted 5 July 2007, accessed 6 July 2007.

Hayward, G., Hodgson, A., Johnson, J., Oancea, A., Pring, R., Spours, K., Wilde, S. and Wright, S. (2005), *The Nuffield Review of 14–19 Education and Training: Annual Report 2004–05*, University of Oxford Department of Educational Studies, Oxford.

Heath, S. and Kenyon, L. (2001), 'Single young professionals and shared household living', *Journal of Youth Studies*, 4, 83–100.

Hesmondhalgh, D. (2002), *The Cultural Industries*, Sage, London.

Hidy, P. (1982), *Who are being Entertained?*, Institute for Culture, Budapest.

Hoffman, D. F. (2002), *The Oligarchs: Wealth and Power in the New Russia*, Public Affairs Limited, Oxford.

Holland, J., Reynolds, T. and Weller, S. (2007), 'Transitions, networks and communities: the significance of social capital in the lives of children and young people', *Journal of Youth Studies*, 10. 97–116.

Holdsworth, C. (2004), 'Family support during the transition out of the parental home in Britain, Spain and Norway', *Sociology*, 38, 909–26.

Holdsworth, C. (2005), '"When will the children leave home!" Family culture and delayed transitions in Spain', *European Societies*, 7, 547–66.

Hussain, Y. and Bagguley, P. (2005), 'Citizenship, ethnicity and identity: Britain's Pakistanis after the 2001 riots', *Sociology*, 39, 407–25.

Hutson, S. and Liddiard, M. (1994), *Youth Homelessness*, Macmillan, Basingstoke.

Igityan, H. (2003), 'Possibilities and risks of Armenian economic development in view of European business: implications for the Armenian legislature', in *Armenian Parliament: Role, Significance, Challenges*, seminar proceedings, Writers' House, Tsakhkadezor, 21–33.

Ilyin, V. (1998), 'The new middle strata in modern Russia', in M. Kivinen (ed.), *The Kalamari Union: Middle Class in East and West*, Ashgate, Aldershot, 118–29.

Inglehart, R. (1977), *The Silent Revolution*, Princeton University Press, New Jersey.

Inglehart, R. (1997), *Modernization and Postmodernization: Cultural, Economic and Political Change in 43 Societies*, Princeton University Press, New Jersey.

International Labour Office (2002), *Global Employment Trends for Youth*, International Labour Office, Geneva.

International Labour Office (2006), *Global Employment Trends for Youth*, International Labour Office, Geneva.

International Organisation for Migration – Azerbaijan (2002), *Shattered Dreams: Report on Trafficking in Persons in Azerbaijan*, International Organisation for Migration, Geneva.

Inui, A. (2003), 'Restructuring youth: recent problems of Japanese youth in its contextual origin', *Journal of Youth Studies*, 6, 219–33.

Ivacovou, M. (2004), 'Life chances: childhood experience and later life outcomes', in I. Stewart and R. Vaitilingham (eds), *The Seven Ages of Man and Woman: A Look at Life in Britain in the Second Elizabethan Age*, Economic and Social Research Council, Swindon, 12–15.

Ivacovou, M. and Berthoud, R. (2001), *Young People's Lives: A Map of Europe*, Institute for Social and Economic Research, University of Essex, Colchester.

Jacoby, S. (1975), *Inside Soviet Schools*, Schocken Books, New York.

Jamieson, L., Anderson, M., McCrone, D., Bechhofer, F., Stewart, R. and Li, Y. (2002), 'Cohabitation and commitment: partnership plans of young men and women', *Sociological Review*, 50, 356–77.

Jarvinen, M. and Grundelach, P. (2007), 'Teenage drinking: symbolic capital and distinction', *Journal of Youth Studies*, 10, 55–71.

Jenkins, R. (1983), *Lads, Citizens and Ordinary Kids*, Routledge, London.

Jones, G. (1995), *Leaving Home*, Open University Press, Buckingham.

Jung, B. (1990), 'The impact of the crisis on leisure patterns in Poland', *Leisure Studies*, 9, 95–105.

Jung, B. (1994), 'For what leisure? The role of culture and recreation in post-communist Poland', *Leisure Studies*, 13, 1–15.

Jung, B. (1996), 'Current evidence on leisure participation in Poland', in A. J. Veal, G. Cushman and J. Zuzanek (eds), *World Leisure Participation: Free Time in the Global Village*, CABI, Oxford.

Jung, B. (1997), 'Initial analysis of the lifestyle of young unemployed and young self-employed – Bulgaria, Hungary, Poland and Slovakia', in L. Machacek and K. Roberts (eds), *Youth Unemployment and Self-Employment in East-Central Europe*, Slovak Academy of Sciences, Bratislava, 27–44.

Jung, B. and Moleda-Zdziech, M. (1998), 'Central and Eastern European cultural policies, media reform and the development of media markets in the 1990s', *Leisure Studies*, 17, 69–93.

Kahn, R. M. and Bowers, W. J. (1970), 'The social context of the rank and file student activist', *Sociology of Education*, 43, 38–55.

Kandelaki, G. (2005), 'Education: a drag on Georgia's reforms', www.eurasianet.org. Posted 14 April 2005, accessed 16 April 2005.

Keeley, G. (2008), 'Spanish parents faking divorce to get children into best schools', *The Guardian*, 19 March.

Kelly, P. (2006), 'The entrepreneurial self and "youth at risk": exploring the horizons of identity in the twenty-first century', *Journal of Youth Studies*, 9, 17–32.

Khachatrian, H. (2002), 'Armenia: repatriation may not solve problems of exodus', www.eurasianet.org. Posted 12 December 2002, accessed 15 December 2002.

Khachatrian, H. (2006), 'Central bank holds firm on fiscal policy', www.eurasianet.org. Posted 31 August 2006, accessed 4 September 2006.

Kharchenko, I. I. (1998), 'High school students plan their future: changes in the 1990s in Western Siberia', paper presented at *International Sociological Association Congress*, Montreal.

Khmelko, V. (2002), 'Macrosocial change in Ukraine: the years of independence', *Sisyphus*, 16, 125–35.

Kivinen, M. (ed.) (1998), *The Kalamari Union: Middle Class in East and West*, Ashgate, Aldershot.

Klein, J. (1965), *Samples from English Cultures*, 2 vols, Routledge, London.

Kogan, I. and Unt, M. (2005), 'Transition from school to work in the transition economies', *European Societies*, 7, 219–53.

Kohler, H.-D. (1999), 'Adjustment problems between human resource strategies and public educational systems in Germany and Spain', paper presented to *European Research Network on Transitions in Youth*, Oslo.

Konrad, G. and Szelenyi, I. (1979), *The Intellectuals on the Road to Class Power*, Harvester, Brighton.

Kornai, J. (2006), 'The great transformation of Central Eastern Europe: success and disappointment', *Economics of Transition*, 14, 207–44.

Krug, E. A. (1964), *The Shaping of the American High School*, Harper and Row, New York.

Kuda, E. (1998), 'On the attractiveness of in-company training in the dual system of vocational training in Germany', *TNTT Publications*, 1, 1, <htpp://tntee.umu.se/publications/eng/on_the_attractiveness.html>

Kutsenko, O. (2002), 'Dynamics of class formation process in Ukrainian society', *Sisyphus*, 16, 137–50.

Kutsenko, O. (2004), 'The zigzags of political regime democratisation in Ukraine', *Ukrainian Sociological Review*, 5, 70–87.

Lagree, J.-C. (ed.) (2002), *Rolling Youth, Rocking Society: Youth Take Part in the Post-Modern Debate on Globalization*, UNESCO, Paris.

Lane, D. (1976), *The Socialist Industrial State*, Allen and Unwin, London.

Lane, D. (1982), *The End of Social Inequality?*, Allen and Unwin, London.

Layard, R. (2005), *Happiness: Lessons from a New Science*, Allen Lane, London.

Lehmann, W. (2004), '"For some reason, I get a little scared": structure, agency and risk in school-work transitions', *Journal of Youth Studies*, 7, 379–96.

Lehmann, W. (2005), '"I'm still scrubbing the floors": experiencing youth apprenticeships in Canada and Germany', *Work, Employment and Society*, 19, 107–29.

Leonard, D. (1980), *Sex and Generation*, Tavistock, London.

Lepper, B. and Schule, U. (1999), 'Multinationals' recruitment policy in transition economies and its impact on local labour markets – the case of Moscow', in Faculty of Economics, University of Split, *Enterprise in Transition*, Split-Sibenik, 300–3.

Li, Y., Savage, M. and Pickles, A. (2003), 'Social capital and social exclusion in England and Wales (1972–1999)', *British Journal of Sociology*, 54, 497–526.

Lillis, J. (2007), 'Kazakhstan plans education reform in drive for competitiveness', www.eurasianet.org. Posted 3 March 2007, accessed 8 March 2007.

Lipset, S. M. and Marks, G. (2000), *It Didn't Happen Here: Why Socialism Failed in the United States*, Norton, New York.

Lowe, G. S. and Krahn, H. (2000), 'Work aspirations and attitudes in an era of labour market restructuring: a comparison of two Canadian cohorts', *Work, Employment and Society*, 14, 1–22.

Luping Wu (2002), 'Can traditional values, modern values and post-modernization values co-exist? Modernization, cultural globalization and the structural change of values among the Chinese youth', paper presented at *International Sociological Association Congress*, Brisbane.

MacDonald, R., Mason, P., Shildrick, T., Webster, C., Johnston, L. and Ridley, L. (2001), 'Snakes and ladders: in defence of studies of youth transitions', *Sociological Research Online*, 5, 4.

MacDonald, R. and Marsh, J. (2005), *Disconnected Youth? Growing Up in Britain's Poor Neighbourhoods*, Palgrave Macmillan, Basingstoke.

MacDonald, R. and Shildrick, T. (2007), 'Street corner society: leisure careers, youth (sub)culture and social exclusion', *Leisure Studies*, 26, 339–55.

McDowell, L. (2003), *Redundant Masculinities? Employment Change and White Working Class Youth*, Blackwell, Oxford.

McLaughlin, D. (2006), 'Polish aid teams sent to Britain', *The Observer*, August 13, 28.

MacRae, R. (2004), 'Notions of "us" and "them": markers of stratification in clubbing lifestyles', *Journal of Youth Studies*, 7, 55–71.

Machacek, L. (1994), *Youth Strategies in the Solution of Unemployment in Slovakia*, Slovak Academy of Sciences, Bratislava.

Machacek, L. (1996), *Slovak Youth Attitudes Towards the Market Challenges*, Institute of Sociology, Slovak Academy of Sciences, Bratislava.

Machacek, L. and Roberts, K. (eds) (1997), *Youth Unemployment and Self-Employment in East-Central Europe*, Institute for Sociology, Slovak Academy of Sciences, Bratislava.

Magun, V. S. (1996), 'From 1985 to 1995: revolution of youth's aspirations and life strategies', *Sotsioloicheskyi Zhurnal*, 3/4, 29–48.

Malmberg-Heimonen, I. and Julkunen, I. (2006), 'Out of employment? A comparative analysis of the risks and opportunities longer term unemployed immigrant youth face when entering the labour market', *Journal of Youth Studies*, 9, 575–92.

Mannheim, K. (1952), 'The problem of generations', in *Essays on the Sociology of Knowledge*, Routledge, London.

Marada, R. (2004), 'Social construction of youth and formation of generational awareness after socialism', in P. Mares *et al.*, *Society, Reproduction and Contemporary Challenges*, Barrister and Principal, Brno, 149–68.

Marasovic, S. (2004), 'The young in Croatia – challenges and prospects', *South East Europe Review*, 6, 4, 79–84.

Markowitz, F. (2000), *Coming of Age in Post-Soviet Russia*, University of Illinois Press, Urbana and Chicago.

Mattar, Y. (2003), 'Virtual communities and hip-hop music consumers in Singapore: interplaying global, local and subcultural identities', *Leisure Studies*, 22, 283–300.

Matthews, M. (1972), *Class and Society in Soviet Russia*, Allen Lane, London.

Matthews, M. (1982), *Education in the Soviet Union*, Allen and Unwin, London.

Mead, M. (1935), *Sex and Temperament in Three Primitive Societies*, Routledge, London.

Mead, M. (1971), *The Coming of Age in Samoa*, Penguin, Harmondsworth.

Meek, J. (1998), 'Brown envelopes for young Russians', *The Guardian*, 17 March, p. 11.

Meshkova, E. (1998), 'Education in restructuring Russia: history and tendencies', paper presented at *International Sociological Association Congress*, Montreal.

Michailova, S. and Mills, A. (1998), 'Processual dynamics or organisational transformation in conditions of continuous disequilibrium', paper presented at *14th EGOS Colloquium*, Maastricht.

Milenkova, V. and Molhov, M. (2002), The private school in Bulgaria – its identity and presence in the public space', *Sociological Problems*, 34, 224–36.

Mirzakhanyan, A., Manasyan, H., Suvaryan, Y., Yeganyan, R., Shahnazaryan, N. and Jrbashyan, N. (2002), *Education, Poverty and Economic Activity in Armenia: Situation Analysis Report*, United Nations Office, Yerevan.

Mitev, P.-E. (2004), Bulgarian youth and European perspective', *South East Europe Review*, 6, 4, 49–64.

Molgat, M. (2002), 'Leaving home in Quebec: theoretical and social implications of (im)mobility among youth', *Journal of Youth Studies*, 5, 135–52.

Morley, L. (2007), 'The X factor: employability, elitism and equity in graduate recruitment', *21st Century Society*, 2, 191–207.

Muggleton, D. (2000), *Inside Subculture: The Postmodern Meaning of Style*, Berg, Oxford.

Muljukova, I. A. (2003), 'Transformation of Karelian students' political orientations: an experience of longitudinal study', paper presented at *4th International Youth Research Conference in Karelia*, Niittylahti.

Mussuri, E. (2003), 'Poll shows youth growing more optimistic', *Kyiv Post*, 8, 14, April 3, 4.

Mythen, G. (2004), *Ulrich Beck: A Critical Introduction to the Risk Society*, Pluto Press, London.

Mythen, G. (2005), 'Employment, individualization and insecurity: rethinking the risk society perspective', *Sociological Review*, 53, 129–49.

Nagasawa, T. (2004), 'Employment issues and policies of youth in Japan', paper presented to *Eighth Japanese-German Joint Seminar on Labor Issues*, University of Bremen, Bremen.

National Centre for Social Research (2003), *National Survey of Sexual Attitudes and Lifestyles II*, National Centre for Social Research, London.

Need, A. and Evans, G. (2001), 'Analysing patterns of religious participation in post-communist Eastern Europe', *British Journal of Sociology*, 52, 220–48.

Nilan, P. and Feixa, C. (eds) (2006), *Global Youth? Hybrid Identities, Plural Worlds*, Routledge, London.

Niznik, J. and Skotnicka-Illasiewicz, E. (1992), 'What is Europe for young Poles?' *International Journal of Sociology*, 22, 50–9.

Nossiter, T. (1969), 'How children learn about politics', *New Society*, 31 July, 166–7.

Oksamytna, S. and Khemlko, V. (2004), 'Social exclusion in Ukraine in the initial stages of the restoring capitalism', *Ukrainian Sociological Review*, 4, 179–92.

Oljasz, T. (1998), 'Crime busters', *Warsaw Voice*, 6 December 1998, 16–17.

Omel'chenko, E. (1996), 'Young women in provincial gang culture: a case study in Ul'ianovsk', in H. Pilkington (ed.), *Gender, Generation and Identity in Contemporary Russia*, Routledge, London, 216–35.

Orozco, M. (2006), 'Sending money home: can remittances reduce poverty?' *Insights*, 60, January, 1–2.

Oskarsdottir, G. (1995), 'Dropping out in Scandinavia and the USA: a comparative study of dropout patterns', paper presented to *Workshop on Transitions in Youth: Comparisons Over Time and Across Countries*, Oostvoorne.

Osterman, P. (1980), *Getting Started*, MIT Press, Cambridge, Mass.

Paczynska, A. (2005), 'Inequality, political participation, and democratic deepening in Poland', *East European Politics and Societies*, 19, 573–613.

Pais, J. M. (2003), 'The multiple faces of the future in the labyrinth of life', *Journal of Youth Studies*, 6, 115–26.

Park, A., Phillips, M. and Johnson, M. (2005), *Young People in Britain: The Attitudes and Experiences of 12–19 Year Olds*, Research Report RR564, Department for Education and Skills, Nottingham.

Parker, H., Williams, L. and Aldridge, J. (2002), 'The normalization of "sensible" recreational drug use: further evidence from the north-west England longitudinal study', *Sociology*, 36, 941–64.

Parkin, F. (1968), *Middle Class Radicalism*, Manchester University Press, Manchester.

Parsons, T. (1954), 'Age and sex in the social structure of the United States', in *Essays in Sociological Theory*, Free Press, Chicago.

Parsons, R. (2003), 'Georgia: reputation for tolerance slipping amidst attitudes towards religious minorities', www.eurasianet.org. Posted 30 July 2003.

Pejic, V. (2004), 'Young people in Serbia – attitudes, moral values and perspectives', *South East Europe Review*, 6, 4, 65–78.

Petrov, V. and Kantemirova, I. (2004), 'Designing of disablement in the institutional field', in G. Osadchaya and E. Meshkova (eds), *Methodology of Sociological Analysis of Social Sphere*, Russian State Social University, Moscow, 54–61.

Piirainen, T. (1998), 'From status to class: the emergence of a class society in Russia', in M. Kivinen (ed.), *The Kalamari Union: Middle Class in East and West*, Ashgate, Aldershot, 314–41.

Pilkington, H. (1994), *Russia's Youth and its Culture*, Routledge, London.

Pilkington, H. (1996), 'Farewell to the Tuscova: masculinities and femininities on the Moscow youth scene', in H. Pilkington (ed.), *Gender, Generation and Identity in Contemporary Russia*, Routledge, London.

Pilkington, H. (2004a), 'Youth strategies for glocal living: space, power and communication in everyday cultural practice', in A. Bennett and K. Kahn-Harris (eds), *After Subculture: Critical Studies in Contemporary Youth Culture*, Palgrave, Basingstoke, 119–34.

Pilkington, H. (2004b), *"Everyday" but not "Normal": Drug Use and Youth Cultural Practice in Russia*, Final Report R000239439, Economic and Social Research Council, Swindon.

Pilkington, H., Omel'chenko, E., Flynn, M., Bliudina, U. and Starkova, E. (2002), *Looking West: Cultural Globalization and Russian Youth Cultures*, Pennsylvania State University Press, Pennsylvania.

Pollert, A. (2003), 'Women, work and equal opportunities in post-communist transition', *Work, Employment and Society*, 17, 331–57.

Pollock, G. (1997), 'Uncertain futures: young people in and out of employment since 1940', *Work, Employment and Society*, 11, 615–38.

Ponina, E. (2004), 'The problems of childhood in modern Russia', in G. Osadchaya and E. Meshkova (eds), *Methodology of Sociological Analysis of Social Sphere*, Russian State Social University, Moscow, 91–3.

Poretzkina, E. and Jyrkinen-Pakkasvirta, T. (1995), 'Reconstruction of consumption patterns of St Petersburg families', paper presented at *European Sociological Association Conference*, Budapest.

Predborska, I. (2005), 'The social position of young women in present-day Ukraine', *Journal of Youth Studies*, 8, 349–65.

Predborska, I., Ivaschenko, K. and Roberts, K. (2004), 'Youth transitions in East and West Ukraine', *European Sociological Review*, 20, 403–13.

Puuronen, V., Sinisalo, P., Miljukova, I. and Shvet, L. (2000), *Youth in a Changing Karelia*, Ashgate, Aldershot.

Quintini, G, and Martin, S. (2006), 'Starting well or losing their way? The position of youth in the labour market in OECD countries', *OECD Social, Employment and Migration Working Papers*, No 39, OECD Publications, Paris.

Rainie, L. and Madden, M. (2006), *Not Looking for Love: The State of Romance in America*, www.pewinternet.org. Accessed 13 March 2006.

Ravesloot, J., Du Bois-Reymond, M. and te Poel, Y. (1999), 'Courtship and sexuality of young people in the fifties and the nineties – an intergenerational study from the Netherlands', *Young*, 7, 4. www.alli.fi/nyri/young/1999/articleravesloo99–4.htm.

Reiter, H. (2006), 'The missing link: the transition from education to labour in the Soviet Union revisited', *EUI Working Papers*, SPS No 2006/07, European University Institute, Badia Fiesolana.

Riesman, D. (1952), *The Lonely Crowd: A Study of the Changing American Character*, Yale University Press, New Haven.

Riordan, J. (1980), *Soviet Sport*, Blackwell, Oxford.

Riordan, J. (1982), 'Leisure: the state and the individual in the USSR', *Leisure Studies*, 1, 65–79.

Riordan, J. (1988), 'Problems of leisure and glasnost', *Leisure Studies*, 7, 173–85.

Roberts, K. (1968), 'The entry into employment: an approach towards a general theory', *Sociological Review*, 16, 165–84.

Roberts, K. (2001a), 'Unemployment without social exclusion: evidence from young people in Eastern Europe', *International Journal of Sociology and Social Policy*, 21, 118–44.

Roberts, K. (2001b), 'The new East European model of education, training and youth employment', *Journal of Education and Work*, 14, 315–28.

Roberts, K. (2001c), *Class in Modern Britain*, Palgrave, Basingstoke.

Roberts, K. (2006a), 'The career pathways of young adults in the former USSR', *Journal of Education and Work*, 19, 415–32.

Roberts, K. (2006b, 2nd edition), *Leisure in Contemporary Society*, CABI, Wallingford.

Roberts, K., Adibekian, A., Nemiria, G., Tarkhnishvili, L. and Tholen, J. (1998), 'Traders and Mafiosi: the young self-employed in Armenia, Georgia and Ukraine', *Journal of Youth Studies*, 1, 259–78.

Roberts, K., Clark, S. C., Fagan, C. and Tholen, J. (2000), *Surviving Post-Communism: Young People in the Former Soviet Union*, Edward Elgar, Cheltenham.

Roberts, K., Clark, S. C. and Wallace, C. (1994), 'Flexibility and individualisation: a comparative study of transitions into employment in England and Germany', *Sociology*, 28, 31–54.

Roberts, K. and Fagan, C. (1999), 'Old and new routes into the labour markets in former communist countries', *Journal of Youth Studies*, 2, 153–70.

Roberts, K., Fagan, C., Boutenko, I. and Razlogov, K. (2001), 'Economic polarisation, leisure practices and policies, and the quality of life: a study in post-communist Moscow', *Leisure Studies*, 20, 161–72.

Roberts, K. Fagan, C., Foti, K., Jung, B., Kurzynowski, A., Szumlicz, T., Kovatcheva, S. and Machacek, L. (1997), 'Youth unemployment in East-Central Europe', *Sociologia; Slovak Sociological Review*, 29, 671–84.

Roberts, K., Fagan, C., Tarkhnishvili, L., Ivaschenko, E. and Adibekian, A. (2000), 'Education, employment and social mobility: some evidence from Armenia, Georgia and Ukraine in the 1990s', *European Journal of Education*, 35, 125–36.

Roberts, K. and Jung, B. (1995), *Poland's First Post-Communist Generation*, Avebury, Aldershot.

Roberts, K., Kurzynowski, A., Szumlicz, T. and Jung, B. (1997), 'Employers' workforce formation practices, young people's employment opportunities and labour market behaviour in post-communist Poland', *Communist Economies and Economic Transformation*, 9, 87–98.

Roberts, K., Osadchaya, G., Dsuzev, H. V., Gorodyanenko, V. G. and Tholen, J. (2002), 'Who succeeds and who flounders? Young people in East Europe's new market economies', *Sociological Research Online*, 7, 4.

Roberts, K., Osadchaya, G. I., Dsuzev, K. V., Gorodyanenko, V. G. and Tholen, J. (2003), 'Economic conditions, and the family and housing transitions of young adults in Russia and Ukraine', *Journal of Youth Studies*, 6, 70–88.

Roberts, K., Povall, S. and Tholen, J. (2005), 'Farewell to the intelligentsia: political transformation and changing forms of leisure consumption in the former communist countries of Eastern Europe', *Leisure Studies*, 24, 115–35.

Roberts, K., Predborska, I. and Ivaschenko, K. (2003), 'Youth transitions in East and West Ukraine', paper presented at *European Sociological Association Conference*, Murcia.

Roberts, K. and Szumlicz, T. (1995), 'Education and school-to-work transitions in post-communist Poland', *British Journal of Education and Work*, 8, 54–74.

Rose, R. (1991), *Between State and Market: Key Indicators of Transition in Eastern Europe*, Studies in Public Policy 196, University of Strathclyde, Glasgow.

Rosenbaum, J. (2001), *Beyond College for All: Career Paths for the Forgotten Half*, Sage Foundation, New York.

Roszak, T. (1970), *The Making of a Counter Culture*, Faber, London.

Ruchkin, B. A. (1998), 'The youth as a strategic resource for the development of Russia in the XXI century', paper presented at *International Sociological Association Congress*, Montreal.

Rugg, J., Ford, J. and Burrows, R. (2004), 'Housing advantage? The role of student renting in the constitution of housing biographies in the United Kingdom', *Journal of Youth Studies*, 7, 19–34.

Rumberger, R. W. (1981), *Overeducation in the US Labor Market*, Praeger, New York.

Rumyanyseva, N. (2004), 'Higher education in Kazakhstan: the issue of corruption', *International Higher Education*, Fall, Centre for International Higher Education, Boston College, Boston. www. bc.edu/bc_orhg/avp/soe/cihl/newsletter/News37/text013.htm. Accessed 29 January 2007.

Saar, E. (2005), 'New entrants on the Estonian labour market: a comparison with EU countries', *European Societies*, 7, 513–46.

Salagaev, A. L. and Shashkin, A. V. (2000), 'Peace or war: scenarios of behaviour before a fight', paper presented at conference on *Youth on the Threshold of the 3rd Millennium,* Petrozavodsk.

Salagaev, A. L. and Shashkin, A. V. (2003), 'After effects of the transition: youth criminal careers in Russia', paper presented at *4th International Youth Research Conference in Karelia,* Niittylahti.

Sastry, T. and Bekhradnia, B. (2007), *The Academic Experience of Students in English Universities,* Higher Education Policy Institute, London.

Sattarov, R. M. and Lemberanskaya, L. M. (1998), 'Transitions in social orientations of youth in post-Soviet Azerbaijan', paper presented at *Annual Workshop of the European Network on Transitions in Youth,* Edinburgh.

Sattarov, R. M. and Lemberanskaya, L. M. (1999), 'Changing socioeconomic system and transitions of youth into the labour market in Azerbaijan', in *Transitions and Mobility in the Youth Labour Market: Proceedings of Workshop of the European Network on Transitions in Youth,* Norwegian Social Research, Oslo, 25–34.

Schneider, B. M. and Stevenson, D. (1999), *The Ambitious Generation: America's Teenagers, Motivated but Directionless,* Yale University Press.

Schofield, M. (1973), *The Sexual Behaviour of Young Adults,* Allen Lane, London.

Schuman, H. and Corning, A. G. (2000), 'Collective knowledge of public events: the Soviet era from the Great Purge to glasnost', *American Journal of Sociology,* 105, 913–56.

Schupp, J., Buchtemann, C. F. and Soloff, D. (1994), 'School to work transition patterns – (West) Germany and the United States', *Working Paper of the Network on Transitions in Youth,* European Science Foundation, Strasbourg.

Schwartz, G. (2003), 'Employment restructuring in Russian industrial enterprises: confronting a paradox', *Work, Employment and Society,* 17, 49–72.

Searle-Chatterjee, M. (1999), 'Occupation, biography and new social movements', *Sociological Review,* 47, 258–79.

Sennett, R. (1998), *The Corrosion of Character: The Personal Consequences of Work in the New Capitalism,* Norton, London.

Shahnazarian, N. (2002), 'Aspects of social and political integration of the youth', *Armenia Social Trends,* June, 41–2.

Shavit, Y. and Muller, W. (2000), 'Vocational education: where diversion and where safety net?' *European Societies,* 2, 29–50.

Shildrick, T. and MacDonald, R. (2006), 'In defence of subculture: young people's leisure and social divisions', *Journal of Youth Studies,* 9, 125–40.

Shildrick, T. and MacDonald, R. (2007), 'Biographies of exclusion: poor work and poor transitions', *International Journal of Lifelong Education*, 26, 589–604.

Shimoniak, W. (1970), *Communist Education*, Rand McNally, Chicago.

Shorter, E. (1976), *The Making of the Modern Family*, Collins, London.

Shvets, L. and Rusanova, V. (2003), 'The youth of Karelia in the sphere of leisure time: priorities and subcultures', paper presented at *4th International Youth Research Conference in Karelia*, Niittylahti.

Sikevich, Z. (2003), 'Crisis of ethnic identity: case of Russian youth', paper presented at the 4th *International Youth Research Conference in Karelia*, Niittylahti.

Silbereisen, R. K., Vaskovics, L. A. and Zinneker, J. (1996), *Youth in the Reunited Germany*, Leske and Budrich, Opladen.

Simonchuk, E. (2004), 'The working class in Ukraine: chronicle of losses', *Ukrainian Sociological Review*, 5, 155–78

Simonova, N. (2003), 'The evolution of educational inequalities in the Czech Republic after 1989', *British Journal of the Sociology of Education*, 24, 471–85.

Skeggs, B. (2004), *Class, Self, Culture*, Routledge, London.

Smallwood, S. and Jeffries, J. (2003), 'Family building intentions in England and Wales: trends, outcomes and interpretations', *Populations Trends*, 112, 15–28.

Smith, H. (1976), *The Russians*, Times Books, London.

Smith, N., Lister, R., Middleton, S. and Cox, L. (2005), 'Young people as real citizens: towards an inclusionary understanding of citizenship', *Journal of Youth Studies*, 8, 425–33.

Social Agenda (2006), 'Combating persistent youth unemployment in the EU', 14 July, 7–8.

Solga, H. (2002), 'Stigmatization by negative selection: explaining less educated young people's decreasing employment opportunities', *European Sociological Review*, 18, 159–78.

Spannring, R. (2005), 'Some qualitative findings on young people's attitudes towards political participation', in *The Central European Dimension of Youth Research*, Central European Network of Youth Research, Trnava, 20–35.

State Statistical Committee of the Republic of Azerbaijan (2004), *Men and Women in Azerbaijan 2004*, Baku.

Stenning, A. (2005a), 'Re-placing work: economic transformations and the shape of a community in post-socialist Poland', *Work, Employment and Society*, 19, 235–59.

Stenning, A. (2005b), 'Where is the post-socialist working class? Working class lives in the spaces of (post)-socialism', *Sociology*, 39, 983–99.

Stephenson, S. (2001), 'Street children in Moscow: using and creating social capital', *Sociological Review*, 49, 530–47.

Stokes, H. and Wyn, J. (2007), 'Constructing identities and making careers: young people's perspectives on work and learning', *International Journal of Lifelong Education*, 26, 495–511.

Stolle, D. and Micheletti, M. (2005), 'What motivates political consumers?' paper presented at conference on *Political Consumption – Consumed Politics*, Giessen.

Sumbadze, N. and Trakhan-Mouravi, G. (2003), *Panel Survey of Georgia's Population: October 2002*, Institute of Policy Studies, Tbilisi.

Sweeting, H. and West, P. (2003), 'Young people's leisure and risk-taking behaviours: changes in gender patterning in the West of Scotland during the 1990s', *Journal of Youth Studies*, 6, 391–412.

Szdlik, M. (2002), 'Vocational education and labour markets in deregulated, flexibly coordinated and planned societies', *European Societies*, 4, 79–105.

Szelenyi, I. (1983), *Urban Inequalities under State Socialism*, Oxford University Press, Oxford.

Tanner, J., Asbridge, M. and Wortley, S. (2008), 'Our favourite melodies: musical consumption and teenage lifestyles', *British Journal of Sociology*, 59, 117–44.

Tarkhnishvili, L., Voskanyan, A., Tholen, J. and Roberts, K. (2005), 'Waiting for the market: young adults in Telavi and Vanadzor', *Journal of Youth Studies*, 8, 313–30.

Thornton, S. (1995), *Club Cultures: Music, Media and Subcultural Capital*, Polity Press, Cambridge.

Tilkidjiev, N. (1996), 'Social stratification in post-communist Bulgaria', in J. Coen-Huther (ed.), *Bulgaria at the Crossroads*, Nova Science Publishers, New York.

Tilkidjiev, N. (2004), *New Post-Communist Hierarchies: Blocks, Division and Status Order*, Bulgarian Academy of Sciences, Sofia.

Tomanovic, S. and Ignjatovic, S. (2006), 'The transition of young people in a transition society: the case of Serbia', *Journal of Youth Studies*, 9, 269–85.

Tomev. L. and Daskalova, N. (2004), 'Young people in Bulgaria', *South East Europe Review*, 6, 4, 37–47.

Tomusk, V. (2000), 'Reproduction of the "state nobility" in Eastern Europe: past positions and new practices', *British Journal of Sociology of Education*, 21, 269–82.

Trapido, D. (2007), 'Gendered transition: post-Soviet trends in gender wage inequality among young and full-time workers', *European Sociological Review*, 23, 223–37.

Turner, R. H. (1960), 'Sponsored and contest mobility in the school system', *American Sociological Review*, 25, 855–67.

Tursunkulova, B. (2005), 'Private higher education in Central Asia',

International Higher Education, Winter, Centre for International Higher Education, Boston College, Boston. www.bc.edu/bc_org/avp/soe/cihe/newsletter/News38/text007.htm.

Ule, M. (2005), 'Life and value orientations of contemporary youth: the challenge of change', in *The Central European Dimension in Youth Research*, Central European Network of Youth Research, Trnava, 9–19.

Ule, M. and Kuhar, M. (2003), 'Young adults and a new orientation towards family formation', paper presented at *European Sociological Association Conference*, Murcia.

UNICEF (2007), *Child Poverty in Perspective: An Overview of Child Well-Being in Rich Countries*, Innocenti Report Card 7, UNICEF Innocenti Research Centre, Florence.

United Nations (2007), *World Youth Report 2007. Young People's Transitions to Adulthood: Progress and Challenges*, United Nations, New York.

Vaitkas, R. (2006), 'Transition of Lithuanian universities in the process of creating a common higher education area in Europe', paper presented at *International Conference on Rebuilding Research Universities: Towards European Higher Education and Research Area, Bologna 2010*, Tbilisi.

Vaughan, K. (2005), 'The Pathway Framework meets consumer culture: young people, careers and commitment', *Journal of Youth Studies*, 8, 173–86.

Vickerstaff, S. A. (2003), 'Apprenticeship in the "golden age": were youth transitions really smooth and unproblematic back then?', *Work, Employment and Society*, 17, 269–87.

Vincze, M. (2003), 'The rural employment as an economic and social problem in the post-accession period in Romania', paper presented at *Fifth International Conference on Enterprise in Transition*, Tupeci.

Vinken, H. (2007), 'New life course dynamics? Career orientations, work values and future perceptions of Dutch youth', *Young*, 15, 9–30.

Vitanyi, I. (1981), *The Goals, Methods and Achievements of Cultural Policies as Reflected in the Social Development of Countries*, Institute for Culture, Budapest.

Vries, M. R. de and Wolbers, M. H. J. (2005), 'Non-standard employment and wages among school-leavers in the Netherlands', *Work, Employment and Society*, 19, 503–25.

Walker, C. (2007), 'Navigating a "zombie" system: youth transitions from vocational education in post-Soviet Russia', *International Journal of Lifelong Education*, 26, 513–31.

Wallace, C. (2002), 'Household strategies: their conceptual relevance and analytical scope in social research', *Sociology*, 36, 275–92.

Wallace, C. and Kovacheva, S. (1998), *Youth In Society: The Construction and Deconstruction of Youth in East and West Europe*, Macmillan, London.

Watson, P. (1993), 'Eastern Europe's silent revolution: gender', *Sociology*, 27, 471–87.

Watson, P. (2006), 'Unequalising citizenship: the politics of Poland's health care change', *Sociology*, 40, 1079–96.

Weller, S. (2006), 'Skateboarding alone? Making social capital discourse relevant to teenagers' lives', *Journal of Youth Studies*, 9, 557–74.

Wesolowski, W. (1969), 'The notions of strata and class in socialist society', in A. Beteille (ed.), *Social Inequality*, Penguin, Harmondsworth.

Williams, C., Chuprov, V. and Zubok, J. (1997), 'The voting behaviour of Russian youth', *Journal of Communist Studies and Transformation Politics*, 13, 145–59.

Willis, P. (1977), *Learning to Labour*, Saxon House, Farnborough.

Willis, P. (1978), *Profane Culture*, Routledge, London.

Wood, R. T. (2003), 'The straightedge youth sub-culture: observations on the complexity of sub-cultural identity', *Journal of Youth Studies*, 6, 33–52.

World Bank (2005), 'Youth service: a strategy for youth and national development', *Children and Youth*, 2, 1.

Wozniakowa, E. T. (1998), 'Leisure in the Polish reality of the 1990s', in J. W. te Kloetze (ed.), *Family and Leisure in Poland and the Netherlands*, Garant, Leuven/Apeldoorn, 133–54.

Wyn, J. and Dwyer, P. (1999), 'New directions in research on youth in transition', *Journal of Youth Studies*, 2, 5–21.

Wyn, J. and White, R. (1997), *Rethinking Youth*, Sage, London.

Wyn, J. and Woodman, D. (2006), 'Generation, youth and social change in Australia', *Journal of Youth Studies*, 9, 495–514.

Yakubovich, V. and Kozina, I. (2000), 'The changing significance of ties: an exploration of hiring channels in the Russian transitional labour market', *International Sociology*, 15, 479–500.

Yanowitch, M. (1977), *Social and Economic Inequality in the Soviet Union*, Martin Robertson, London.

Zaidi, A. and Zolyomi, E. (2007), *Intergenerational Transmission of Disadvantages in EU Member States*, European Centre for Social Welfare Policy and Research, Policy Brief, June, Vienna.

Zajda, J. I. (1980), *Education in the USSR*, Pergamon Press, Oxford.

Zhakenov, G. (n.d.), *Kazakhstan National Report on Higher Education System Development*, www.unesco.kz/he/kazakh/kazakh_eng.htm. Accessed 29 January 2007.

Zinneker, J. (1990) 'What does the future hold? Youth and socio-cultural change in the FRG', in L. Chisholm, P. Buchner, H.-H. Kruger and P. Brown (eds), *Childhood, Youth and Social Change: A Comparative Perspective*, The Palmer Press, Falmer, Basingstoke.

Zubok, J. (1998), *Social Integration of Youth in an Unstable Society* (in Russian), Institute of Youth, Moscow.

Zuev, A. E. (1997), 'Socio-economic situation of the youth in a labour sphere', paper presented at conference on *Youth Unemployment in East-Central Europe*, Smolenice, Slovakia.

Index

236